CREATED BY DAVID SCHULNER

DAVID SCHULNER
WRITER

JUAN JOSE RYP
ARTIST

FELIX SERRANO
COLORIST

RUS WOOTON
LETTERER

SEAN MACKIEWICZ
EDITOR

JUAN JOSE RYP
AND ANDY TROY
COVER

CREATED BY DAVID SCHULNER

IMAGE COMICS, INC.
Robert Kirkman - chief operating officer
Erik Larsen - chief financial officer
Todd McFarlane - president
Marc Silvestri - chief executive officer
Jim Valentino - vice-president

Eric Stephenson - publisher
Todd Martinez - sales & licensing coordinator
Jennifer de Guzman - pr & marketing director
Branwyn Bigglestone - accounts manager
Emily Miller - administrative assistant
Jamie Parreno - marketing assistant
Sarah deLaine - events coordinator
Kevin Yuen - digital rights coordinator
Jonathan Chan - production manager
Drew Gill - art director
Monica Garcia - production artist
Vincent Kukua - production artist
Jana Cook - production artist
www.imagecomics.com

For SKYBOUND ENTERTAINMENT
Robert Kirkman - CEO
J.J. Didde - President
Sean Mackiewicz - Editorial Director
Shawn Kirkham - Director of Business Development
Helen Leigh - Office Manager
Brian Huntington - Online Editorial Director
Feldman Public Relations LA - Public Relations

For international rights inquiries,
please contact: foreign@skybound.com

WWW.SKYBOUND.COM

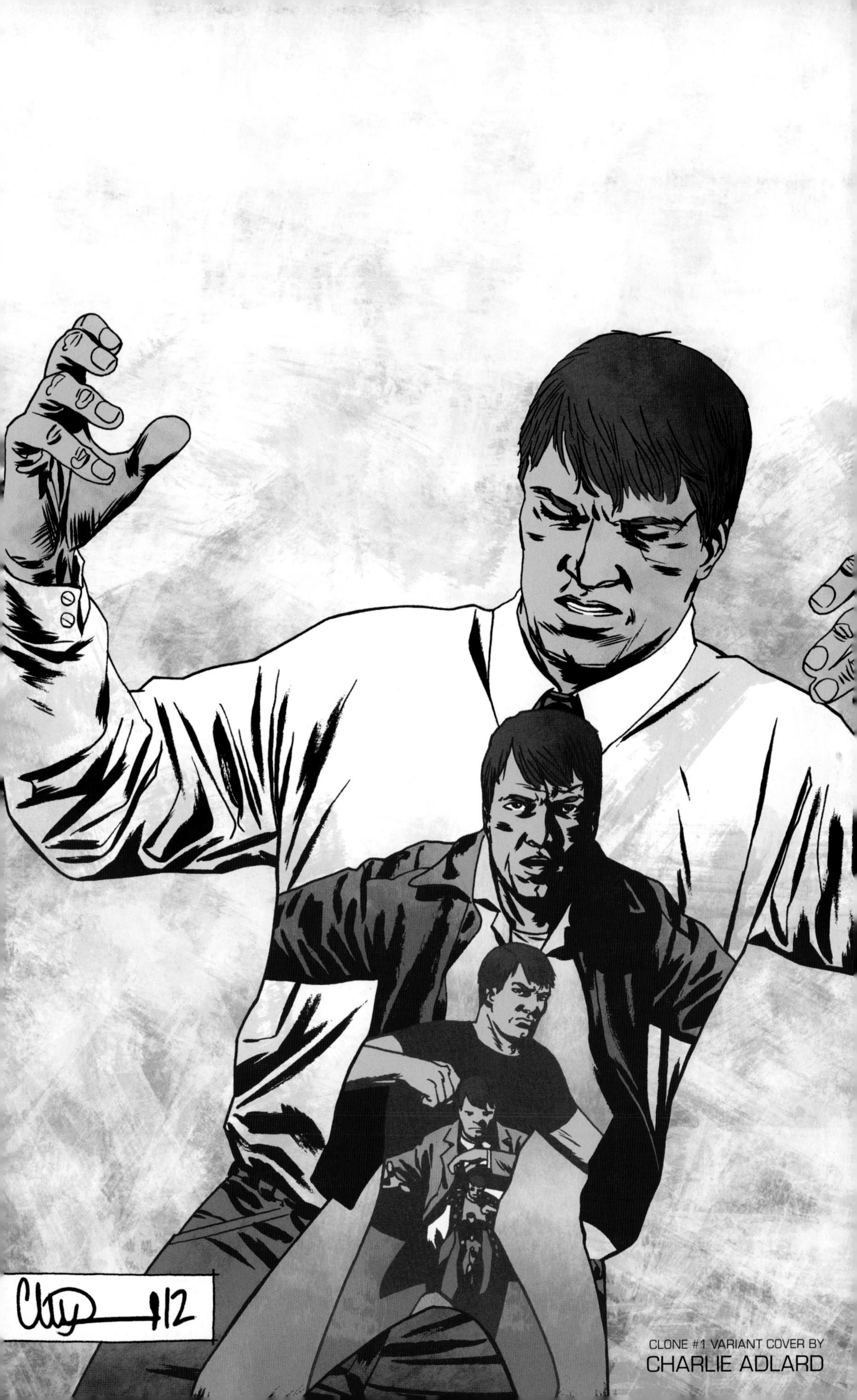

CLONE #1 VARIANT COVER BY
CHARLIE ADLARD

CHAPTER 1

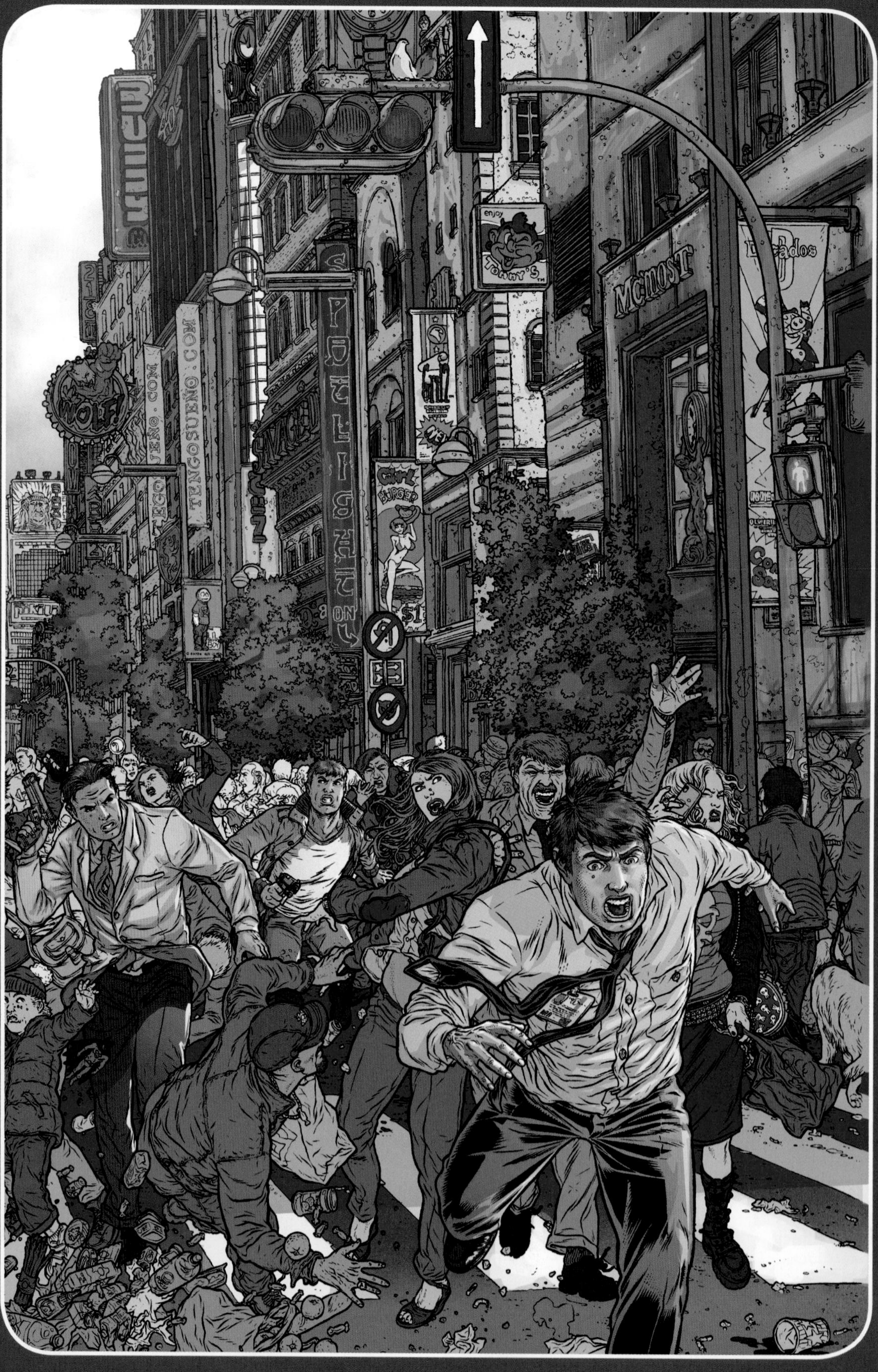
enjoy
TOMMY'S
McMOST
TENGOSUEÑO.COM
WOLF
BURGER
$1

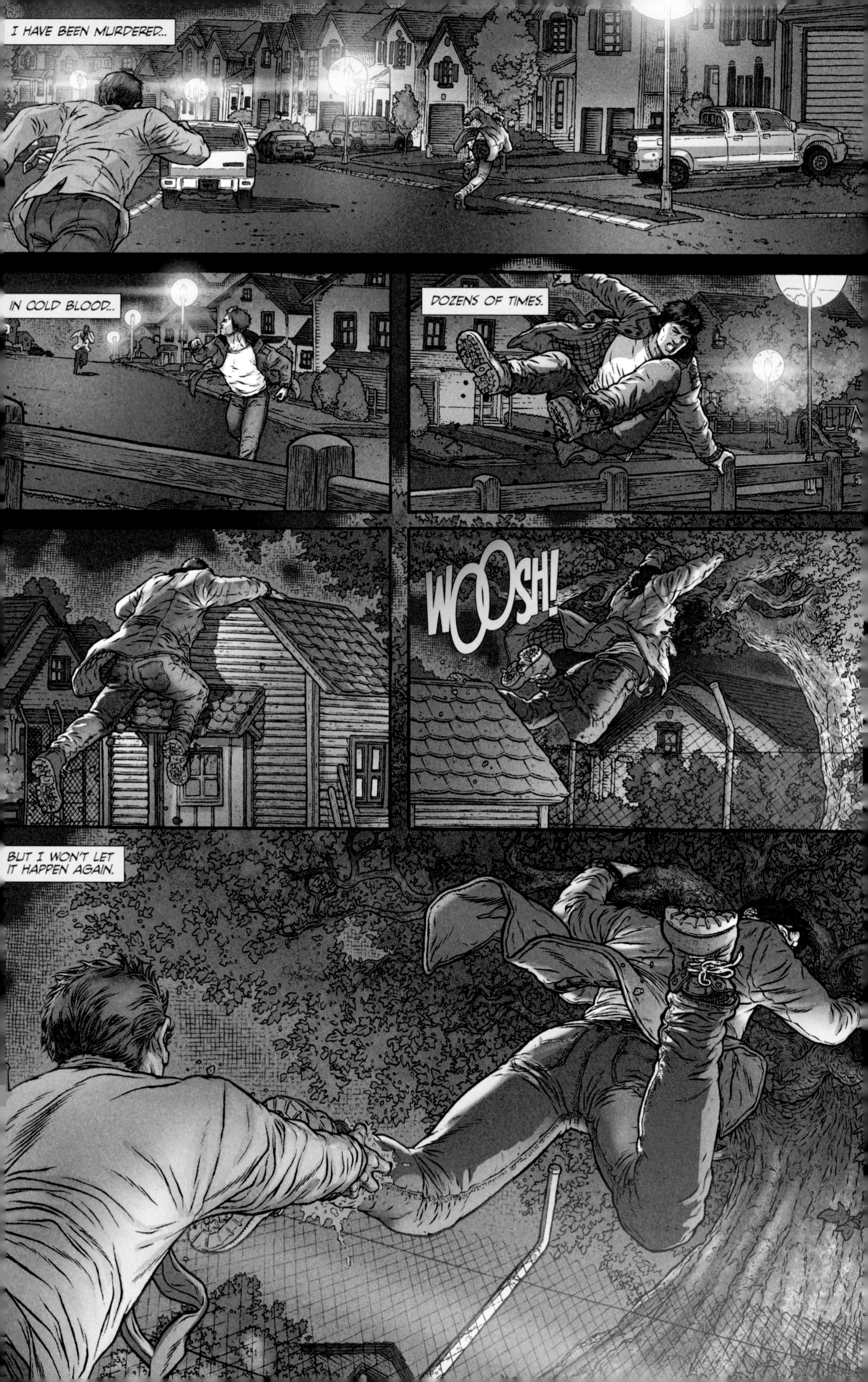
I HAVE BEEN MURDERED...
IN COLD BLOOD...
DOZENS OF TIMES.
WOOSH!
BUT I WON'T LET IT HAPPEN AGAIN.

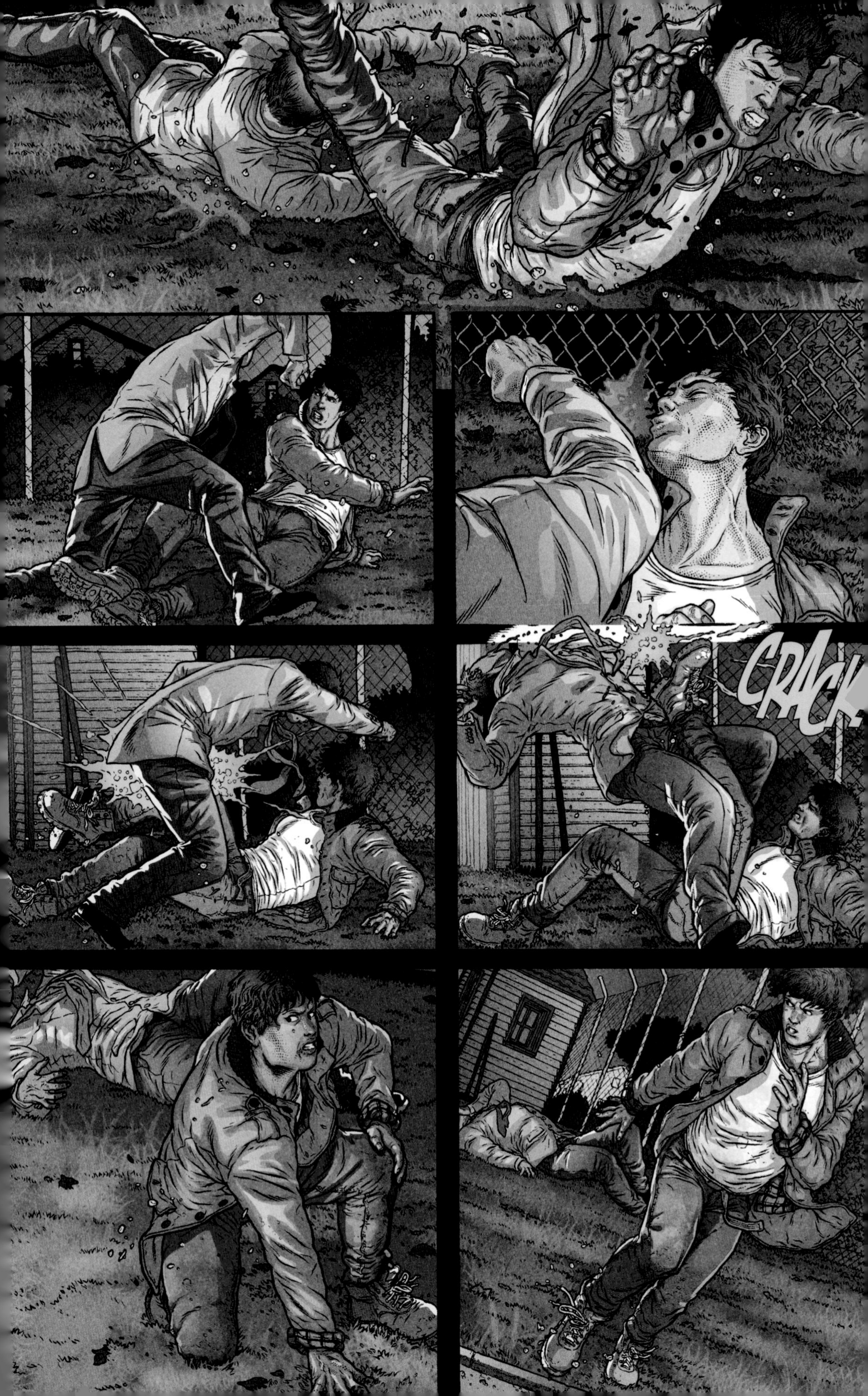
CRACK

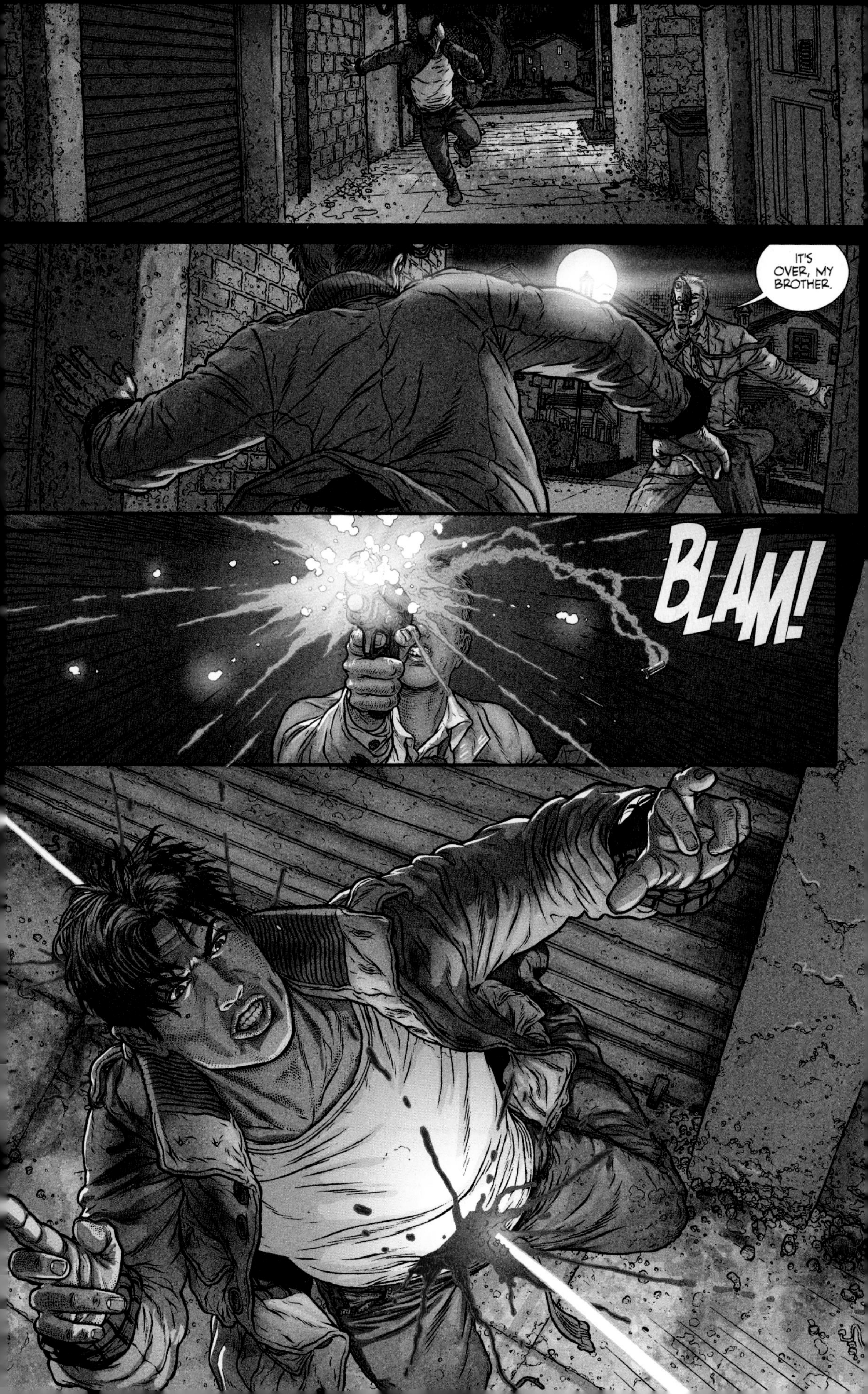
IT'S OVER, MY BROTHER.
BLAM!

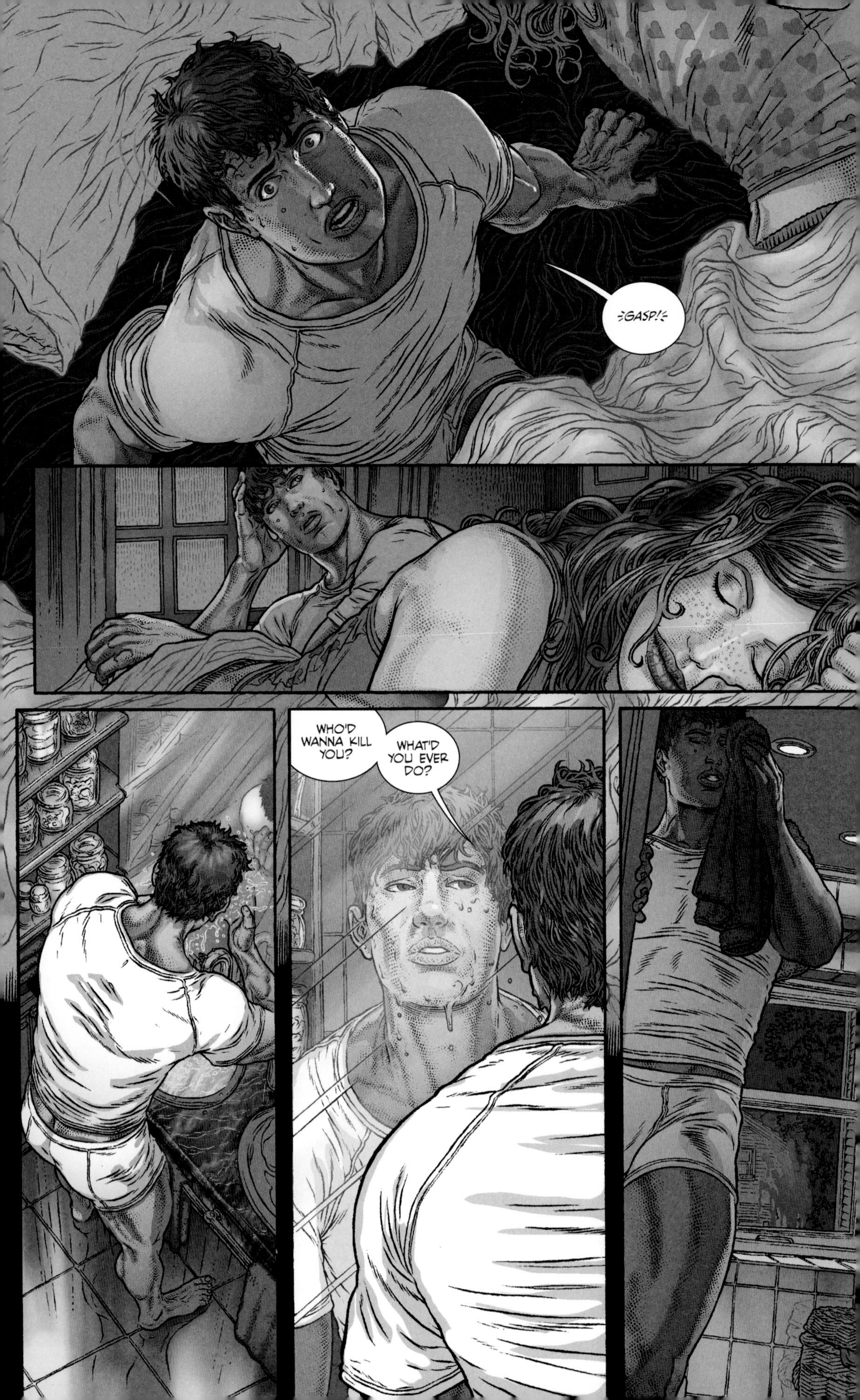
GASP!
WHO'D WANNA KILL YOU?
WHAT'D YOU EVER DO?

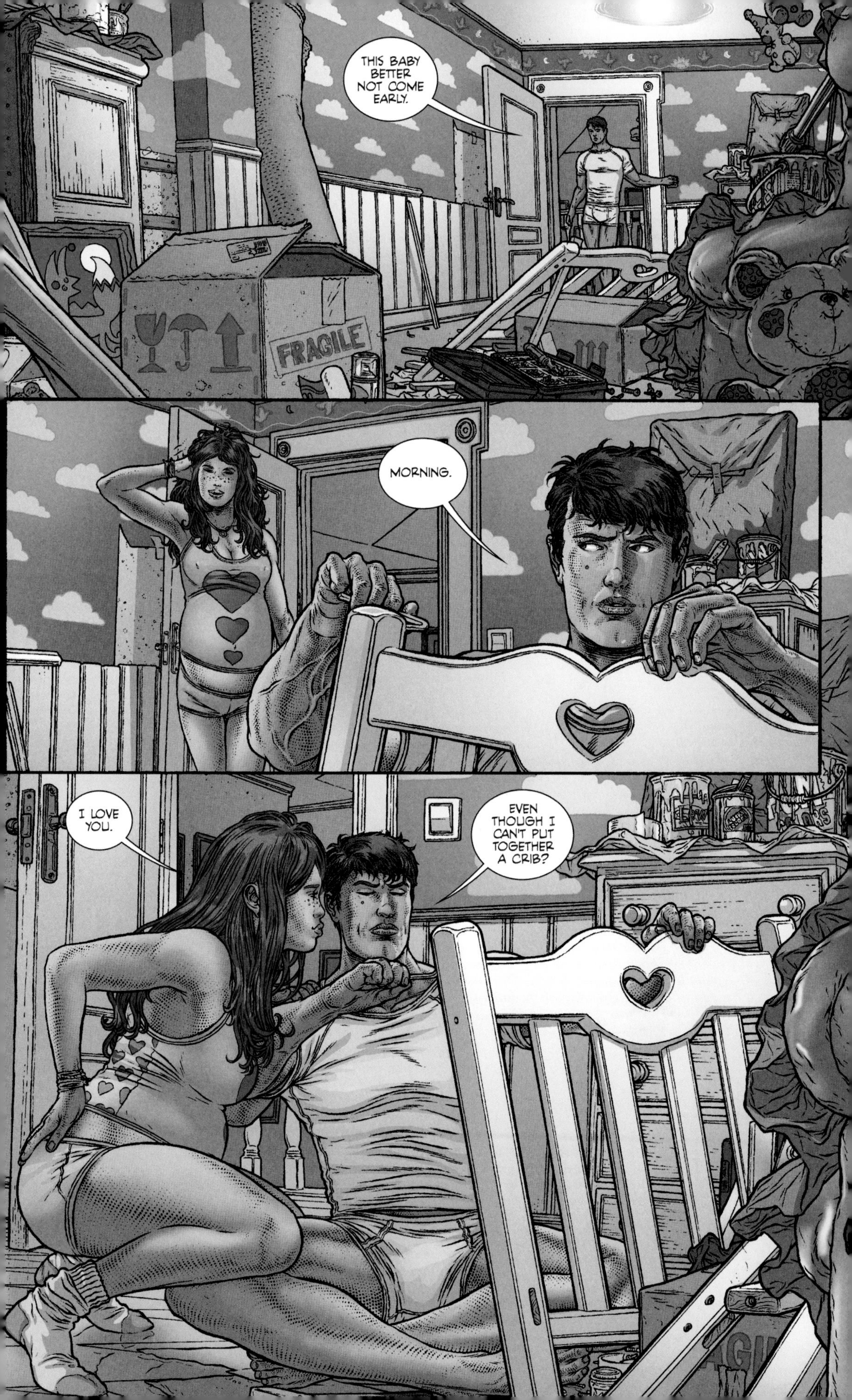
THIS BABY BETTER NOT COME EARLY.
MORNING.
I LOVE YOU.
EVEN THOUGH I CAN'T PUT TOGETHER A CRIB?
FRAGILE

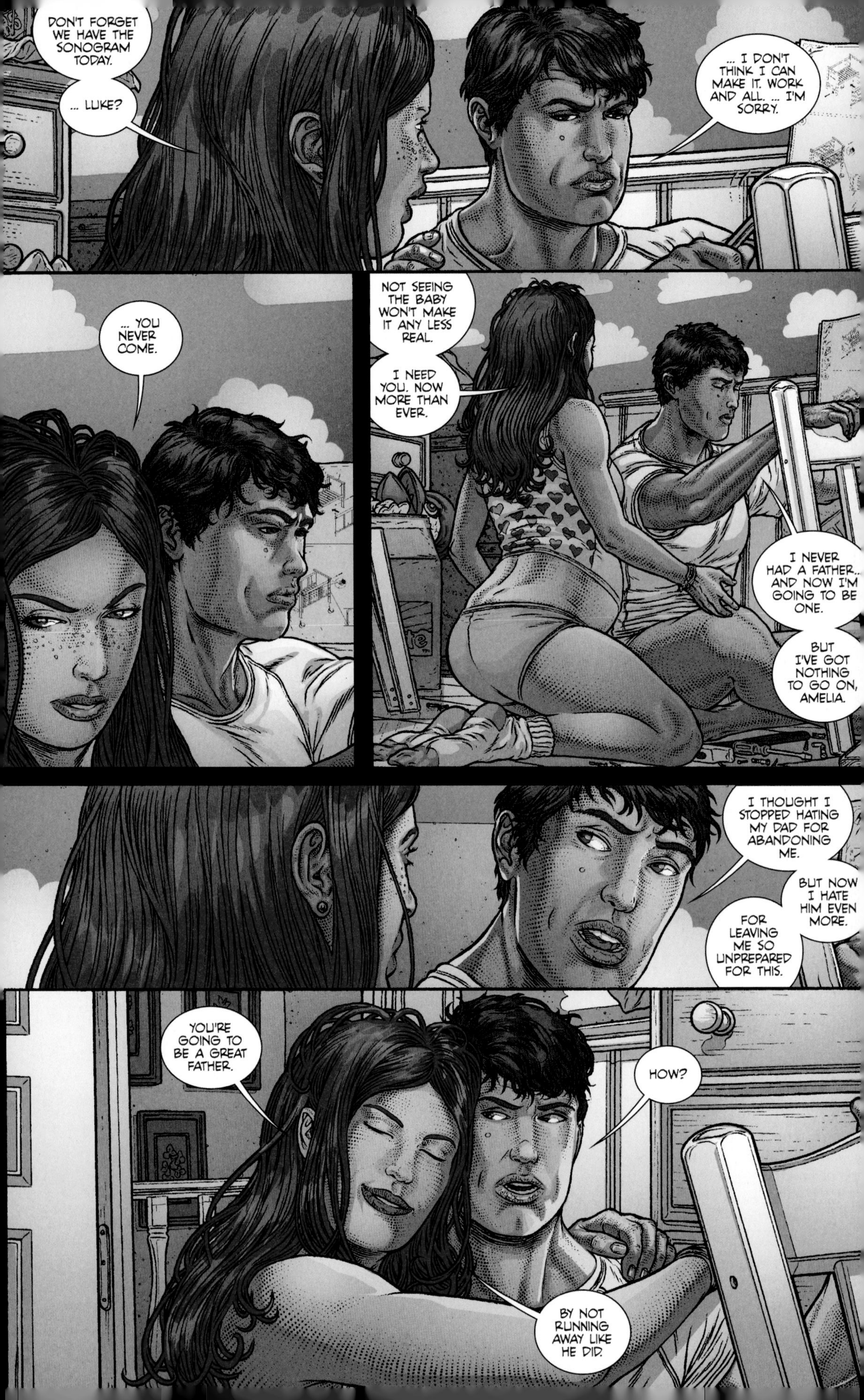
DON'T FORGET WE HAVE THE SONOGRAM TODAY.
... LUKE?
... I DON'T THINK I CAN MAKE IT. WORK AND ALL. ... I'M SORRY.
... YOU NEVER COME.
NOT SEEING THE BABY WON'T MAKE IT ANY LESS REAL.
I NEED YOU. NOW MORE THAN EVER.
I NEVER HAD A FATHER... AND NOW I'M GOING TO BE ONE.
BUT I'VE GOT NOTHING TO GO ON, AMELIA.
I THOUGHT I STOPPED HATING MY DAD FOR ABANDONING ME.
BUT NOW I HATE HIM EVEN MORE.
FOR LEAVING ME SO UNPREPARED FOR THIS.
YOU'RE GOING TO BE A GREAT FATHER.
HOW?
BY NOT RUNNING AWAY LIKE HE DID.

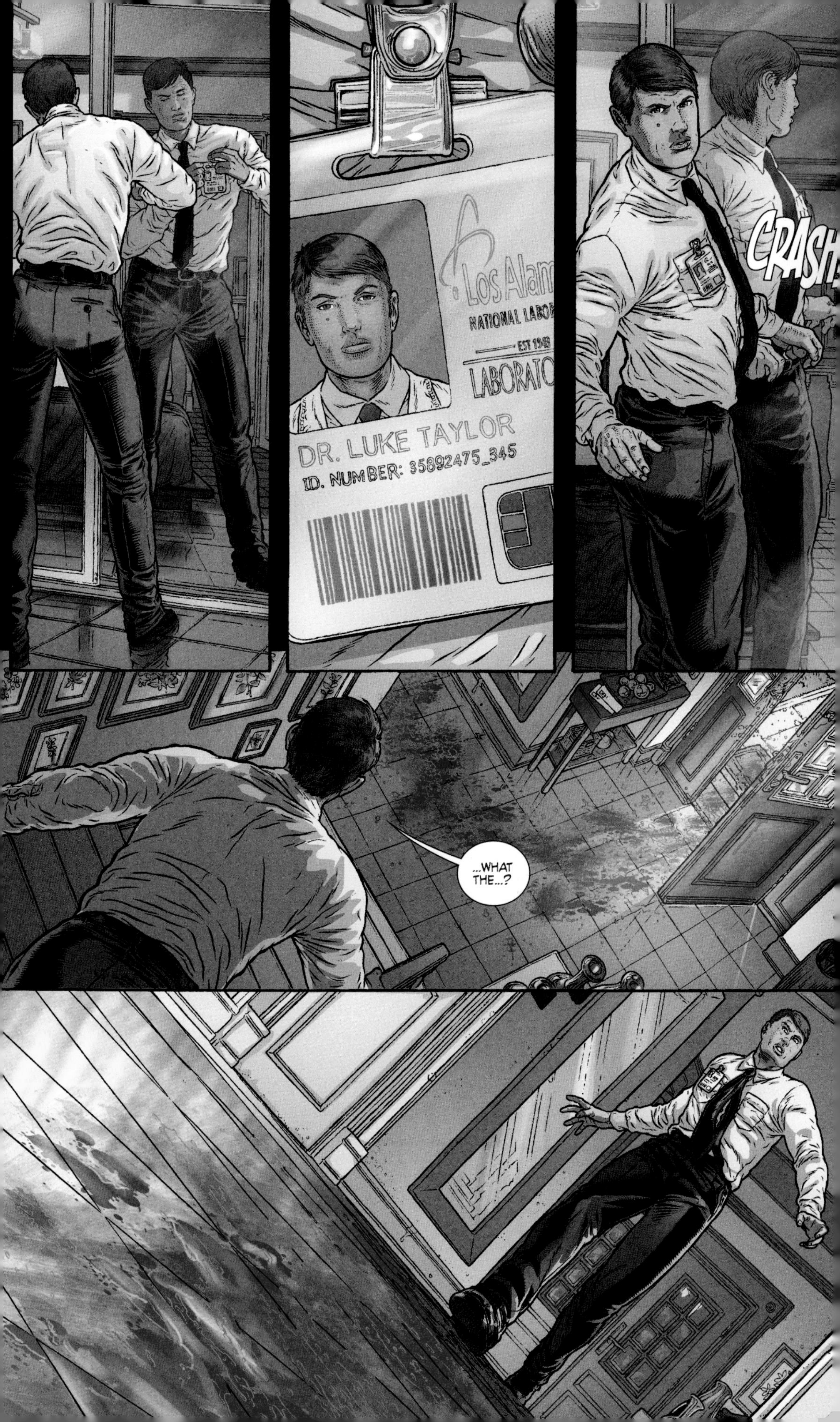
Los Alam
NATIONAL LABO
EST 1943
LABORATO
DR. LUKE TAYLOR
ID. NUMBER: 35892475_345
CRASH
...WHAT THE...?

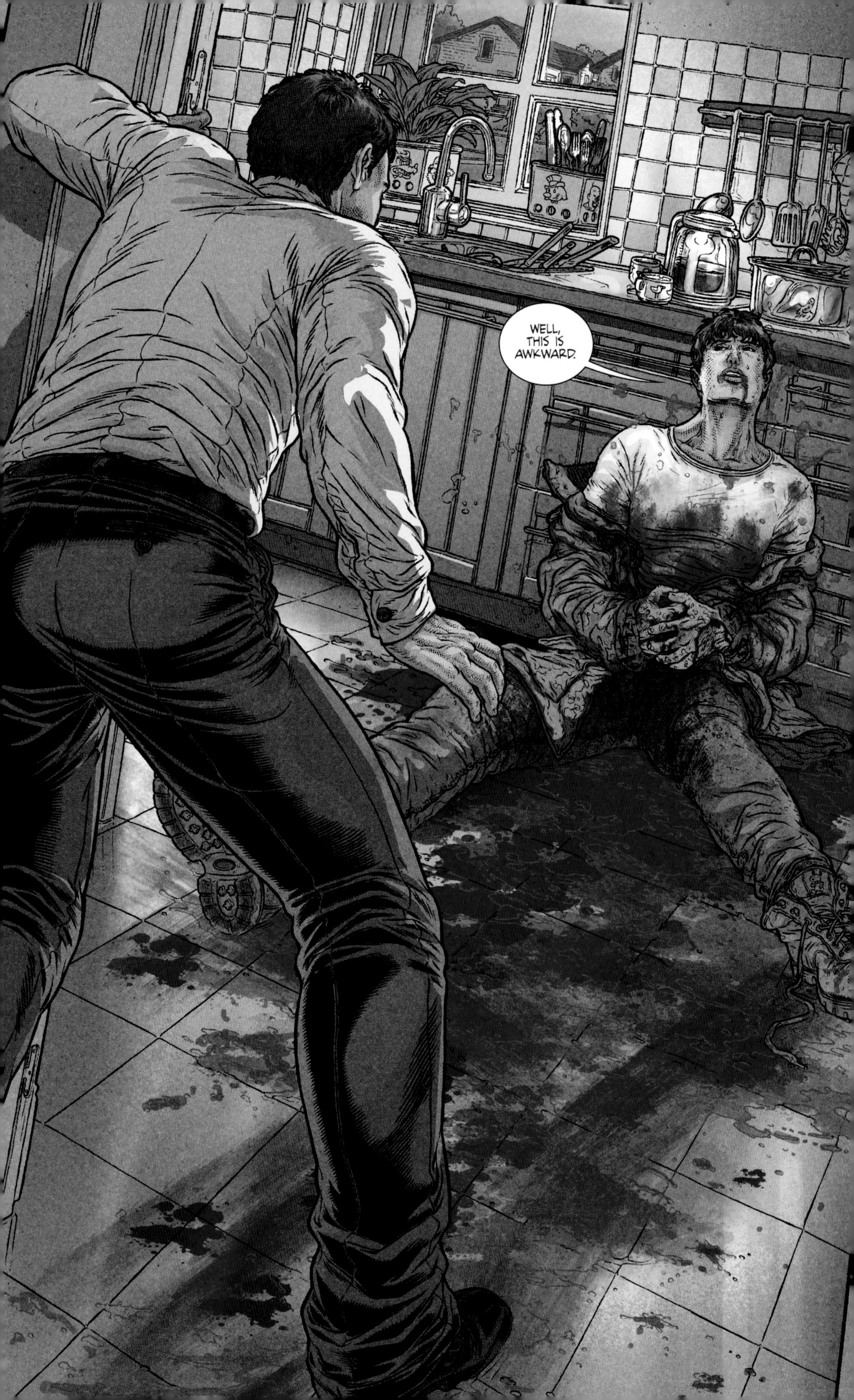
WELL, THIS IS AWKWARD.

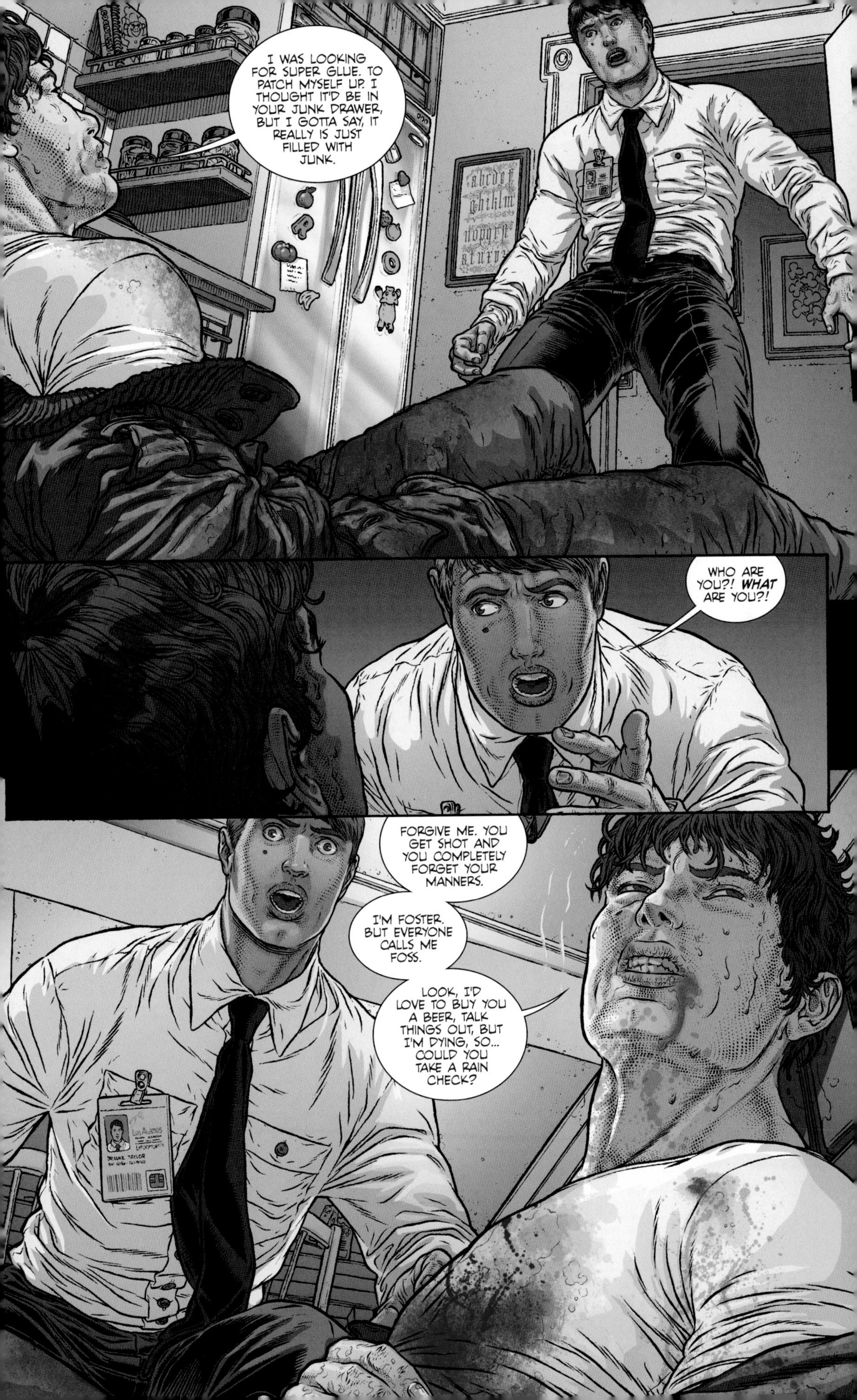
I WAS LOOKING FOR SUPER GLUE. TO PATCH MYSELF UP. I THOUGHT IT'D BE IN YOUR JUNK DRAWER, BUT I GOTTA SAY, IT REALLY IS JUST FILLED WITH JUNK.
WHO ARE YOU?! **WHAT** ARE YOU?!
FORGIVE ME. YOU GET SHOT AND YOU COMPLETELY FORGET YOUR MANNERS.
I'M FOSTER. BUT EVERYONE CALLS ME FOSS.
LOOK, I'D LOVE TO BUY YOU A BEER, TALK THINGS OUT, BUT I'M DYING, SO... COULD YOU TAKE A RAIN CHECK?

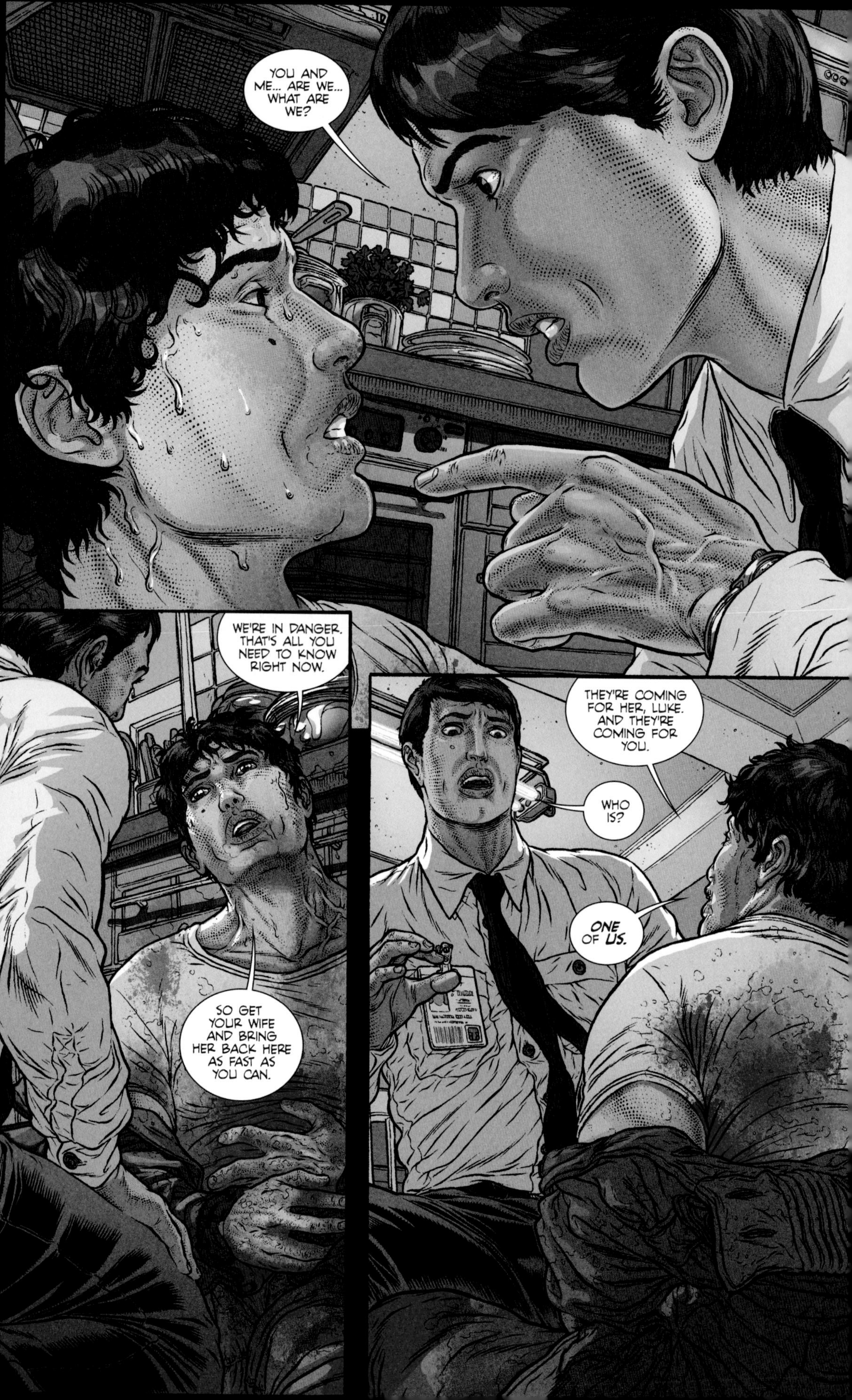
YOU AND ME... ARE WE... WHAT ARE WE?
WE'RE IN DANGER. THAT'S ALL YOU NEED TO KNOW RIGHT NOW.
SO GET YOUR WIFE AND BRING HER BACK HERE AS FAST AS YOU CAN.
THEY'RE COMING FOR HER, LUKE. AND THEY'RE COMING FOR YOU.
WHO IS?
ONE OF US.

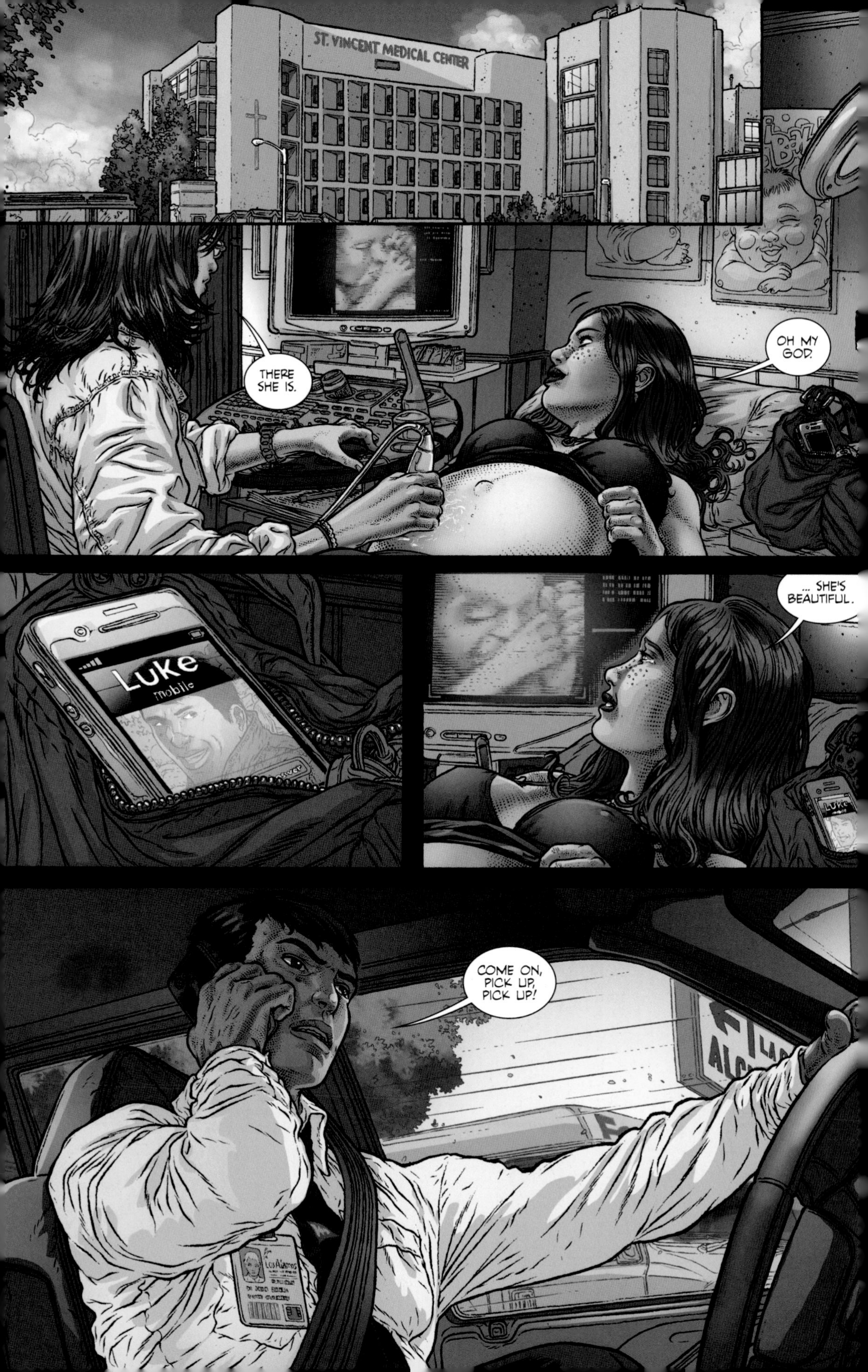
ST. VINCENT MEDICAL CENTER
THERE SHE IS.
OH MY GOD.
Luke
mobile
... SHE'S BEAUTIFUL.
COME ON, PICK UP, PICK UP!

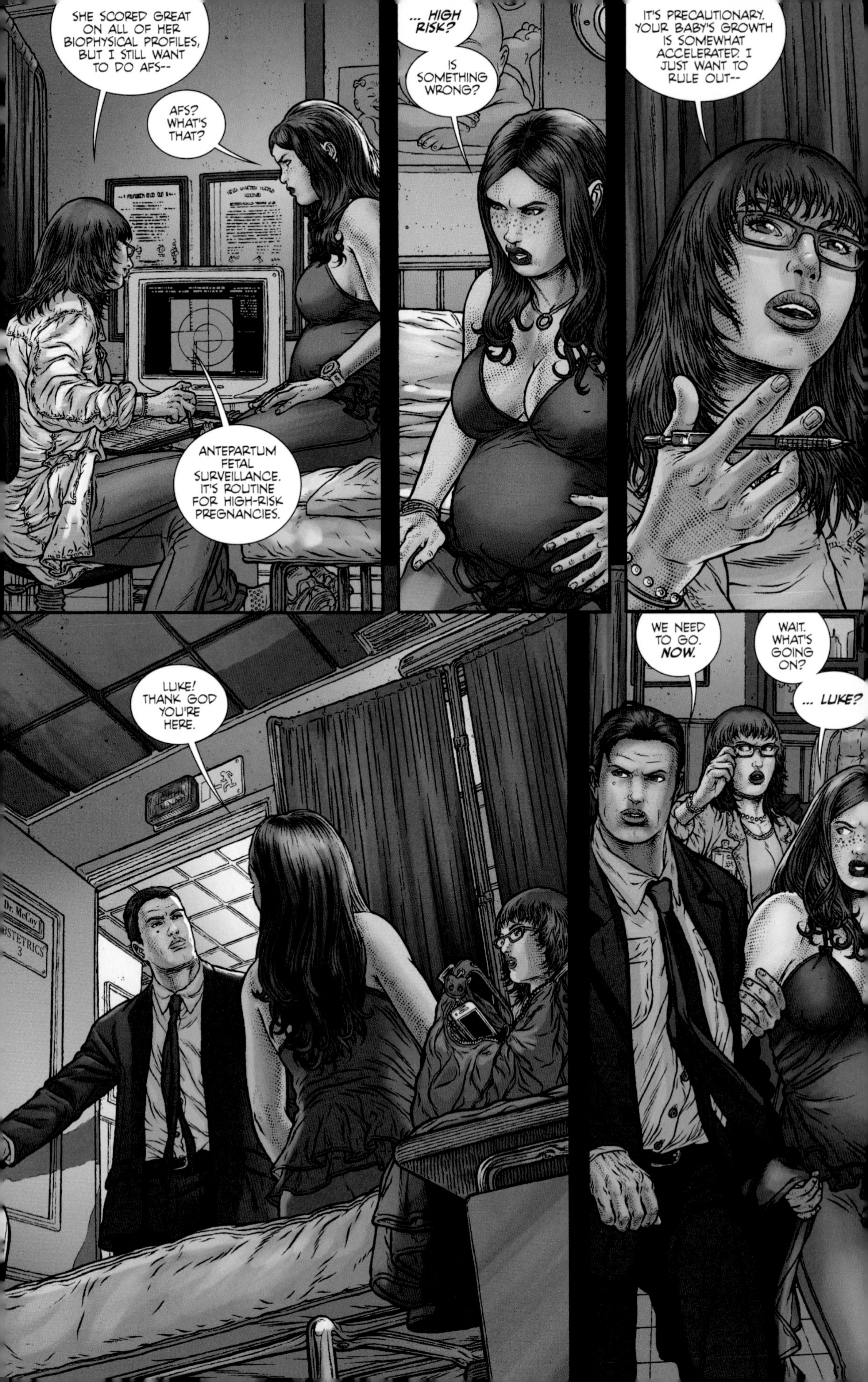
SHE SCORED GREAT ON ALL OF HER BIOPHYSICAL PROFILES, BUT I STILL WANT TO DO AFS--
AFS? WHAT'S THAT?
ANTEPARTUM FETAL SURVEILLANCE. IT'S ROUTINE FOR HIGH-RISK PREGNANCIES.
... HIGH RISK?
IS SOMETHING WRONG?
IT'S PRECAUTIONARY. YOUR BABY'S GROWTH IS SOMEWHAT ACCELERATED. I JUST WANT TO RULE OUT--
LUKE! THANK GOD YOU'RE HERE.
Dr. McCoy
BSTETRICS 3
WE NEED TO GO. NOW.
WAIT. WHAT'S GOING ON?
... LUKE?

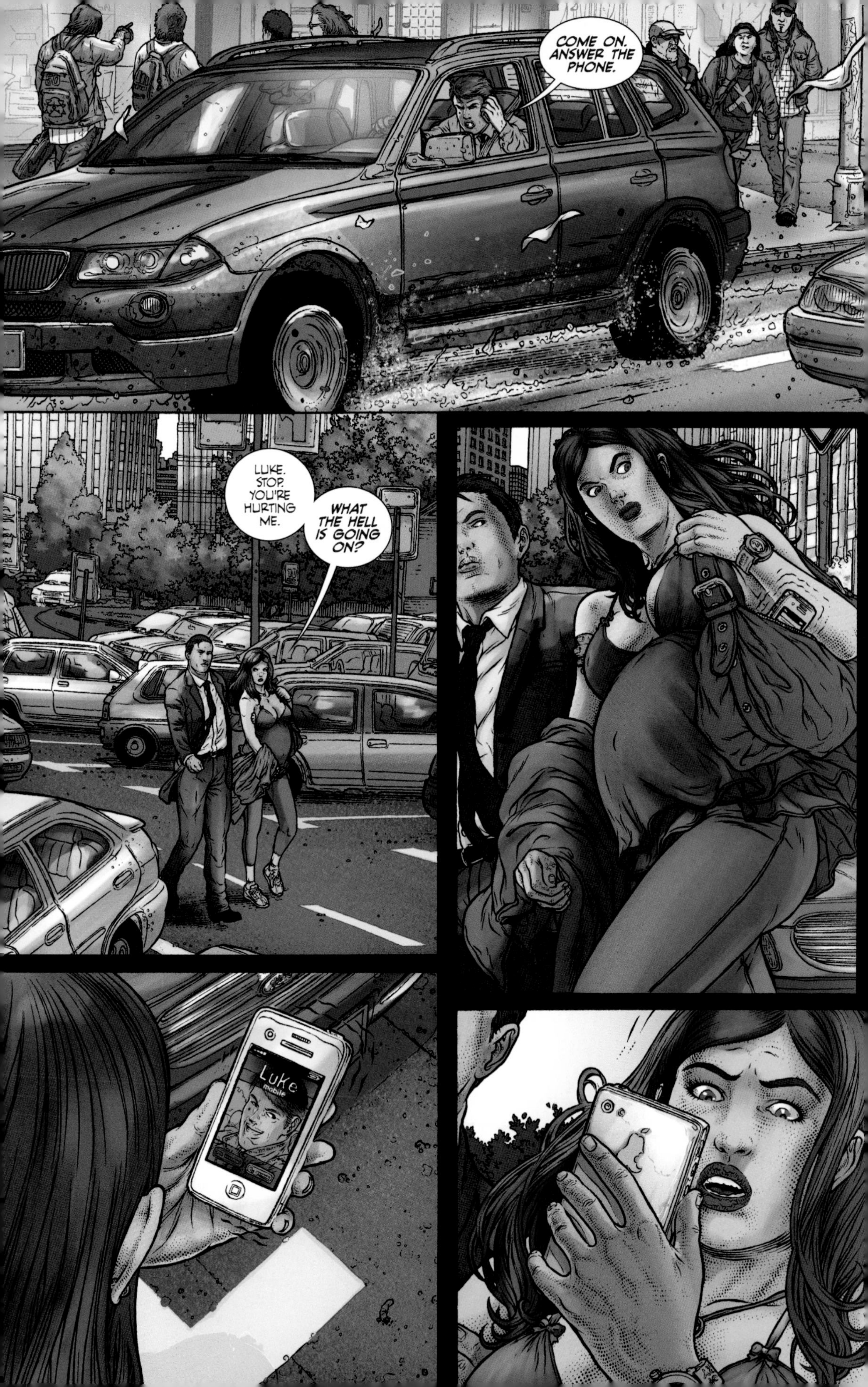
COME ON. ANSWER THE PHONE.
LUKE. STOP. YOU'RE HURTING ME.
WHAT THE HELL IS GOING ON?
Luke mobile

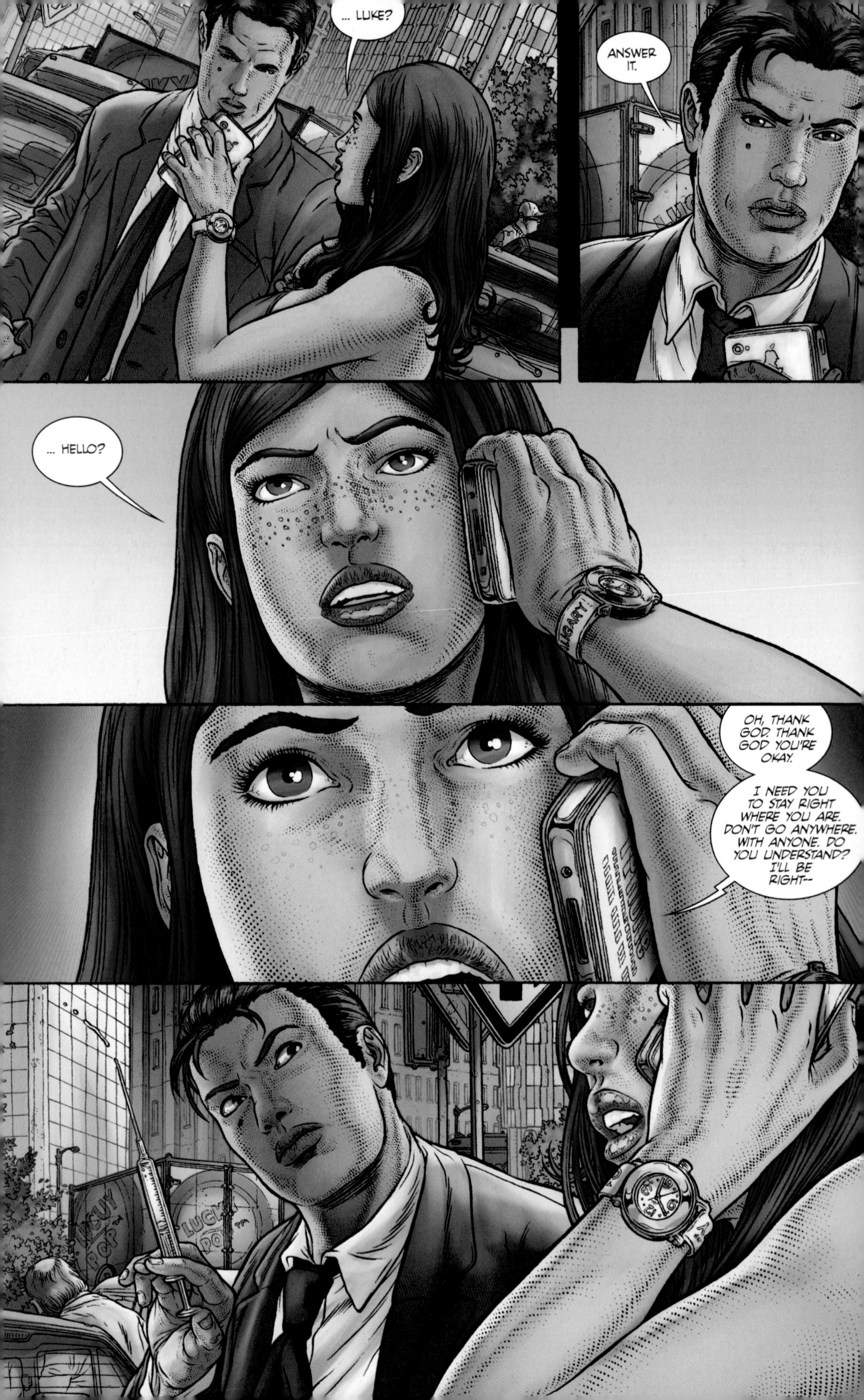
... LUKE?
ANSWER IT.
... HELLO?
OH, THANK GOD. THANK GOD YOU'RE OKAY.
I NEED YOU TO STAY RIGHT WHERE YOU ARE. DON'T GO ANYWHERE. WITH ANYONE. DO YOU UNDERSTAND? I'LL BE RIGHT--

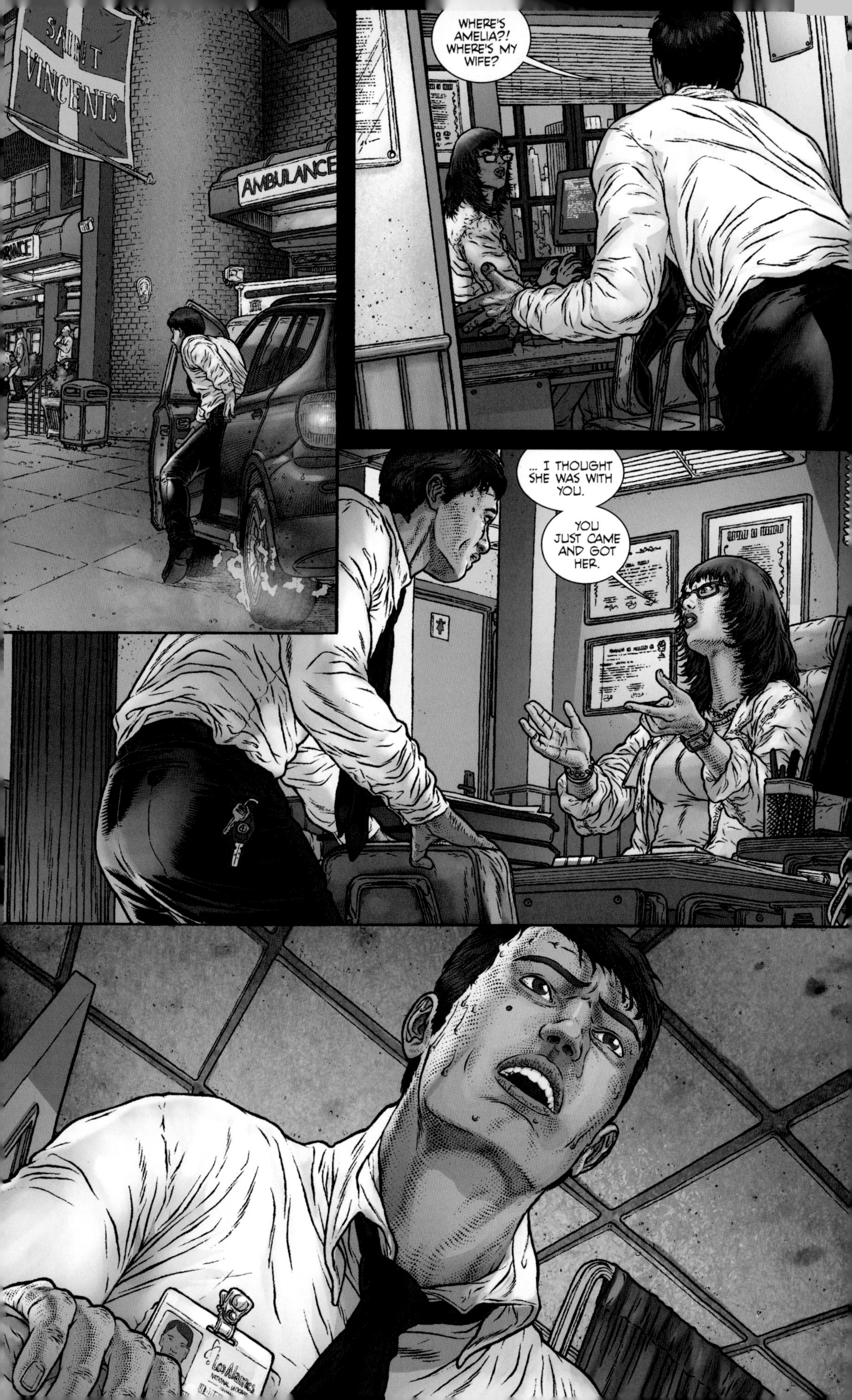
SAINT VINCENTS
AMBULANCE
WHERE'S AMELIA?! WHERE'S MY WIFE?
... I THOUGHT SHE WAS WITH YOU.
YOU JUST CAME AND GOT HER.
Los Alamos

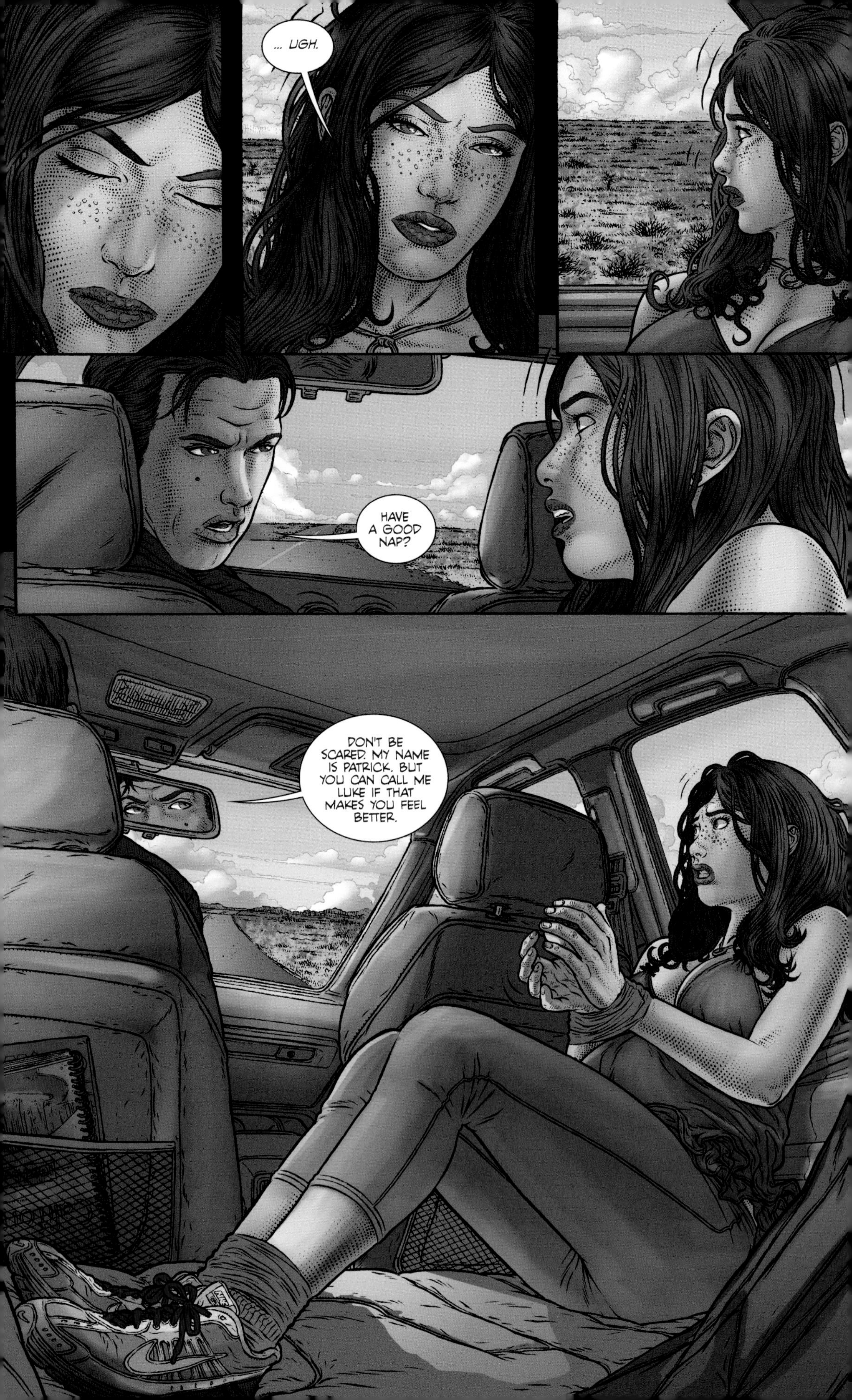
... UGH.
HAVE A GOOD NAP?
DON'T BE SCARED. MY NAME IS PATRICK. BUT YOU CAN CALL ME LUKE IF THAT MAKES YOU FEEL BETTER.

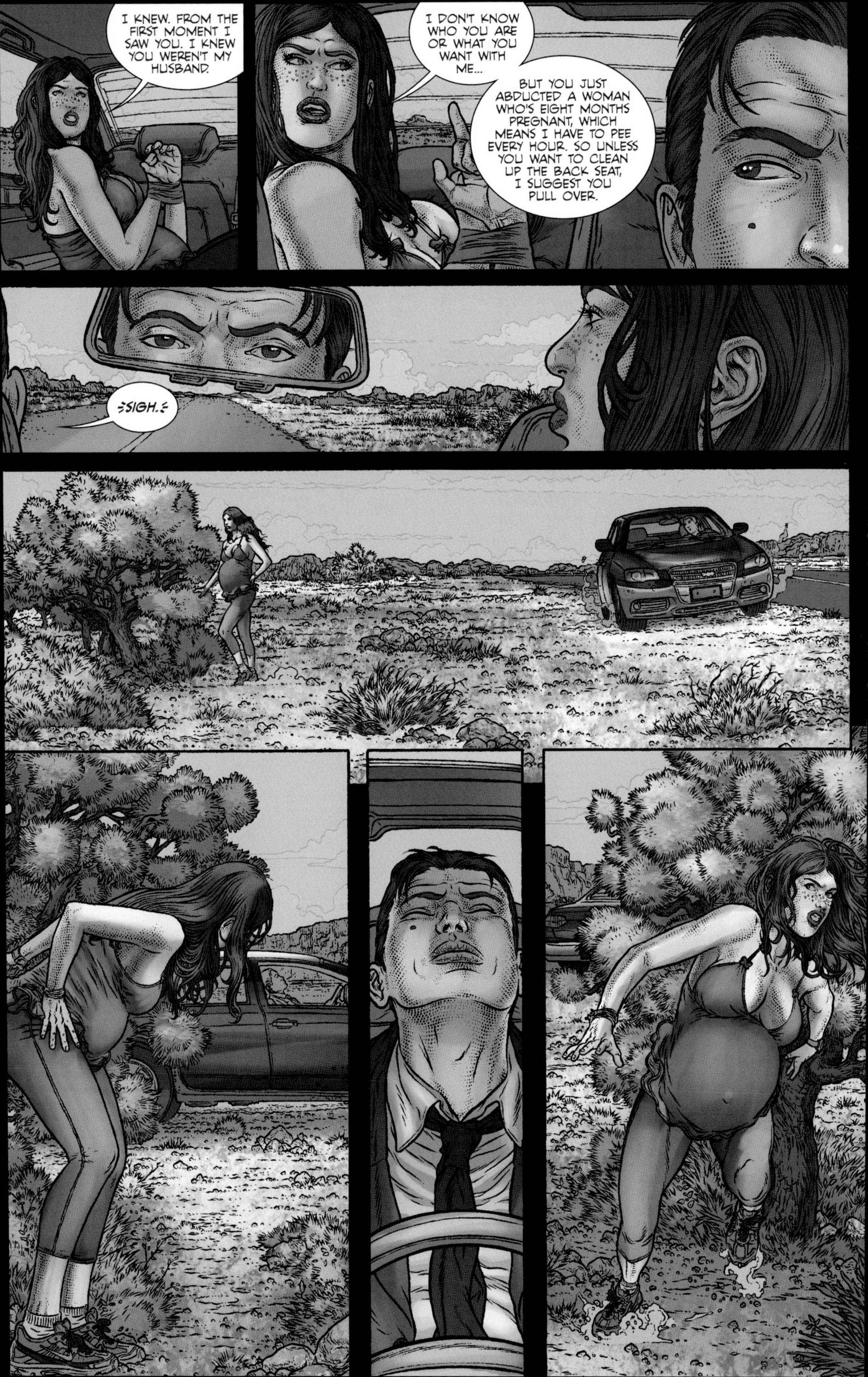
I KNEW. FROM THE FIRST MOMENT I SAW YOU. I KNEW YOU WEREN'T MY HUSBAND.
I DON'T KNOW WHO YOU ARE OR WHAT YOU WANT WITH ME...
BUT YOU JUST ABDUCTED A WOMAN WHO'S EIGHT MONTHS PREGNANT, WHICH MEANS I HAVE TO PEE EVERY HOUR. SO UNLESS YOU WANT TO CLEAN UP THE BACK SEAT, I SUGGEST YOU PULL OVER.
SIGH.

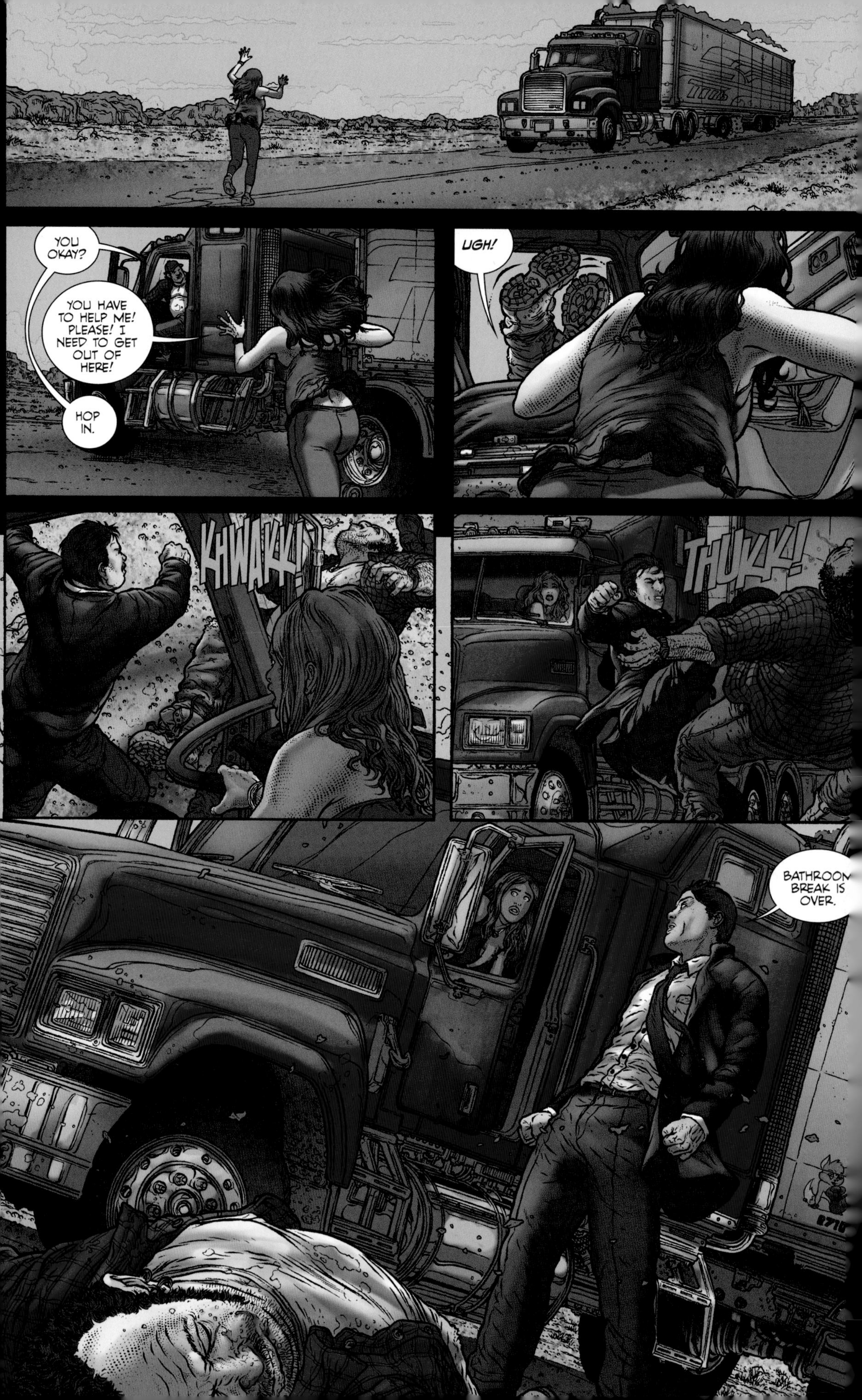
YOU OKAY?
YOU HAVE TO HELP ME! PLEASE! I NEED TO GET OUT OF HERE!
HOP IN.
UGH!
KHWAKK!
THUKK!
BATHROOM BREAK IS OVER.

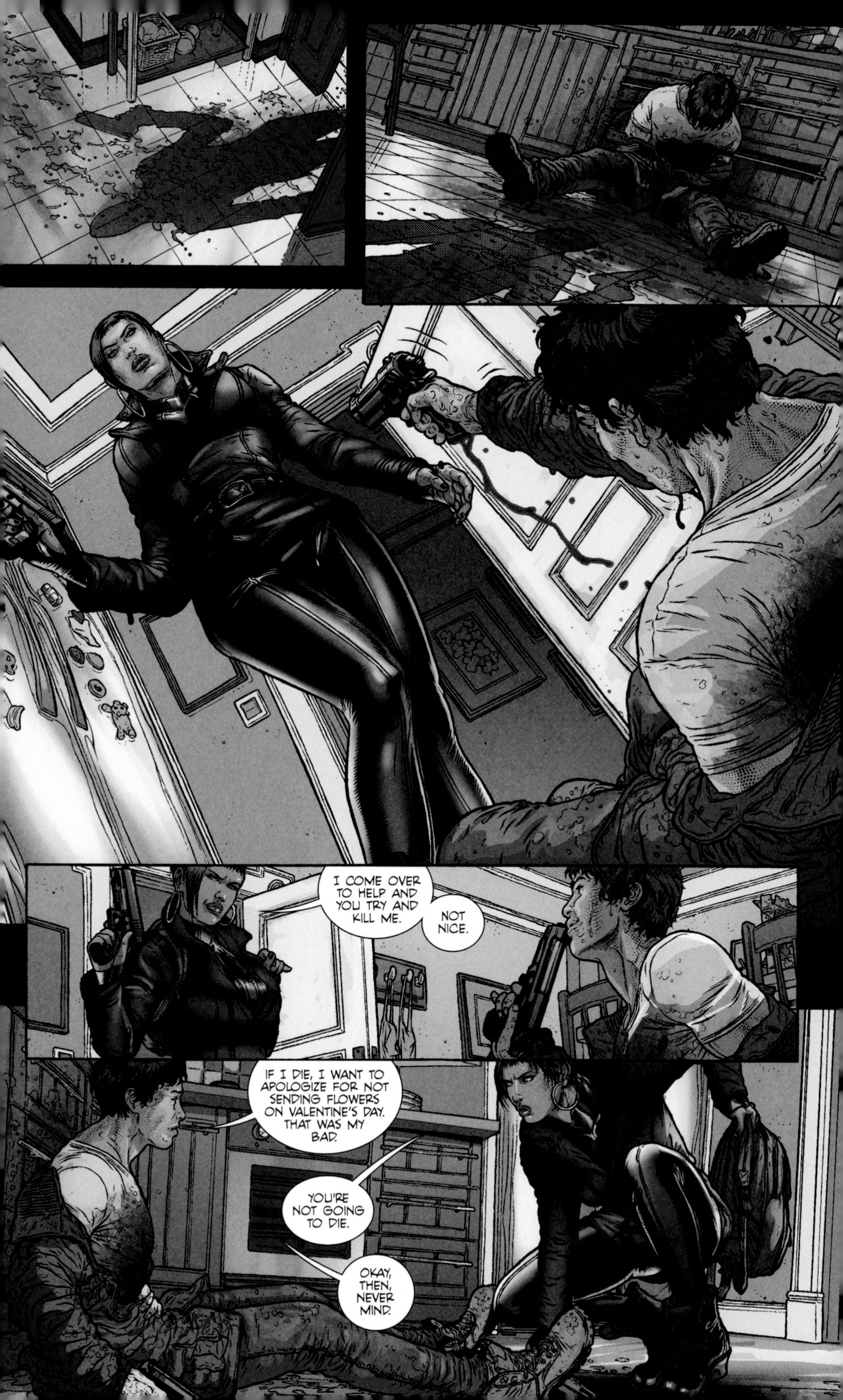
I COME OVER TO HELP AND YOU TRY AND KILL ME.
NOT NICE.
IF I DIE, I WANT TO APOLOGIZE FOR NOT SENDING FLOWERS ON VALENTINE'S DAY. THAT WAS MY BAD.
YOU'RE NOT GOING TO DIE.
OKAY, THEN, NEVER MIND.

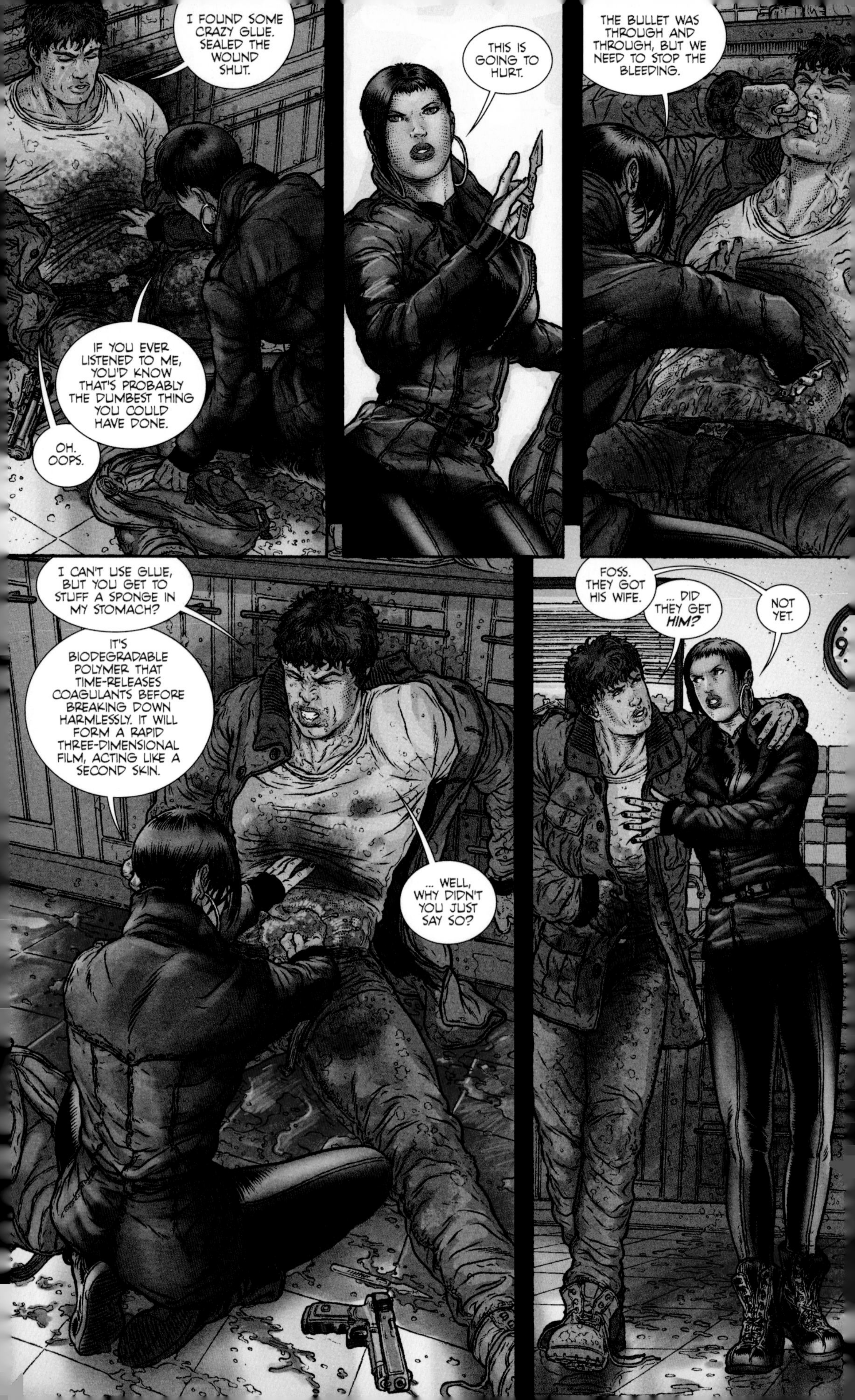
I FOUND SOME CRAZY GLUE. SEALED THE WOUND SHUT.
IF YOU EVER LISTENED TO ME, YOU'D KNOW THAT'S PROBABLY THE DUMBEST THING YOU COULD HAVE DONE.
OH. OOPS.
THIS IS GOING TO HURT.
THE BULLET WAS THROUGH AND THROUGH, BUT WE NEED TO STOP THE BLEEDING.
I CAN'T USE GLUE, BUT YOU GET TO STUFF A SPONGE IN MY STOMACH?
IT'S BIODEGRADABLE POLYMER THAT TIME-RELEASES COAGULANTS BEFORE BREAKING DOWN HARMLESSLY. IT WILL FORM A RAPID THREE-DIMENSIONAL FILM, ACTING LIKE A SECOND SKIN.
... WELL, WHY DIDN'T YOU JUST SAY SO?
FOSS. THEY GOT HIS WIFE.
... DID THEY GET *HIM?*
NOT YET.

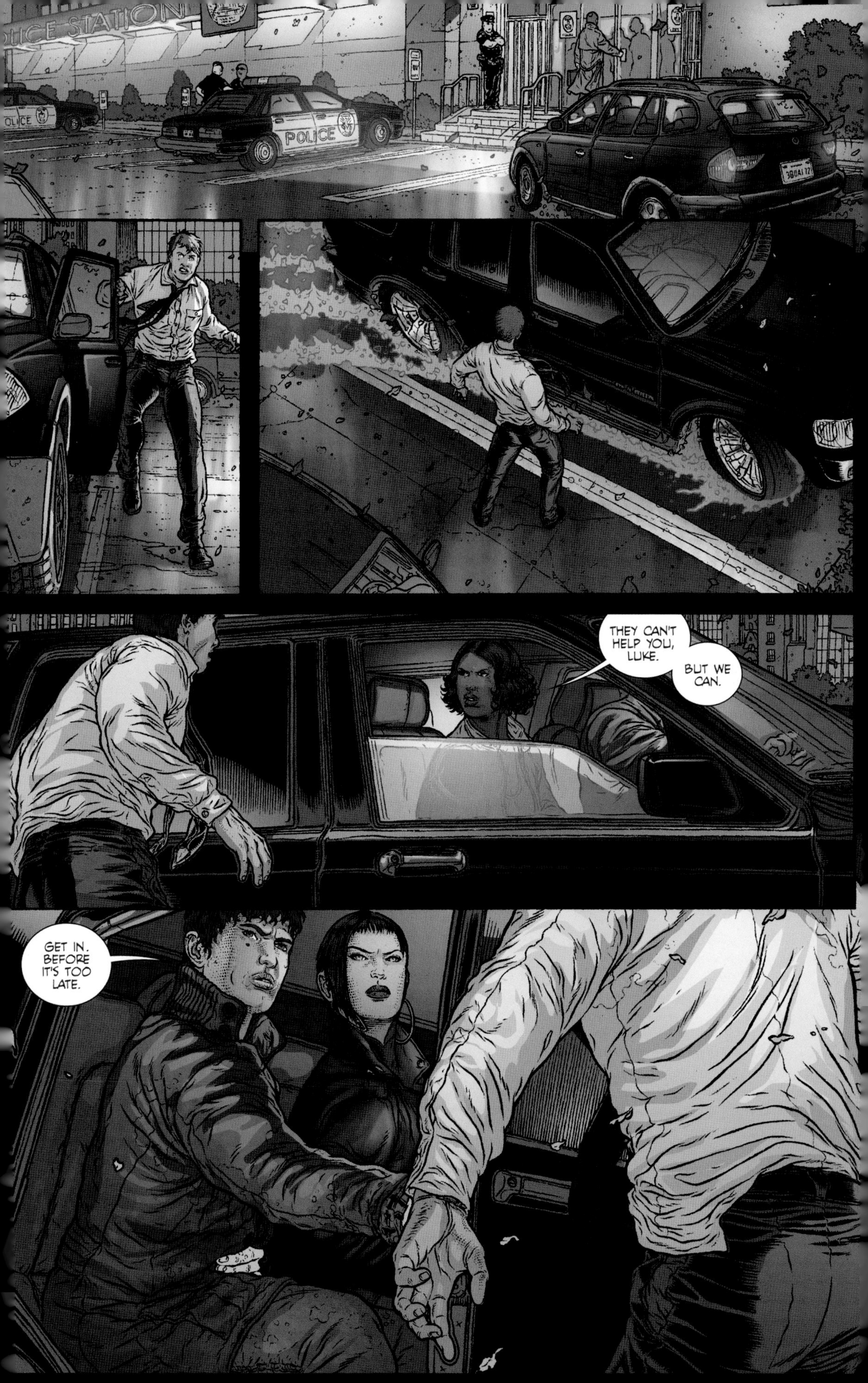
POLICE STATION
POLICE
THEY CAN'T HELP YOU, LUKE.
BUT WE CAN.
GET IN. BEFORE IT'S TOO LATE.

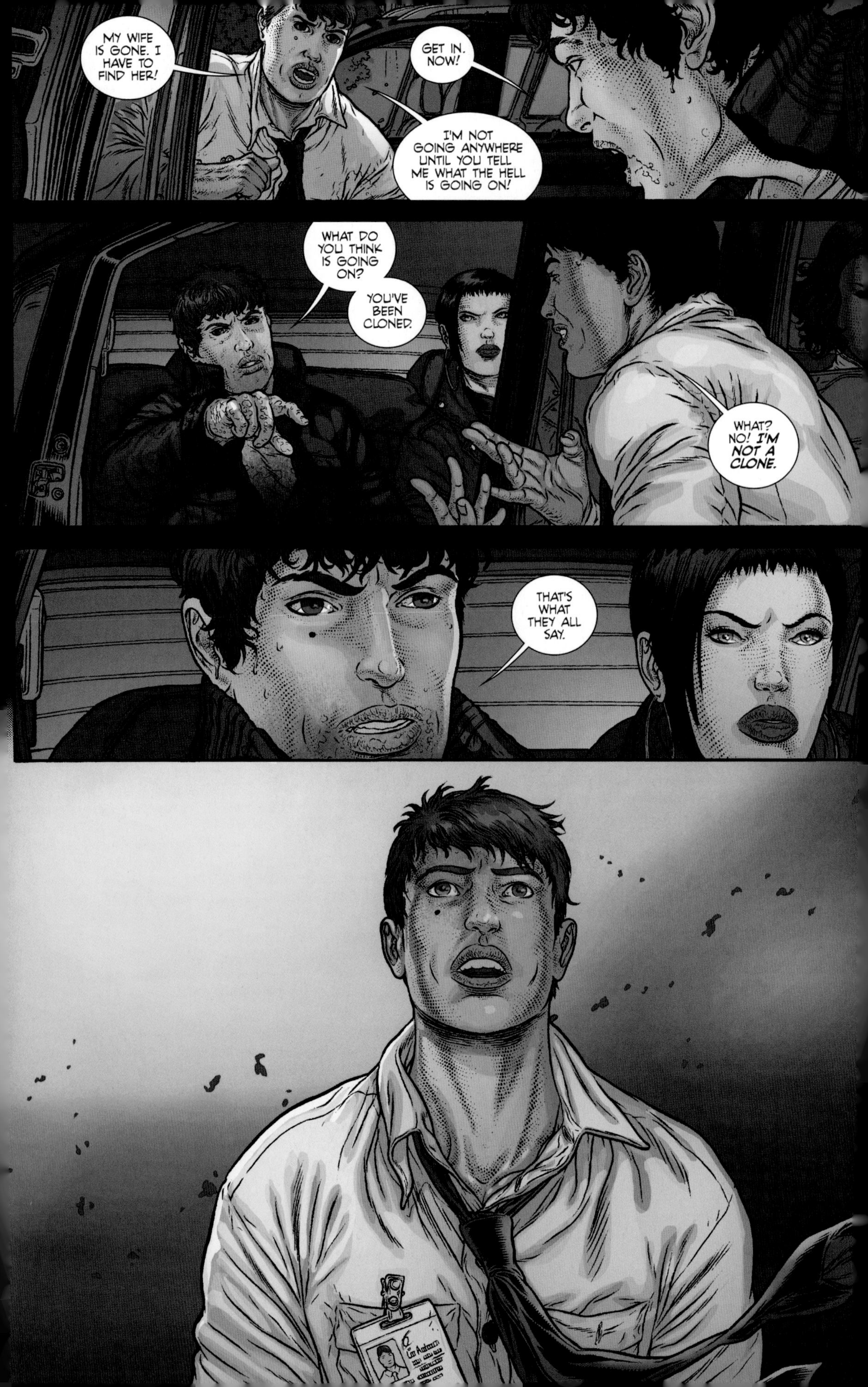
MY WIFE IS GONE. I HAVE TO FIND HER!
GET IN. NOW!
I'M NOT GOING ANYWHERE UNTIL YOU TELL ME WHAT THE HELL IS GOING ON!
WHAT DO YOU THINK IS GOING ON?
YOU'VE BEEN CLONED.
WHAT? NO! I'M NOT A CLONE.
THAT'S WHAT THEY ALL SAY.

CHAPTER 2

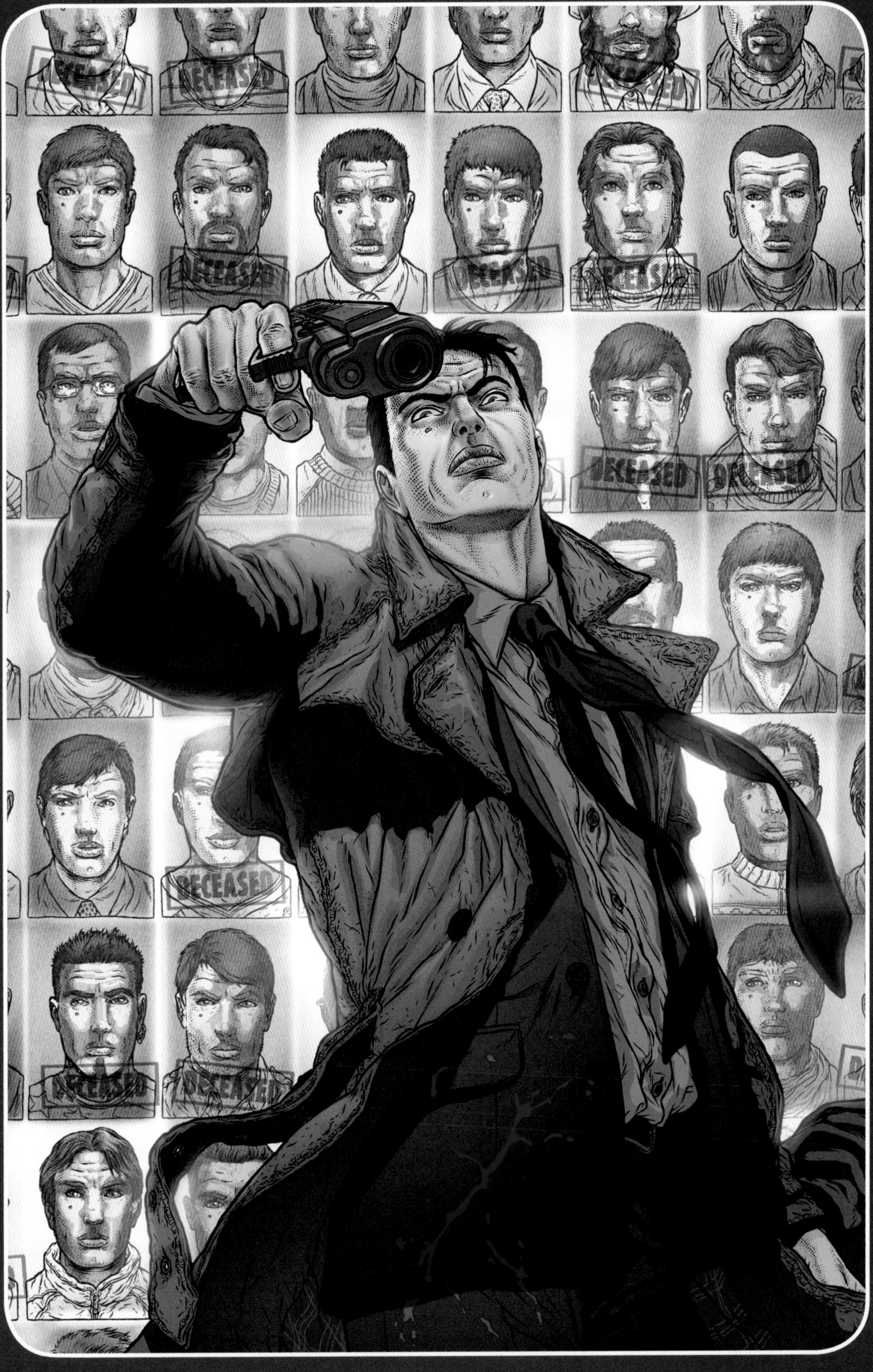
DECEASED
DECEASED
DECEASED
DECEASED
DECEASED
DECEASED
DECEASED
DECEASED
DECEASED
DECEASED
DECEASED

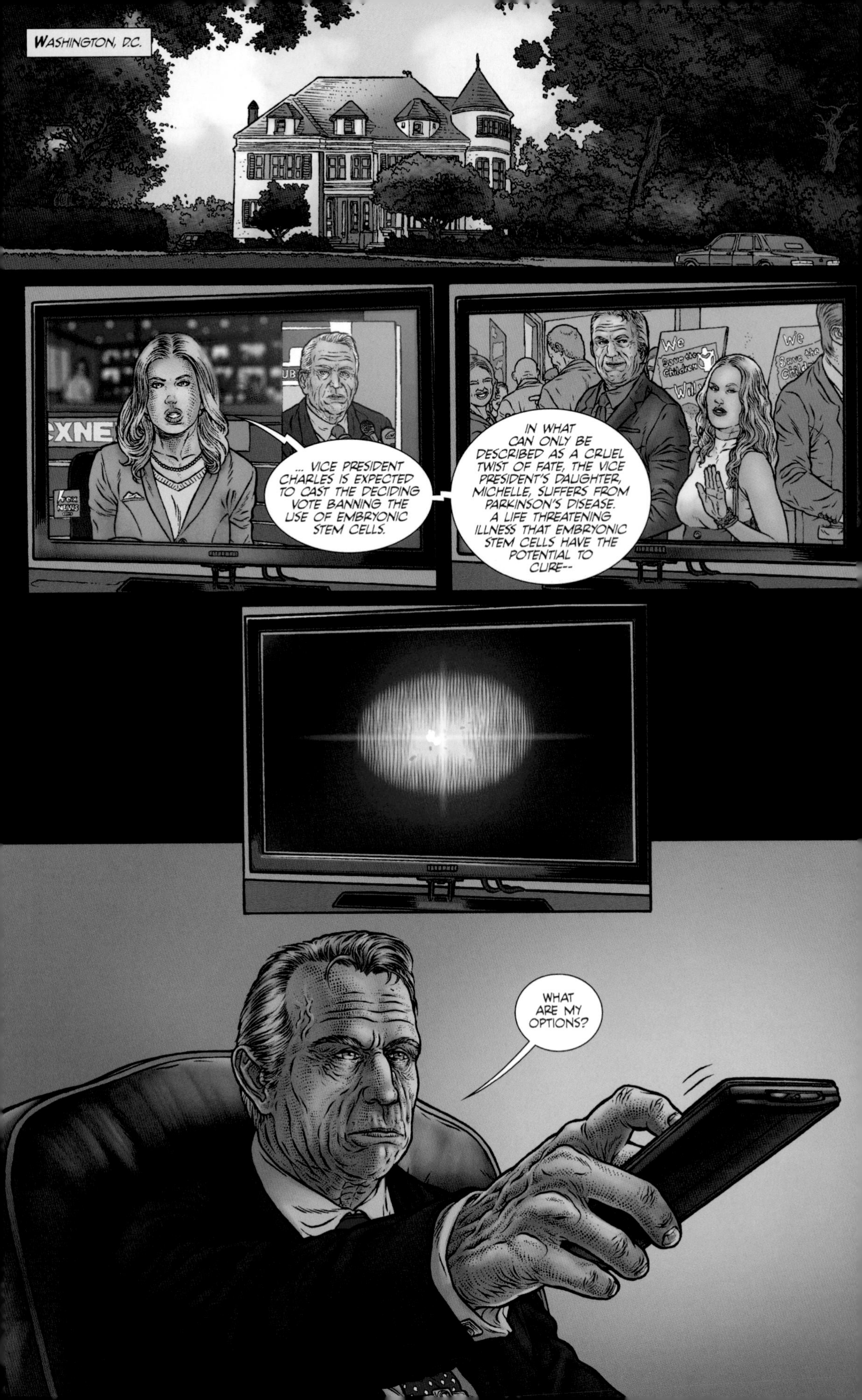
WASHINGTON, D.C.
... VICE PRESIDENT CHARLES IS EXPECTED TO CAST THE DECIDING VOTE BANNING THE USE OF EMBRYONIC STEM CELLS.
IN WHAT CAN ONLY BE DESCRIBED AS A CRUEL TWIST OF FATE, THE VICE PRESIDENT'S DAUGHTER, MICHELLE, SUFFERS FROM PARKINSON'S DISEASE. A LIFE THREATENING ILLNESS THAT EMBRYONIC STEM CELLS HAVE THE POTENTIAL TO CURE--
WHAT ARE MY OPTIONS?

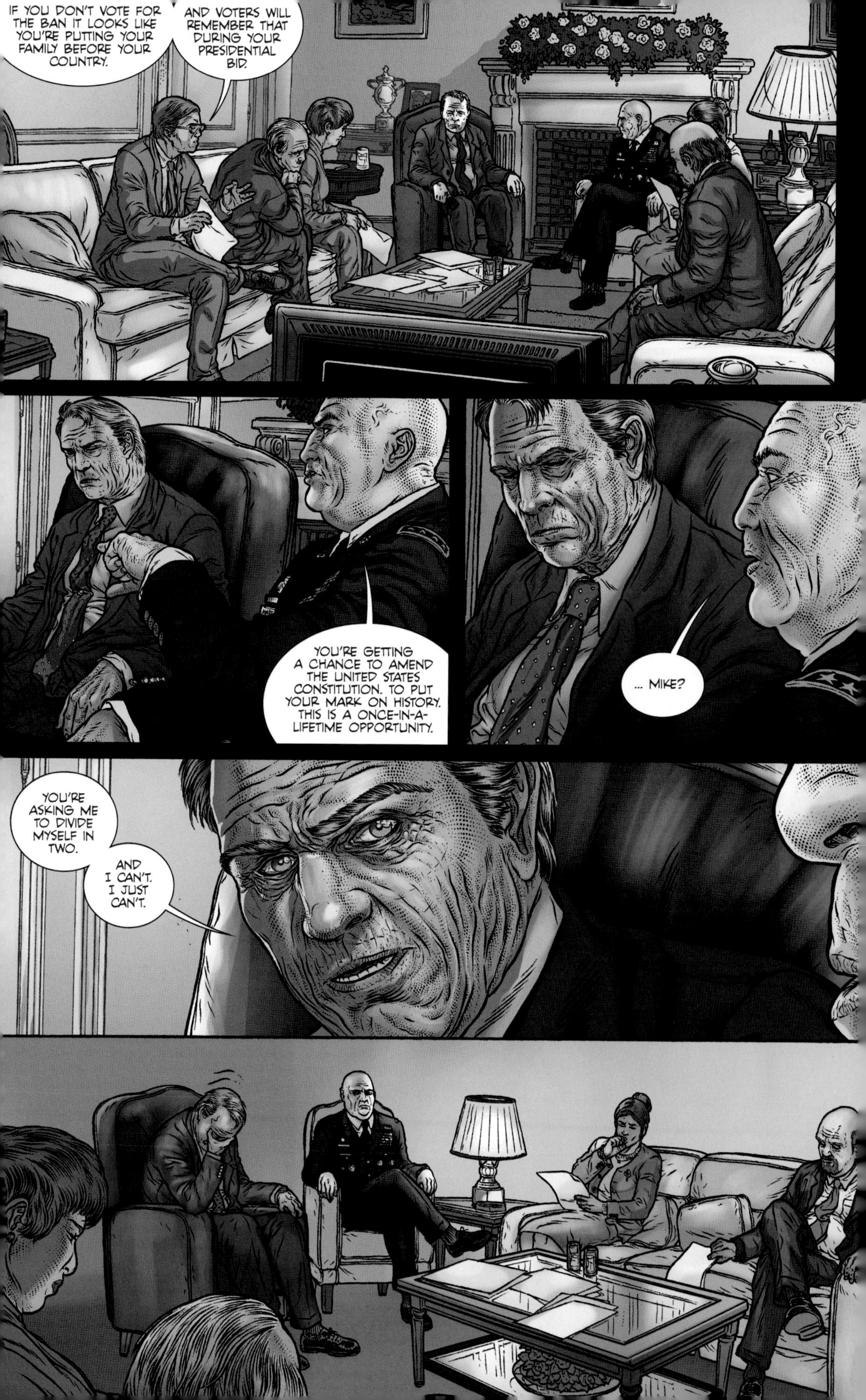
IF YOU DON'T VOTE FOR THE BAN IT LOOKS LIKE YOU'RE PUTTING YOUR FAMILY BEFORE YOUR COUNTRY.
AND VOTERS WILL REMEMBER THAT DURING YOUR PRESIDENTIAL BID.
YOU'RE GETTING A CHANCE TO AMEND THE UNITED STATES CONSTITUTION. TO PUT YOUR MARK ON HISTORY. THIS IS A ONCE-IN-A-LIFETIME OPPORTUNITY.
... MIKE?
YOU'RE ASKING ME TO DIVIDE MYSELF IN TWO.
AND I CAN'T. I JUST CAN'T.

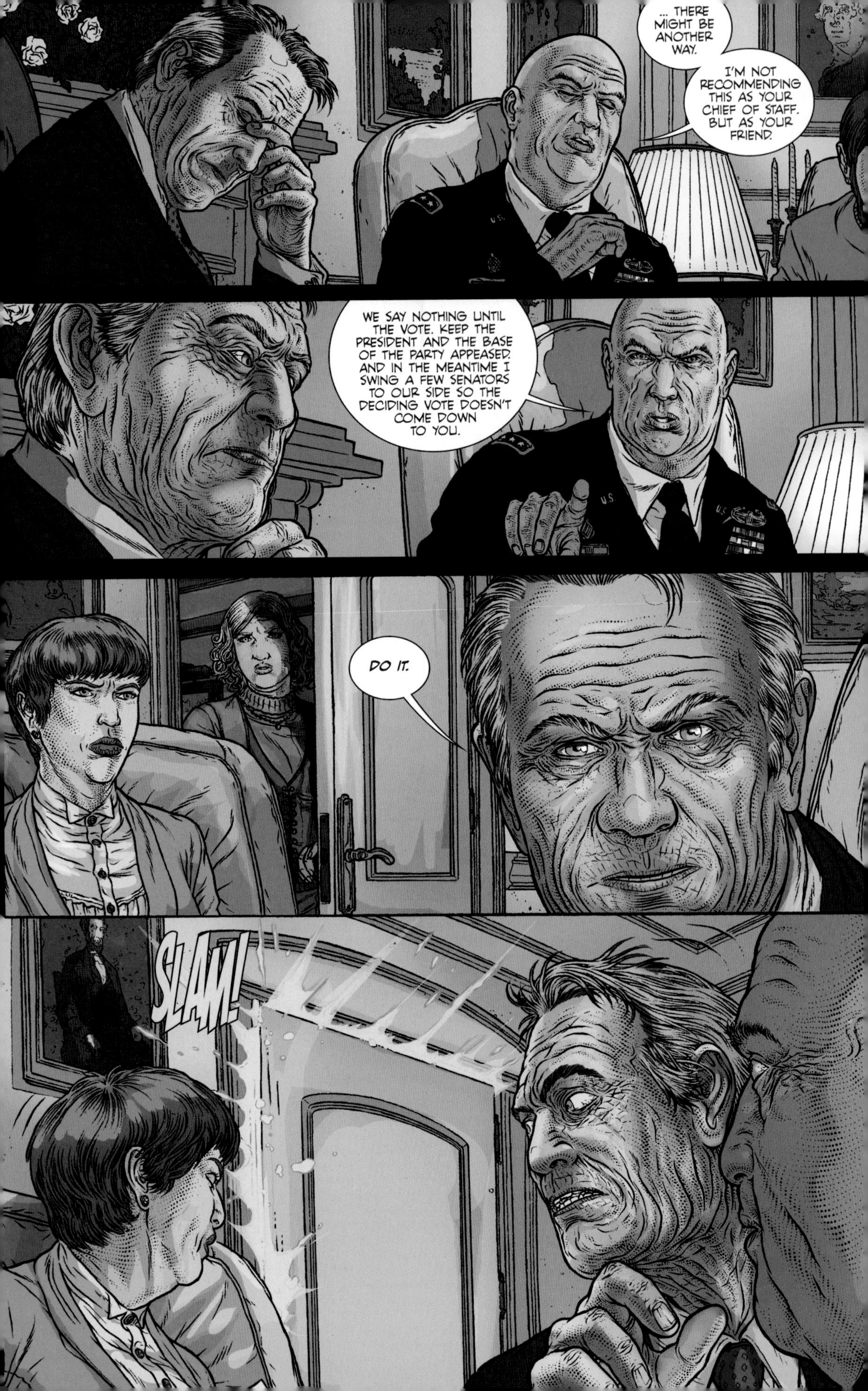
... THERE MIGHT BE ANOTHER WAY.
I'M NOT RECOMMENDING THIS AS YOUR CHIEF OF STAFF. BUT AS YOUR FRIEND.
WE SAY NOTHING UNTIL THE VOTE. KEEP THE PRESIDENT AND THE BASE OF THE PARTY APPEASED. AND IN THE MEANTIME I SWING A FEW SENATORS TO OUR SIDE SO THE DECIDING VOTE DOESN'T COME DOWN TO YOU.
DO IT.
SLAM!

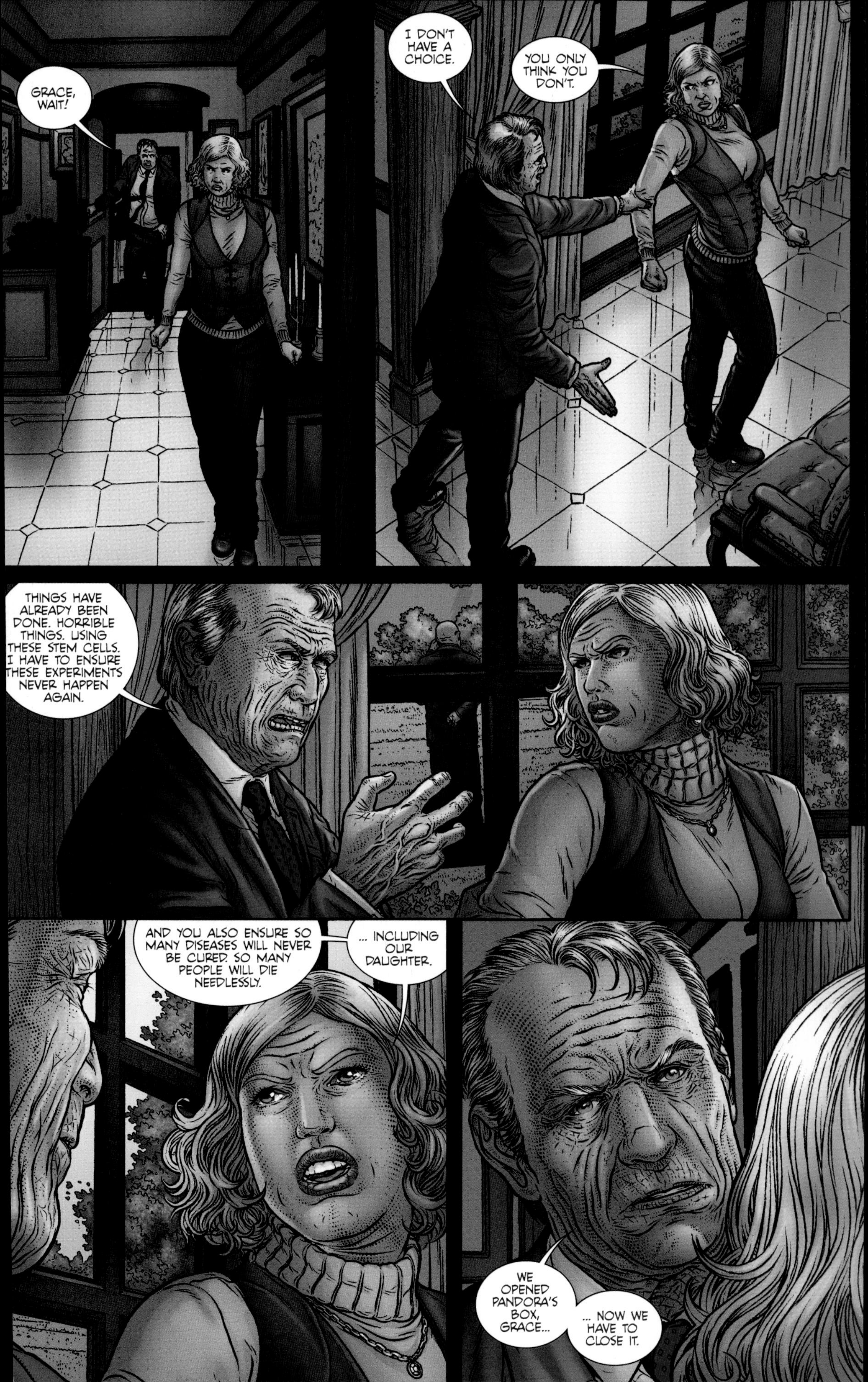
GRACE, WAIT!
I DON'T HAVE A CHOICE.
YOU ONLY THINK YOU DON'T.
THINGS HAVE ALREADY BEEN DONE. HORRIBLE THINGS. USING THESE STEM CELLS. I HAVE TO ENSURE THESE EXPERIMENTS NEVER HAPPEN AGAIN.
AND YOU ALSO ENSURE SO MANY DISEASES WILL NEVER BE CURED. SO MANY PEOPLE WILL DIE NEEDLESSLY.
... INCLUDING OUR DAUGHTER.
WE OPENED PANDORA'S BOX, GRACE...
... NOW WE HAVE TO CLOSE IT.

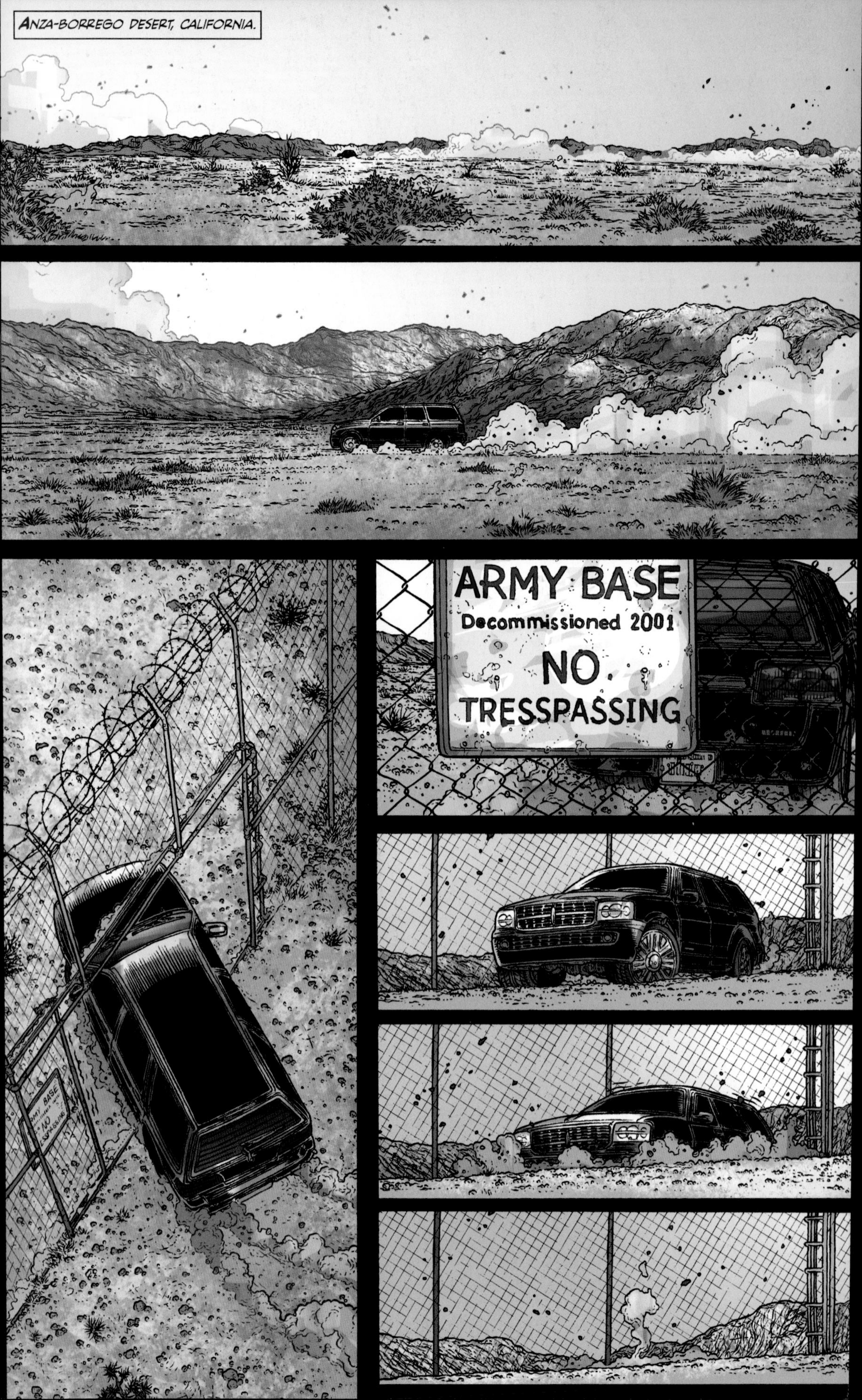
ANZA-BORREGO DESERT, CALIFORNIA.
ARMY BASE
Decommissioned 2001
NO
TRESSPASSING

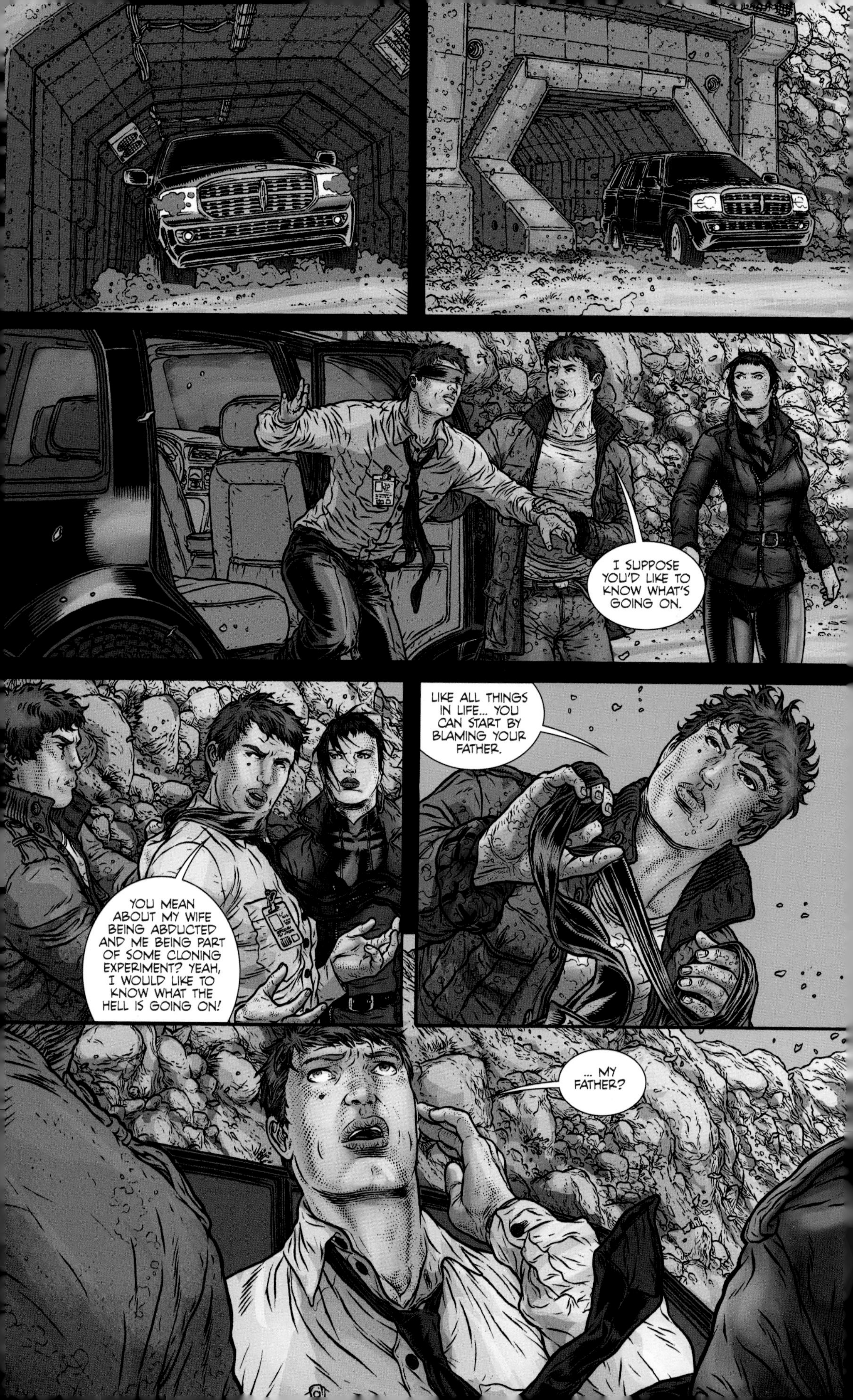
I SUPPOSE YOU'D LIKE TO KNOW WHAT'S GOING ON.
YOU MEAN ABOUT MY WIFE BEING ABDUCTED AND ME BEING PART OF SOME CLONING EXPERIMENT? YEAH, I WOULD LIKE TO KNOW WHAT THE HELL IS GOING ON!
LIKE ALL THINGS IN LIFE... YOU CAN START BY BLAMING YOUR FATHER.
... MY FATHER?

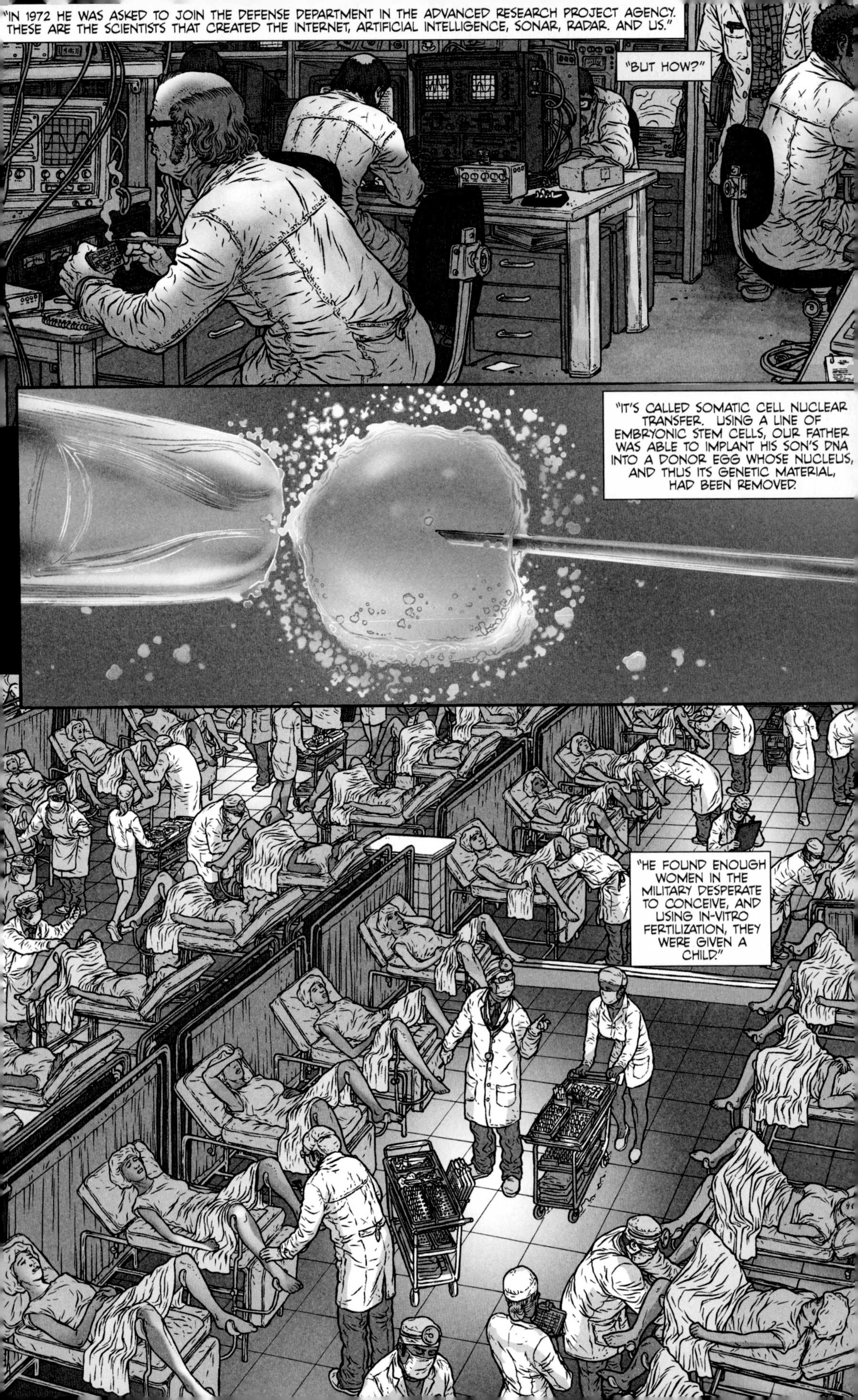
"IN 1972 HE WAS ASKED TO JOIN THE DEFENSE DEPARTMENT IN THE ADVANCED RESEARCH PROJECT AGENCY. THESE ARE THE SCIENTISTS THAT CREATED THE INTERNET, ARTIFICIAL INTELLIGENCE, SONAR, RADAR. AND US."
"BUT HOW?"
"IT'S CALLED SOMATIC CELL NUCLEAR TRANSFER. USING A LINE OF EMBRYONIC STEM CELLS, OUR FATHER WAS ABLE TO IMPLANT HIS SON'S DNA INTO A DONOR EGG WHOSE NUCLEUS, AND THUS ITS GENETIC MATERIAL, HAD BEEN REMOVED.
"HE FOUND ENOUGH WOMEN IN THE MILITARY DESPERATE TO CONCEIVE, AND USING IN-VITRO FERTILIZATION, THEY WERE GIVEN A CHILD."

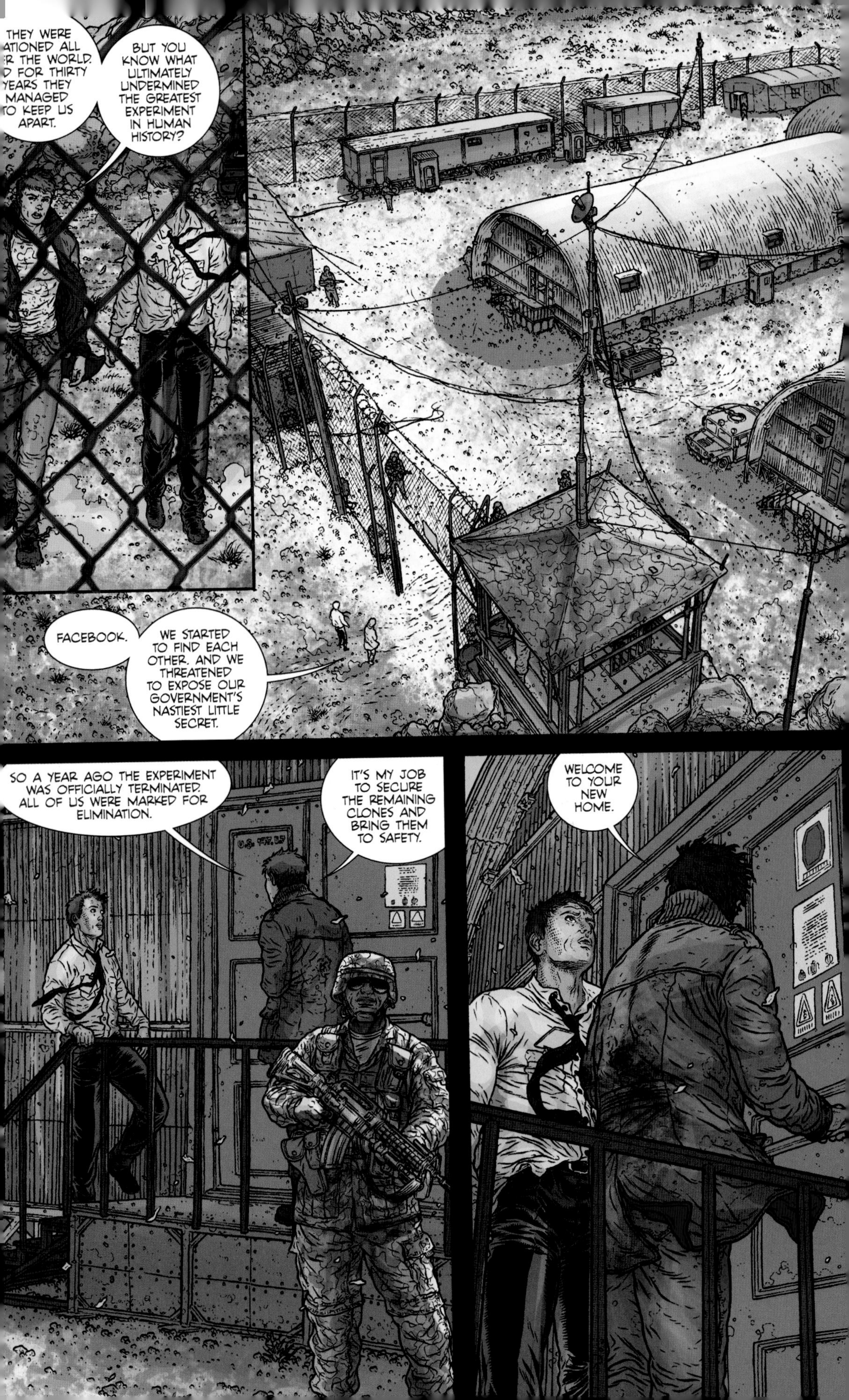
THEY WERE ATIONED ALL R THE WORLD. D FOR THIRTY YEARS THEY MANAGED TO KEEP US APART.
BUT YOU KNOW WHAT ULTIMATELY UNDERMINED THE GREATEST EXPERIMENT IN HUMAN HISTORY?
FACEBOOK.
WE STARTED TO FIND EACH OTHER. AND WE THREATENED TO EXPOSE OUR GOVERNMENT'S NASTIEST LITTLE SECRET.
SO A YEAR AGO THE EXPERIMENT WAS OFFICIALLY TERMINATED. ALL OF US WERE MARKED FOR ELIMINATION.
IT'S MY JOB TO SECURE THE REMAINING CLONES AND BRING THEM TO SAFETY.
WELCOME TO YOUR NEW HOME.

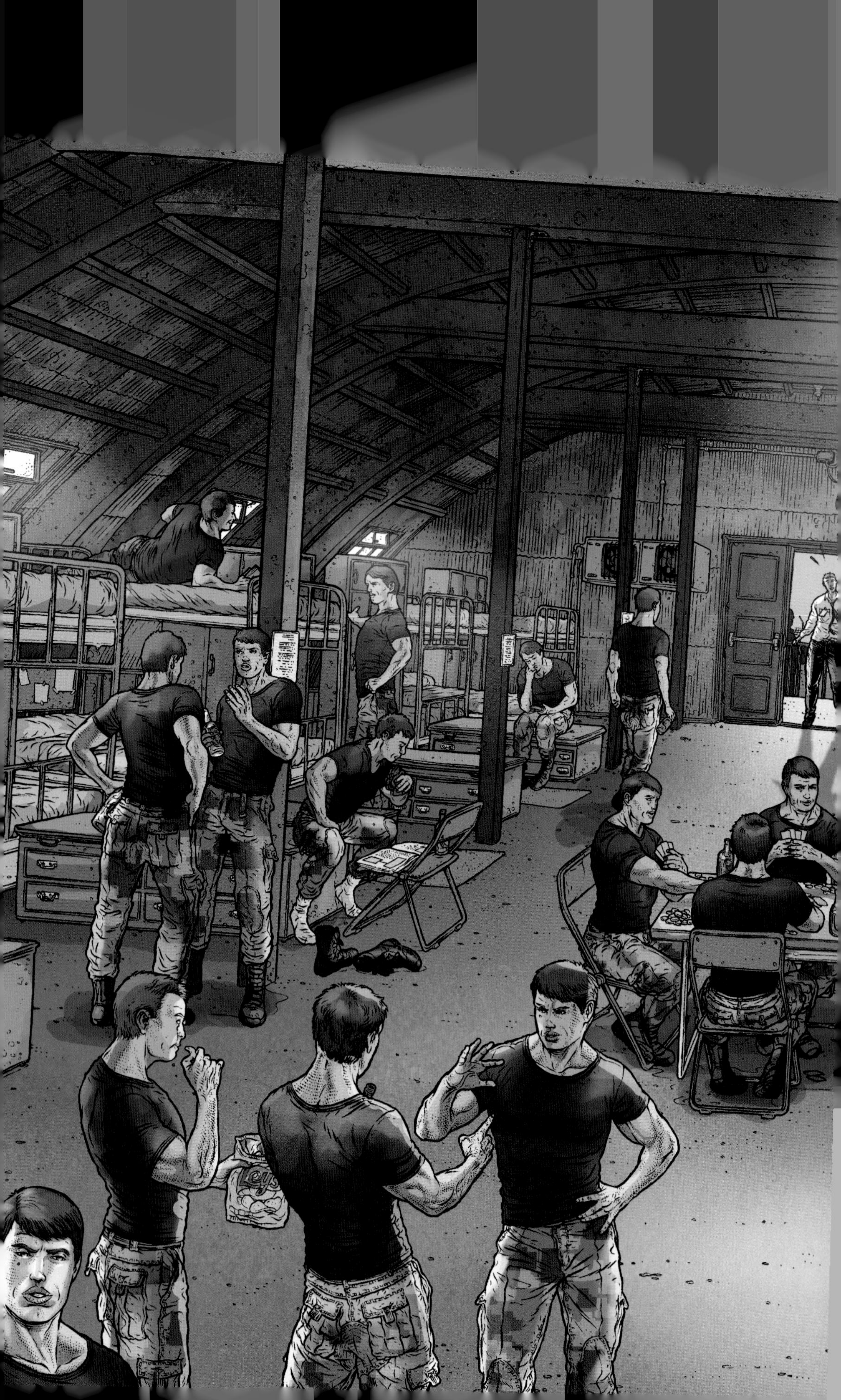

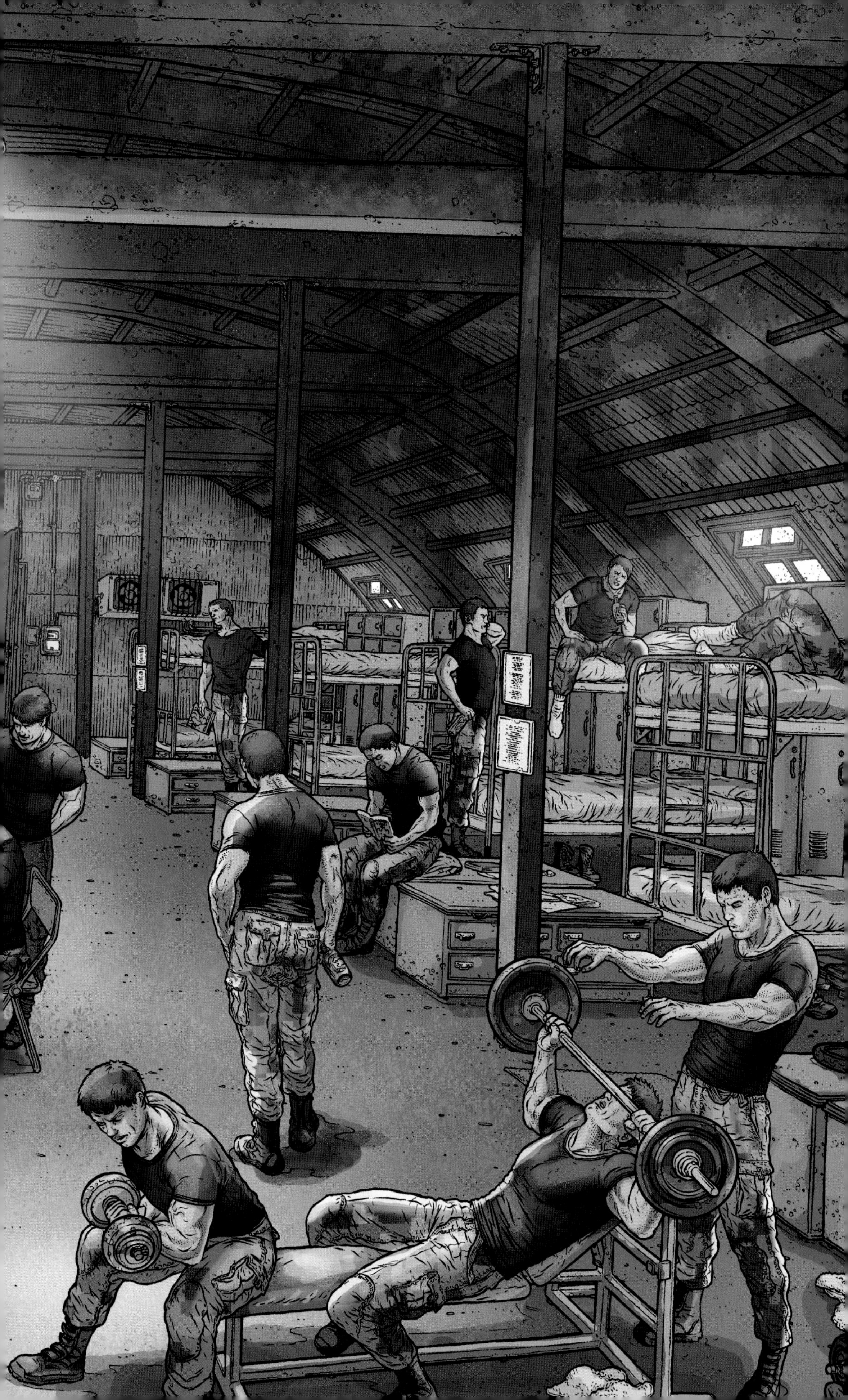

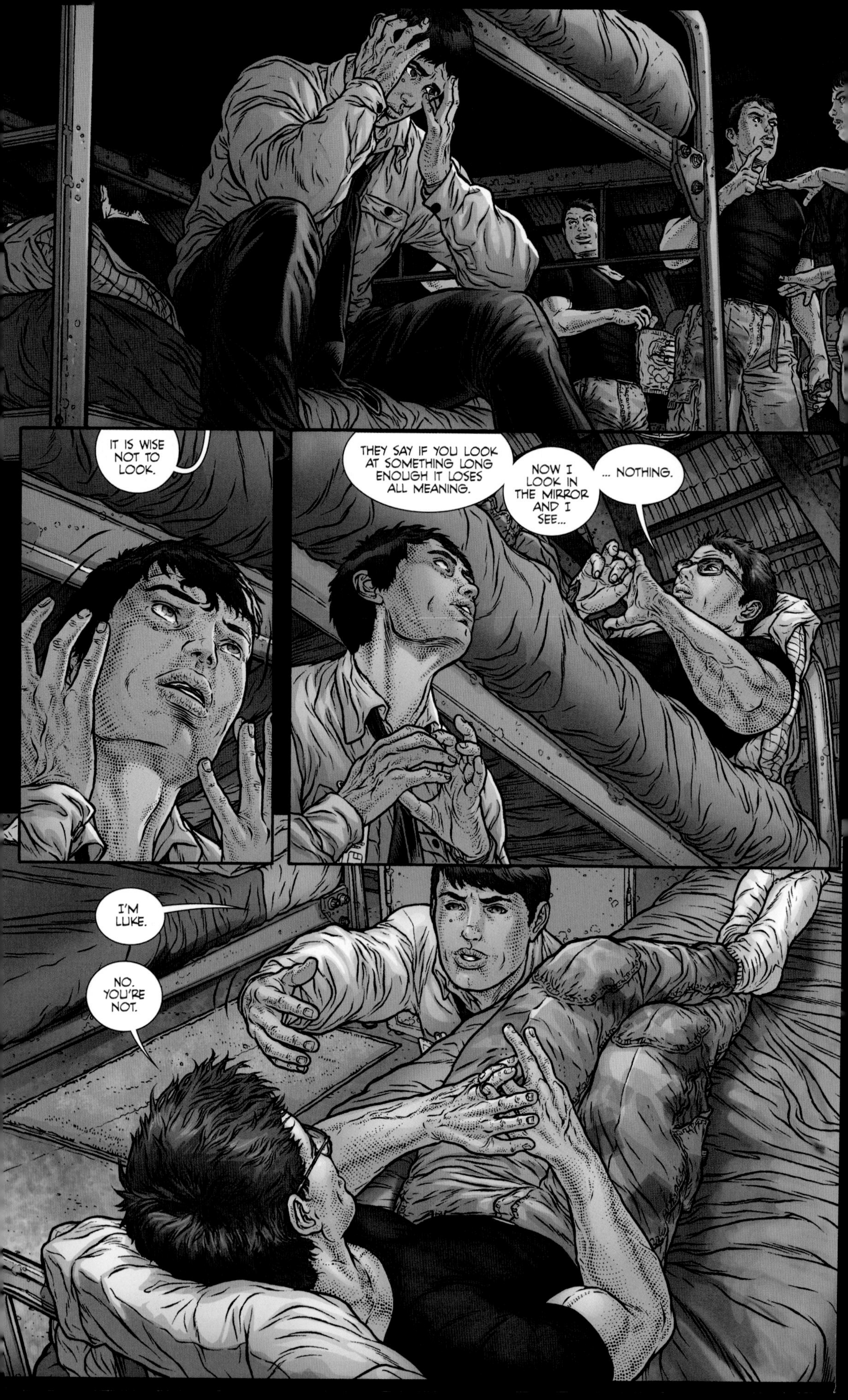
IT IS WISE NOT TO LOOK.
THEY SAY IF YOU LOOK AT SOMETHING LONG ENOUGH IT LOSES ALL MEANING.
NOW I LOOK IN THE MIRROR AND I SEE...
... NOTHING.
I'M LUKE.
NO. YOU'RE NOT.

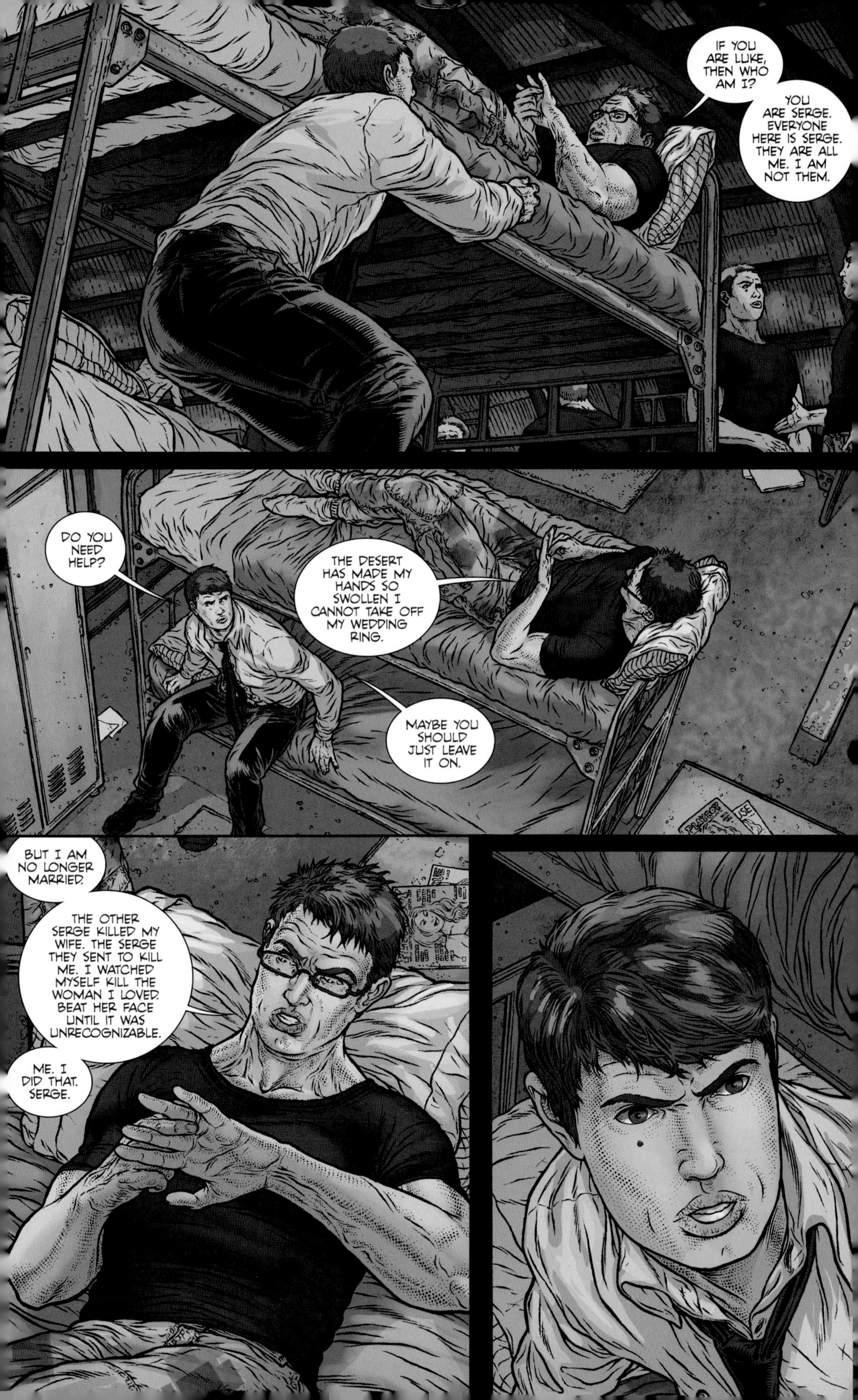
IF YOU ARE LUKE, THEN WHO AM I?
YOU ARE SERGE. EVERYONE HERE IS SERGE. THEY ARE ALL ME. I AM NOT THEM.
DO YOU NEED HELP?
THE DESERT HAS MADE MY HANDS SO SWOLLEN I CANNOT TAKE OFF MY WEDDING RING.
MAYBE YOU SHOULD JUST LEAVE IT ON.
BUT I AM NO LONGER MARRIED.
THE OTHER SERGE KILLED MY WIFE. THE SERGE THEY SENT TO KILL ME. I WATCHED MYSELF KILL THE WOMAN I LOVED. BEAT HER FACE UNTIL IT WAS UNRECOGNIZABLE.
ME. I DID THAT. SERGE.

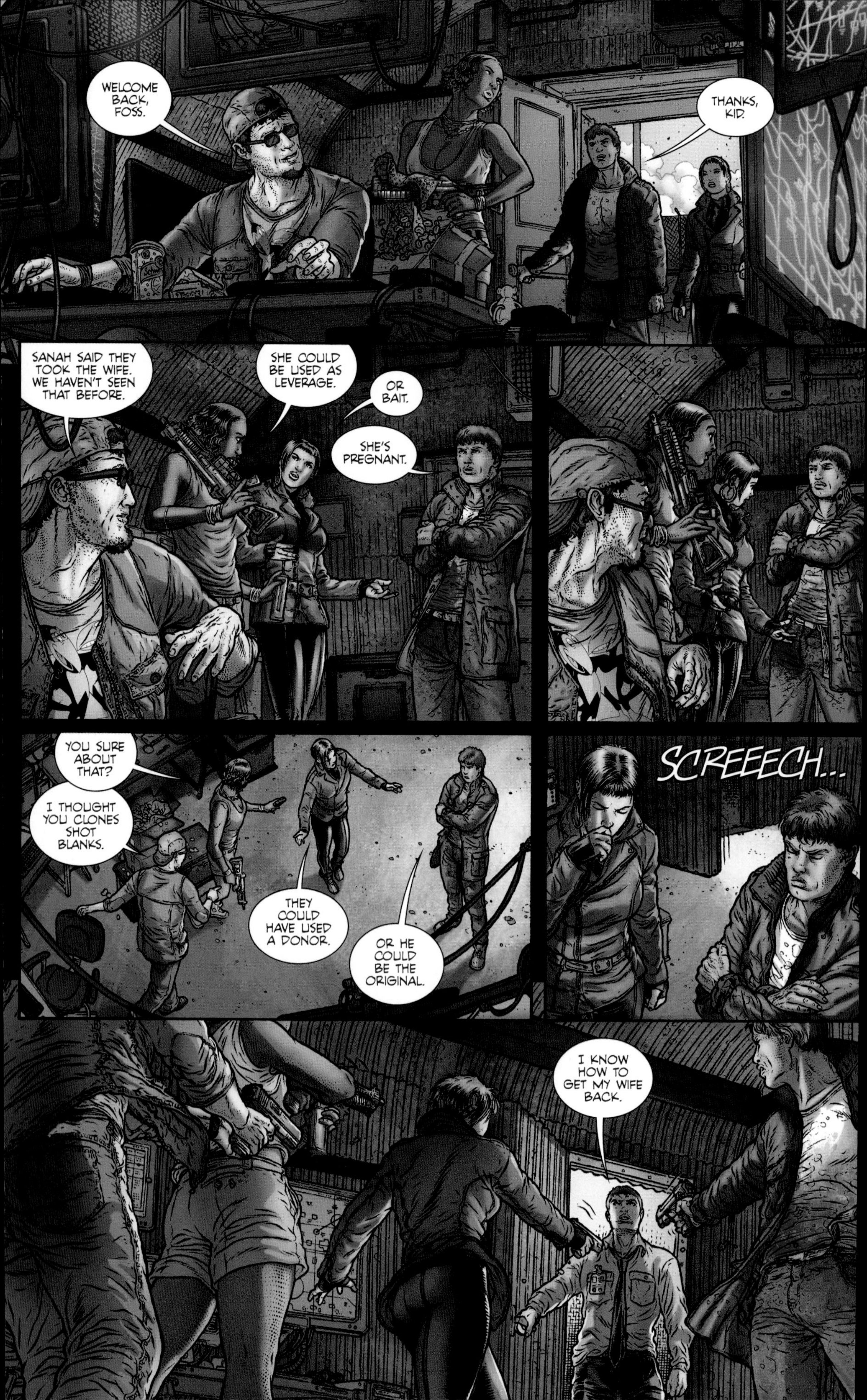
WELCOME BACK, FOSS.
THANKS, KID.
SANAH SAID THEY TOOK THE WIFE. WE HAVEN'T SEEN THAT BEFORE.
SHE COULD BE USED AS LEVERAGE.
OR BAIT.
SHE'S PREGNANT.
YOU SURE ABOUT THAT?
I THOUGHT YOU CLONES SHOT BLANKS.
THEY COULD HAVE USED A DONOR.
OR HE COULD BE THE ORIGINAL.
SCREEECH...
I KNOW HOW TO GET MY WIFE BACK.

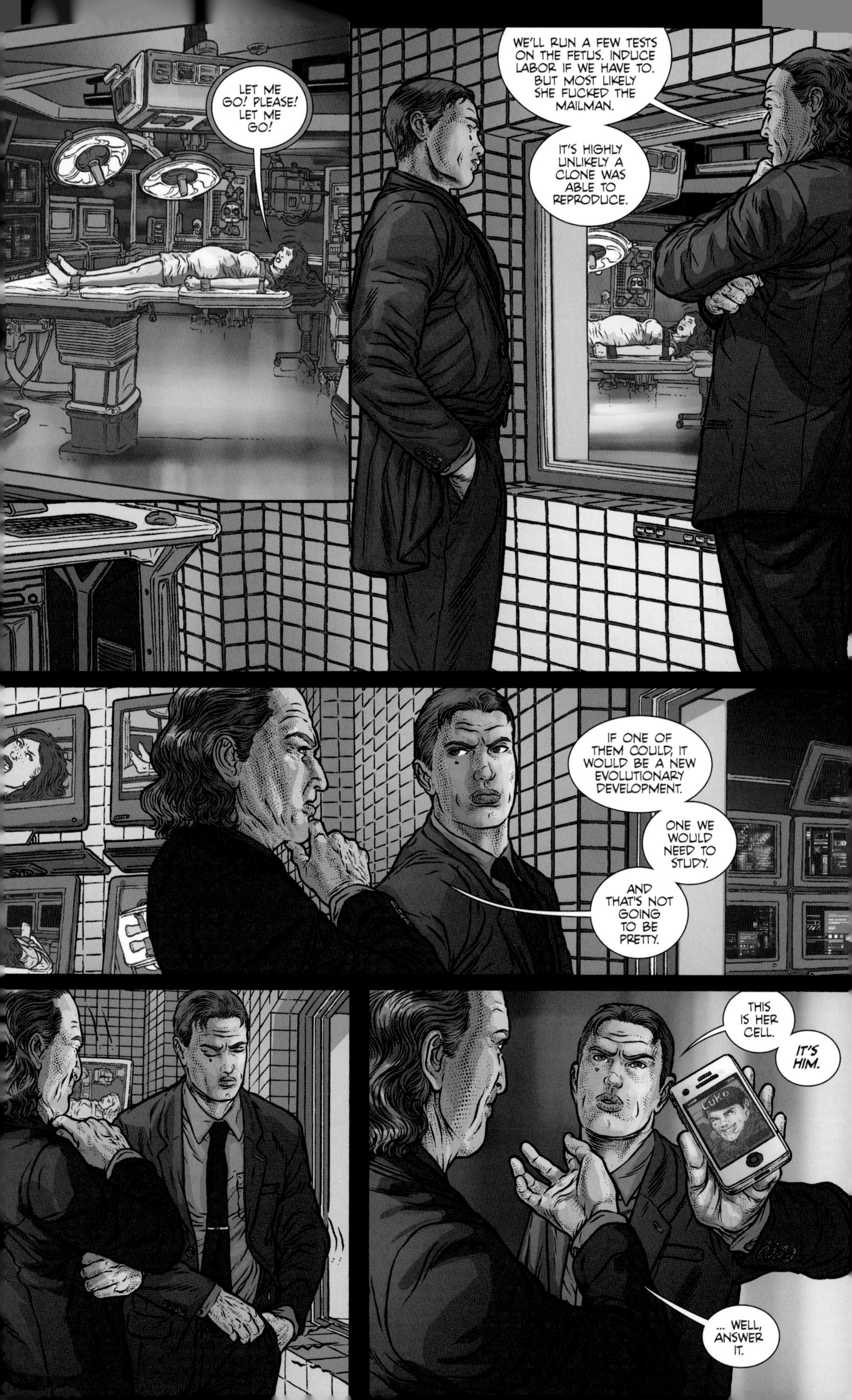
LET ME GO! PLEASE! LET ME GO!
WE'LL RUN A FEW TESTS ON THE FETUS. INDUCE LABOR IF WE HAVE TO. BUT MOST LIKELY SHE FUCKED THE MAILMAN.
IT'S HIGHLY UNLIKELY A CLONE WAS ABLE TO REPRODUCE.
IF ONE OF THEM COULD, IT WOULD BE A NEW EVOLUTIONARY DEVELOPMENT.
ONE WE WOULD NEED TO STUDY.
AND THAT'S NOT GOING TO BE PRETTY.
THIS IS HER CELL.
IT'S HIM.
Luke
... WELL, ANSWER IT.

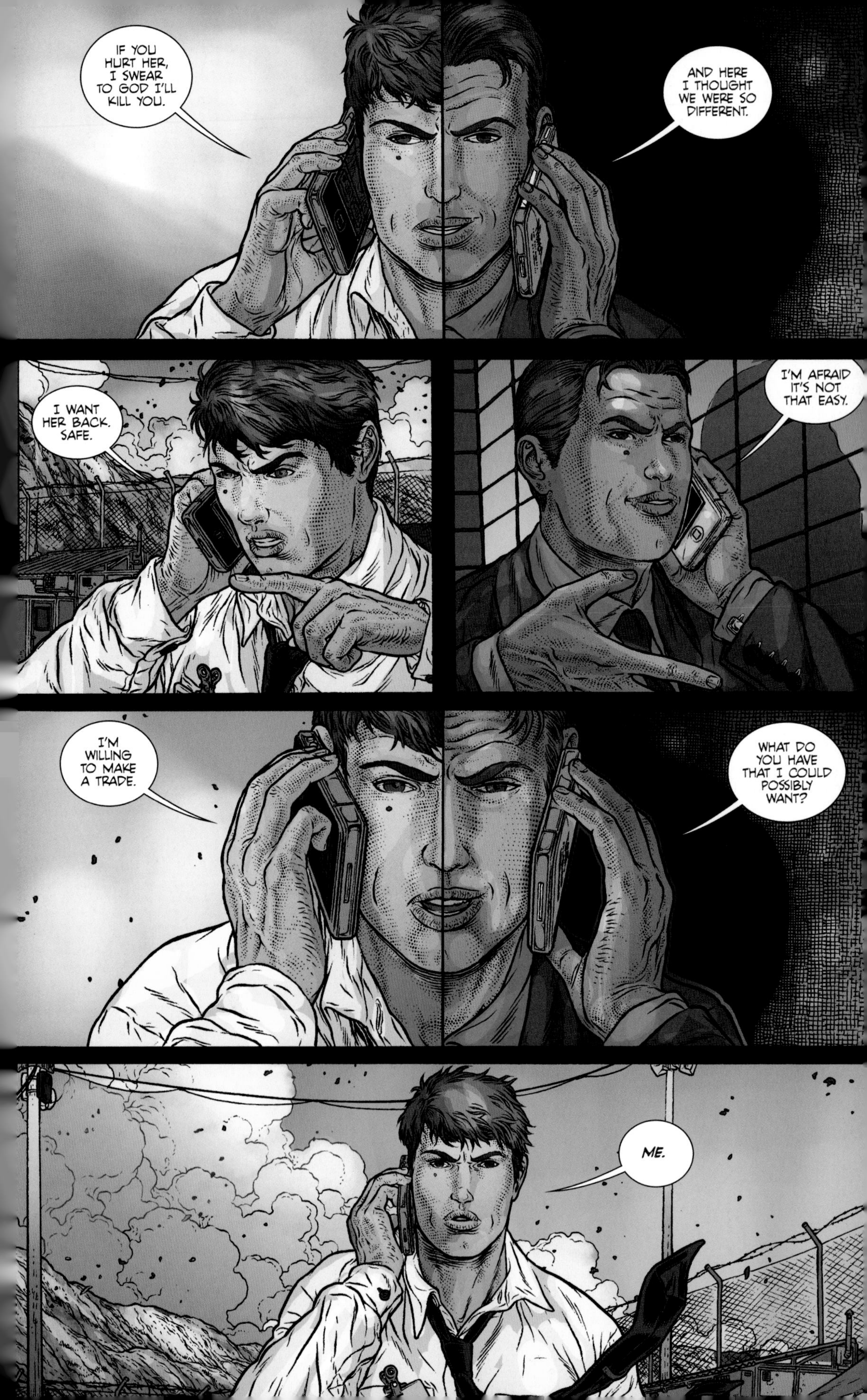
IF YOU HURT HER, I SWEAR TO GOD I'LL KILL YOU.
AND HERE I THOUGHT WE WERE SO DIFFERENT.
I WANT HER BACK. SAFE.
I'M AFRAID IT'S NOT THAT EASY.
I'M WILLING TO MAKE A TRADE.
WHAT DO YOU HAVE THAT I COULD POSSIBLY WANT?
ME.

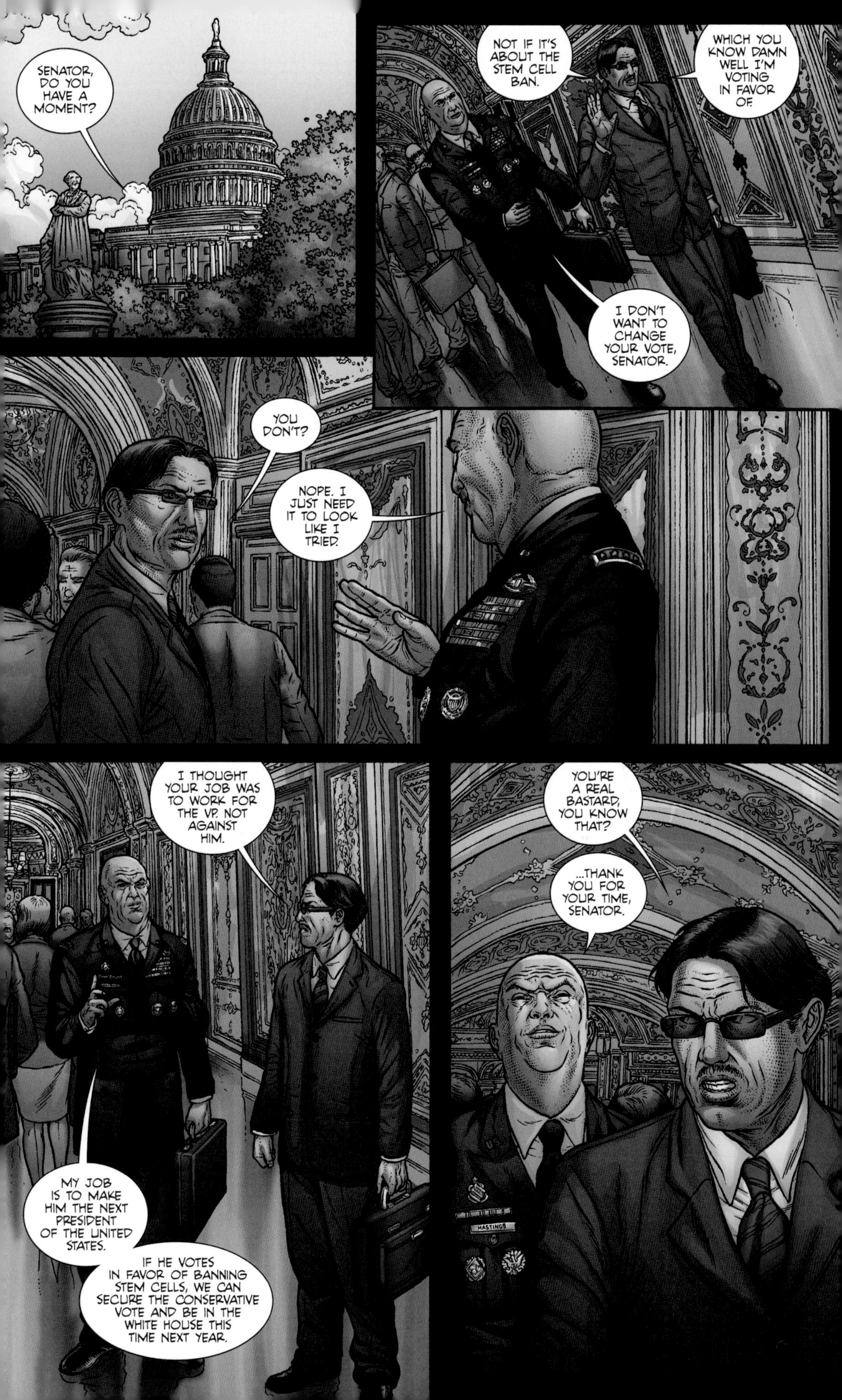
SENATOR, DO YOU HAVE A MOMENT?
NOT IF IT'S ABOUT THE STEM CELL BAN.
WHICH YOU KNOW DAMN WELL I'M VOTING IN FAVOR OF.
I DON'T WANT TO CHANGE YOUR VOTE, SENATOR.
YOU DON'T?
NOPE. I JUST NEED IT TO LOOK LIKE I TRIED.
I THOUGHT YOUR JOB WAS TO WORK FOR THE V.P. NOT AGAINST HIM.
MY JOB IS TO MAKE HIM THE NEXT PRESIDENT OF THE UNITED STATES.
IF HE VOTES IN FAVOR OF BANNING STEM CELLS, WE CAN SECURE THE CONSERVATIVE VOTE AND BE IN THE WHITE HOUSE THIS TIME NEXT YEAR.
YOU'RE A REAL BASTARD, YOU KNOW THAT?
...THANK YOU FOR YOUR TIME, SENATOR.
HASTINGS

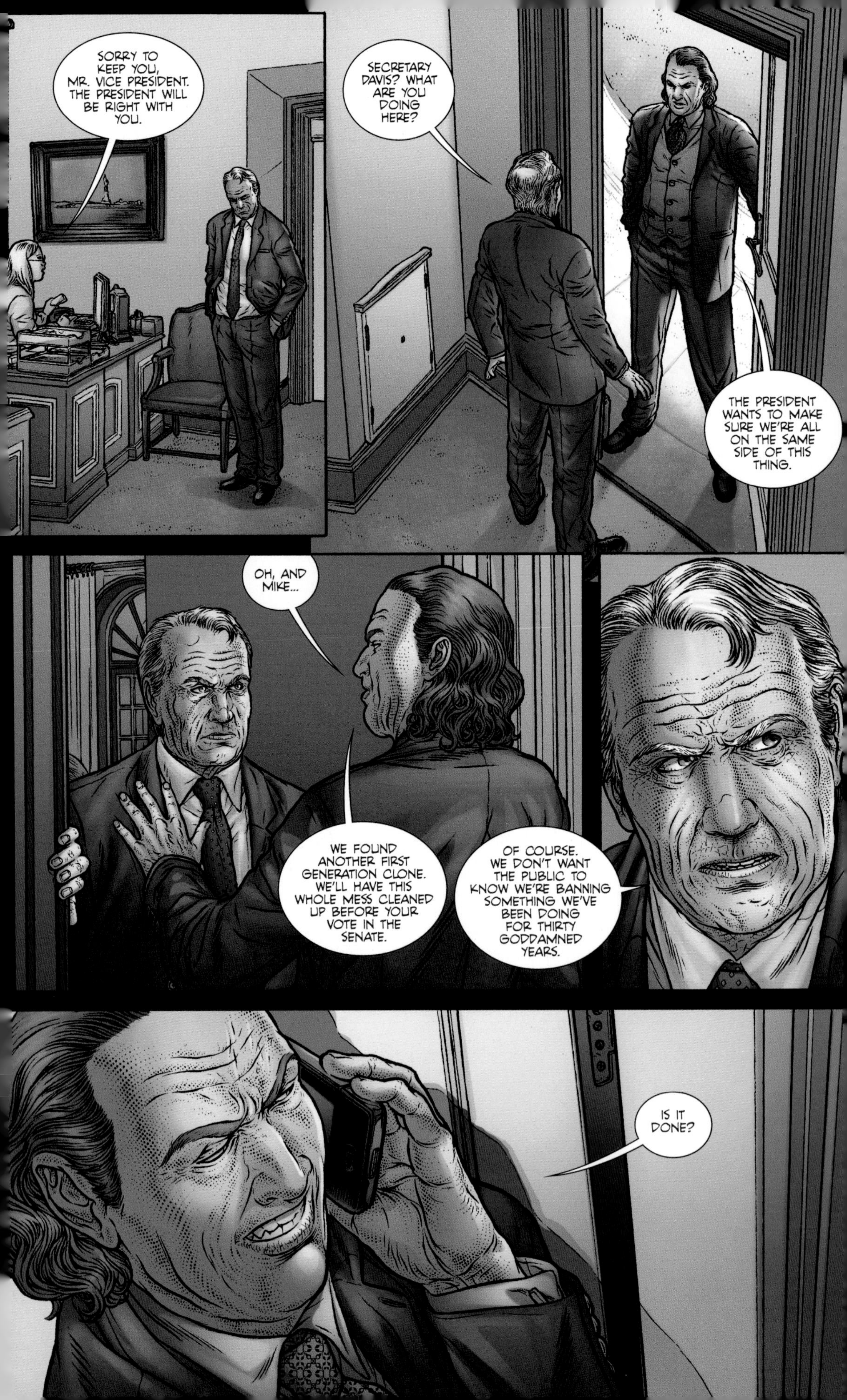
SORRY TO KEEP YOU, MR. VICE PRESIDENT. THE PRESIDENT WILL BE RIGHT WITH YOU.
SECRETARY DAVIS? WHAT ARE YOU DOING HERE?
THE PRESIDENT WANTS TO MAKE SURE WE'RE ALL ON THE SAME SIDE OF THIS THING.
OH, AND MIKE...
WE FOUND ANOTHER FIRST GENERATION CLONE. WE'LL HAVE THIS WHOLE MESS CLEANED UP BEFORE YOUR VOTE IN THE SENATE.
OF COURSE. WE DON'T WANT THE PUBLIC TO KNOW WE'RE BANNING SOMETHING WE'VE BEEN DOING FOR THIRTY GODDAMNED YEARS.
IS IT DONE?

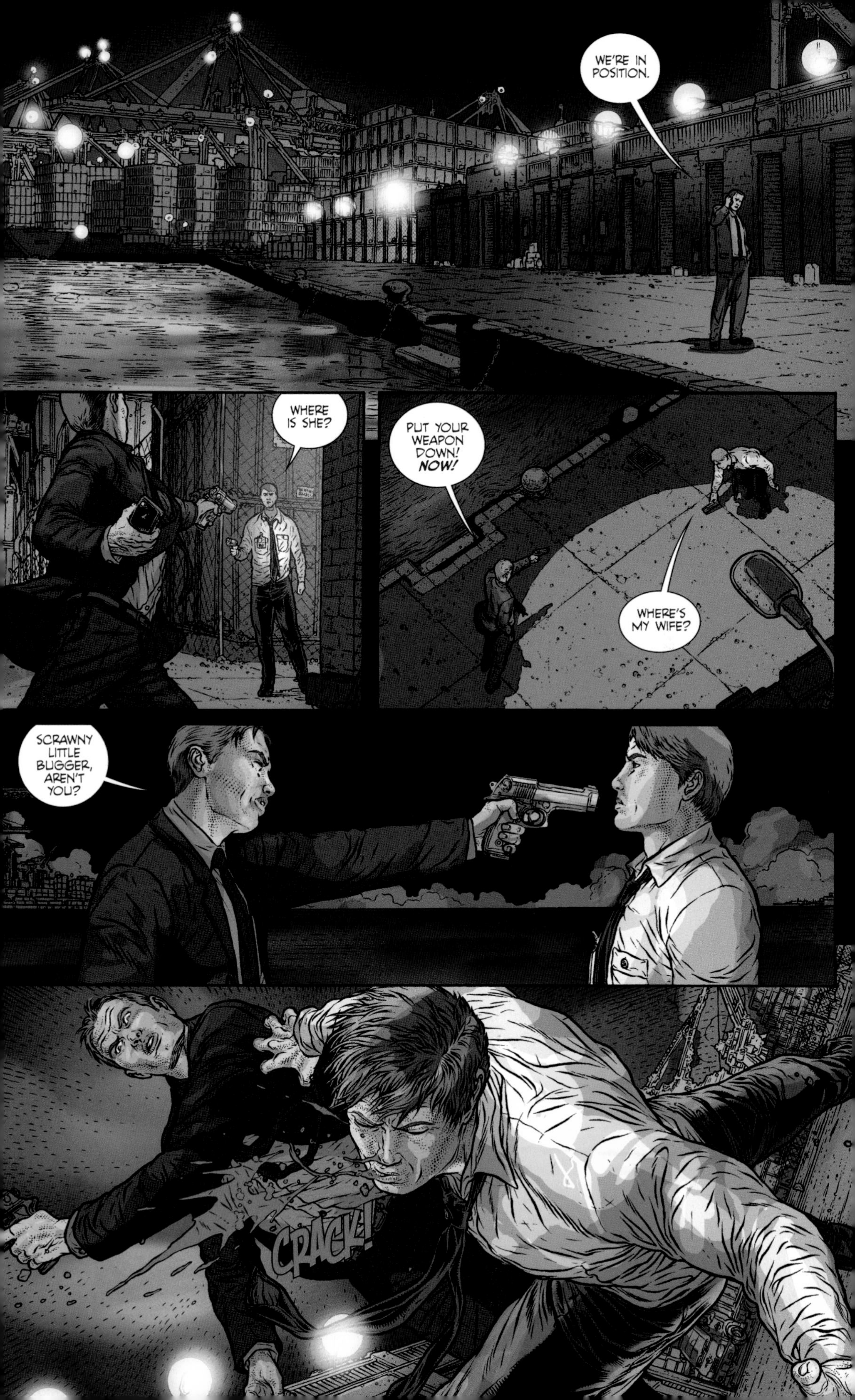
WE'RE IN POSITION.
WHERE IS SHE?
PUT YOUR WEAPON DOWN! **NOW!**
WHERE'S MY WIFE?
SCRAWNY LITTLE BUGGER, AREN'T YOU?
CRACK!

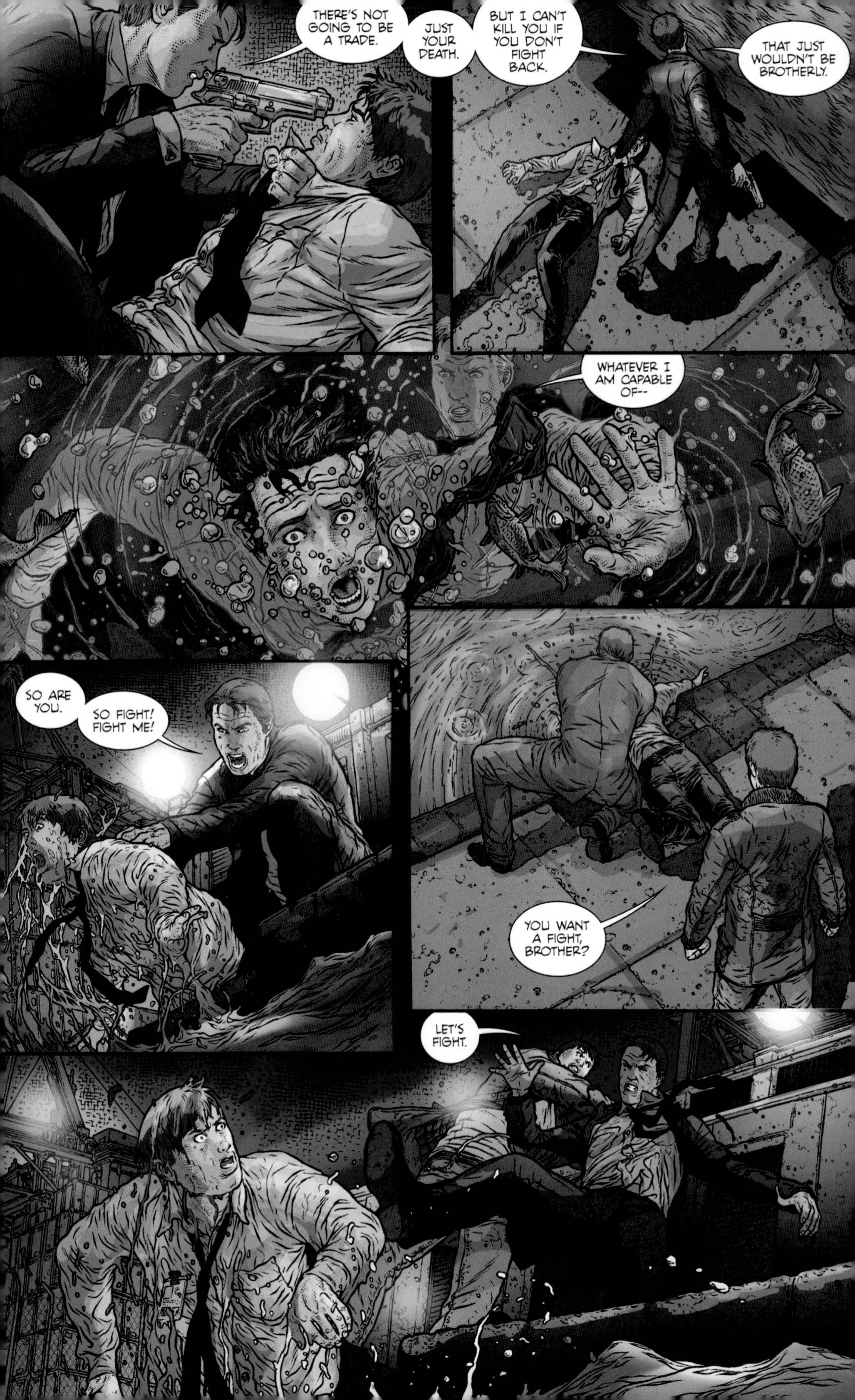
THERE'S NOT GOING TO BE A TRADE.
JUST YOUR DEATH.
BUT I CAN'T KILL YOU IF YOU DON'T FIGHT BACK.
THAT JUST WOULDN'T BE BROTHERLY.
WHATEVER I AM CAPABLE OF--
SO ARE YOU.
SO FIGHT! FIGHT ME!
YOU WANT A FIGHT, BROTHER?
LET'S FIGHT.

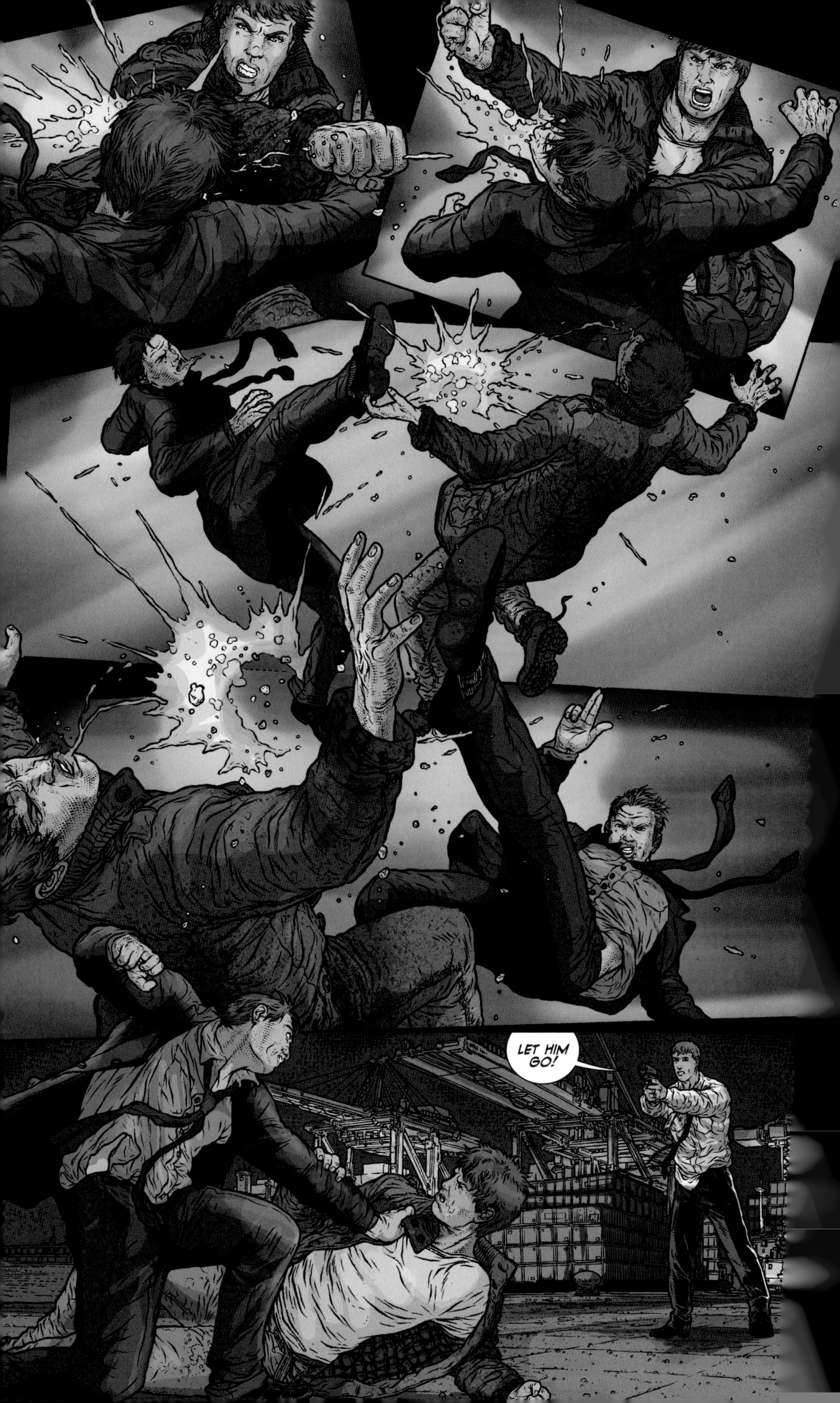
LET HIM GO!

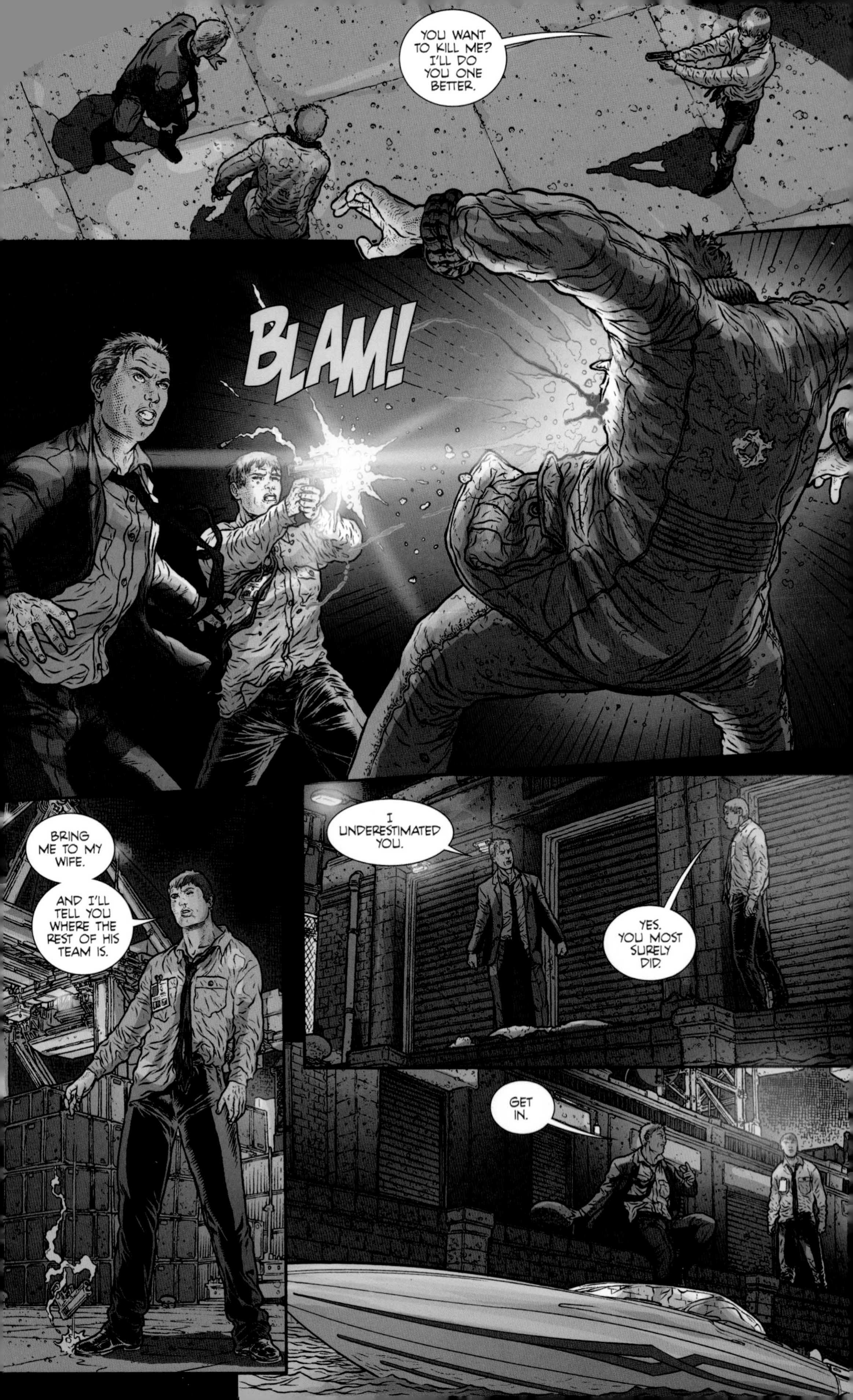
YOU WANT TO KILL ME? I'LL DO YOU ONE BETTER.
BLAM!
BRING ME TO MY WIFE.
AND I'LL TELL YOU WHERE THE REST OF HIS TEAM IS.
I UNDERESTIMATED YOU.
YES. YOU MOST SURELY DID.
GET IN.

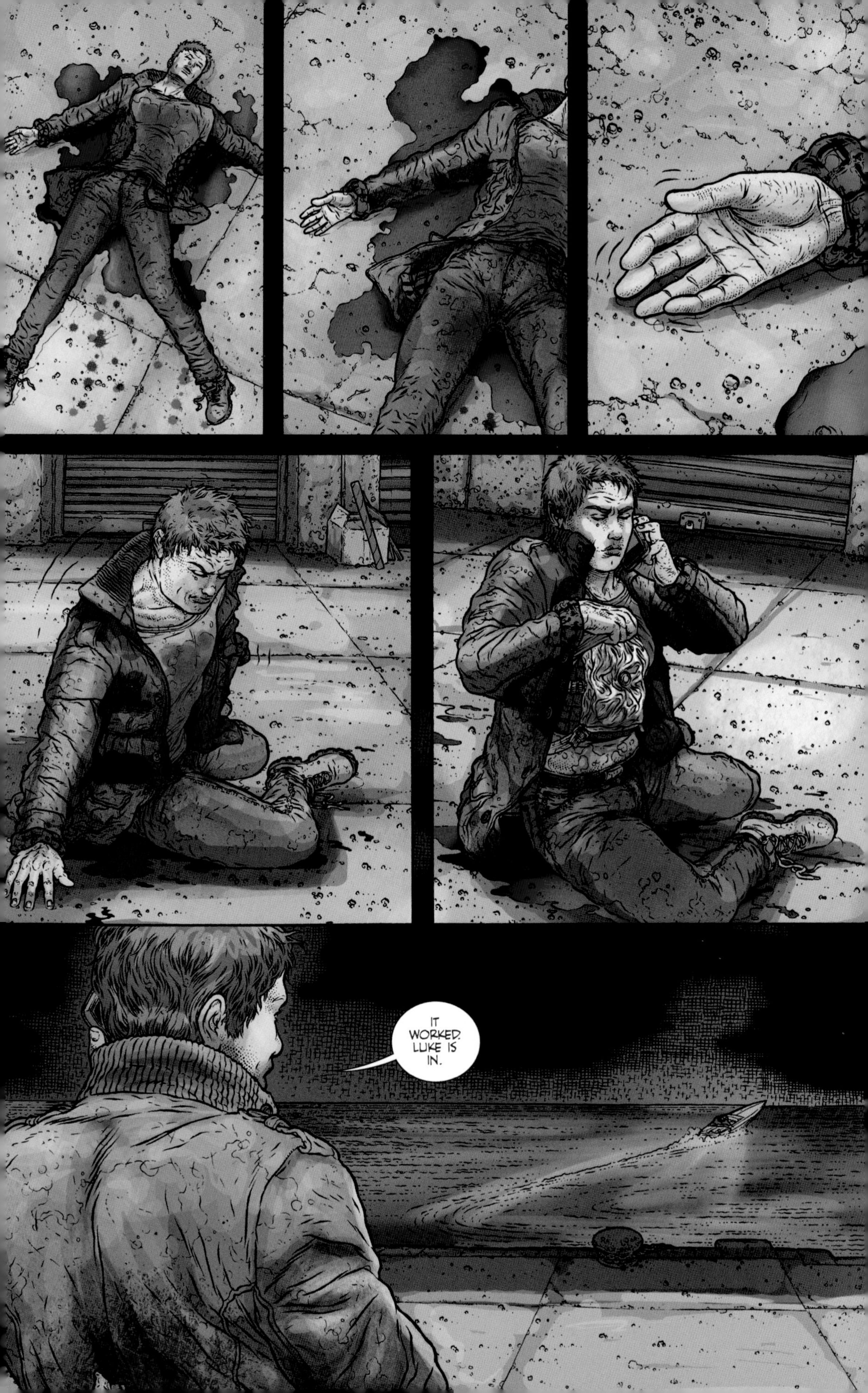
IT WORKED. LUKE IS IN.

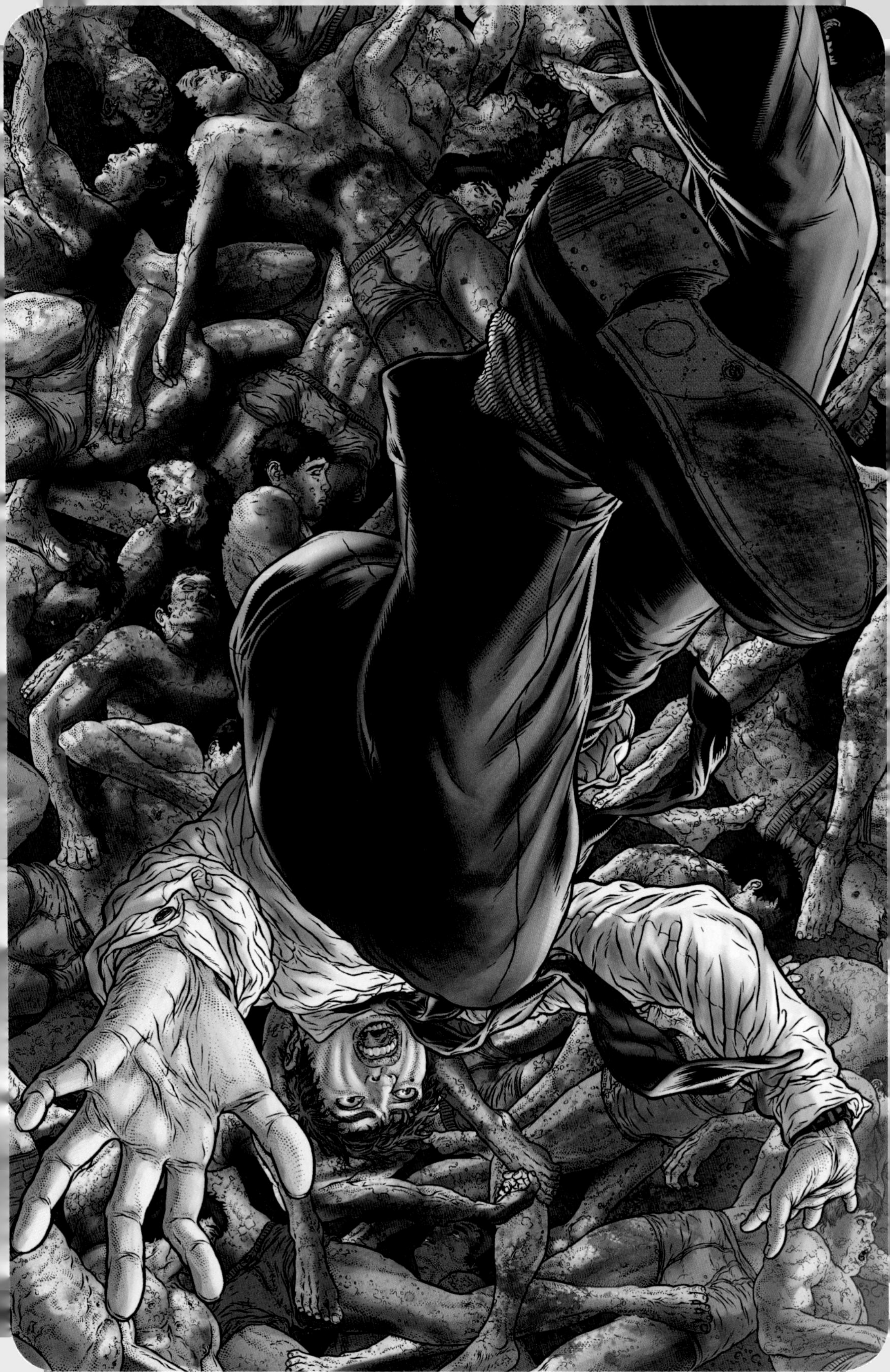

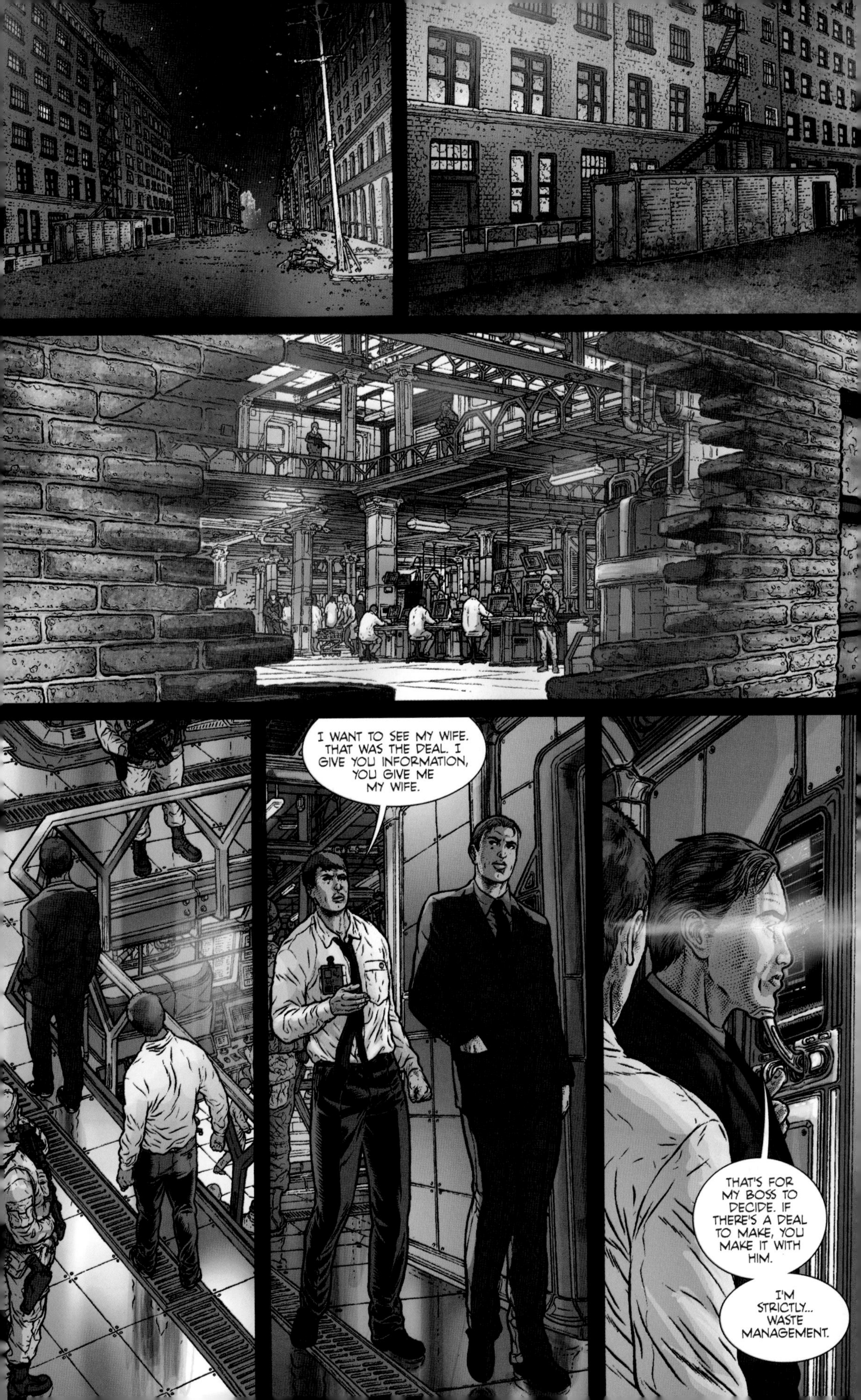
I WANT TO SEE MY WIFE. THAT WAS THE DEAL. I GIVE YOU INFORMATION, YOU GIVE ME MY WIFE.
THAT'S FOR MY BOSS TO DECIDE. IF THERE'S A DEAL TO MAKE, YOU MAKE IT WITH HIM.
I'M STRICTLY... WASTE MANAGEMENT.

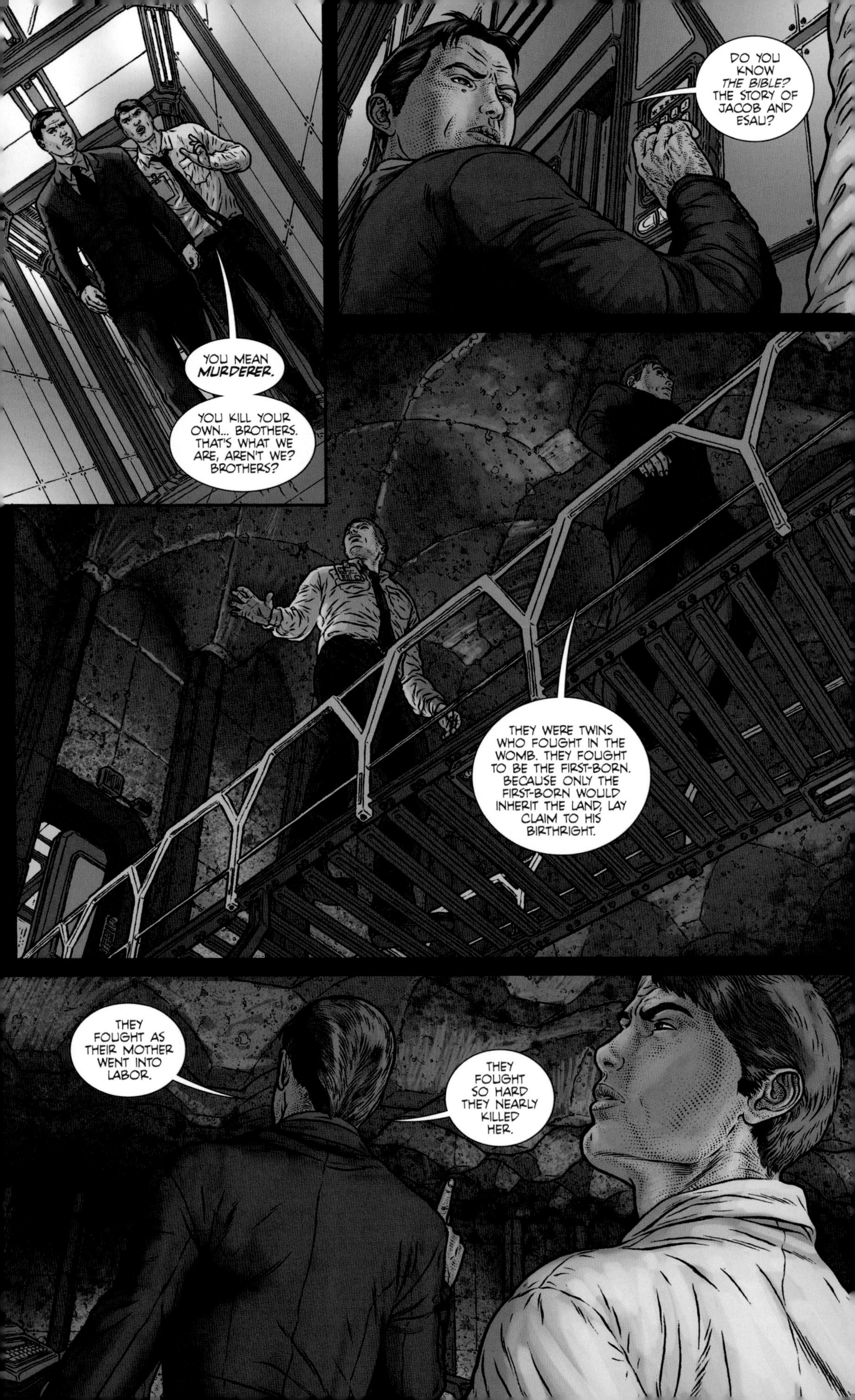
DO YOU KNOW THE BIBLE? THE STORY OF JACOB AND ESAU?
YOU MEAN MURDERER.
YOU KILL YOUR OWN... BROTHERS. THAT'S WHAT WE ARE, AREN'T WE? BROTHERS?
THEY WERE TWINS WHO FOUGHT IN THE WOMB. THEY FOUGHT TO BE THE FIRST-BORN. BECAUSE ONLY THE FIRST-BORN WOULD INHERIT THE LAND, LAY CLAIM TO HIS BIRTHRIGHT.
THEY FOUGHT AS THEIR MOTHER WENT INTO LABOR.
THEY FOUGHT SO HARD THEY NEARLY KILLED HER.

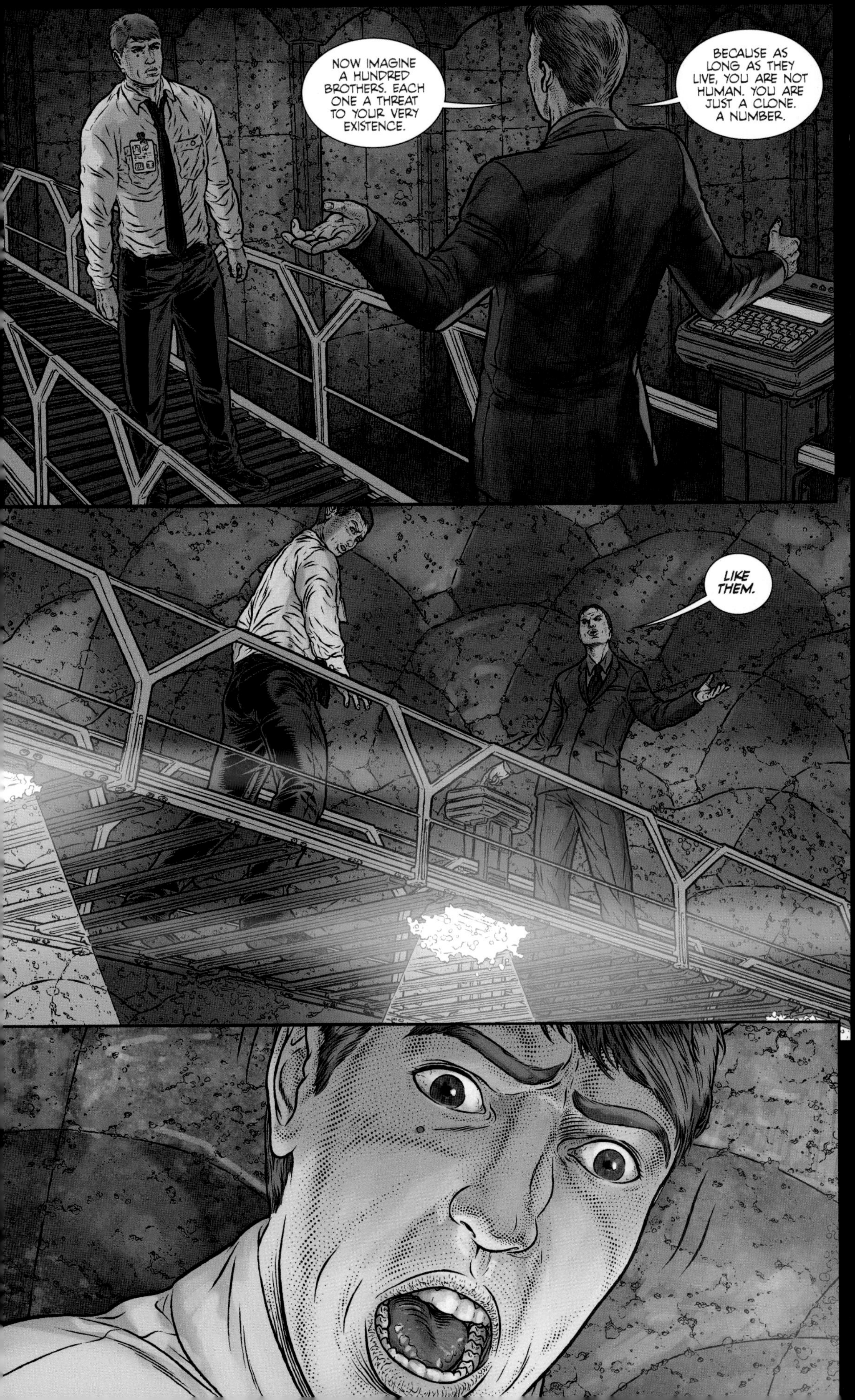
NOW IMAGINE A HUNDRED BROTHERS. EACH ONE A THREAT TO YOUR VERY EXISTENCE.
BECAUSE AS LONG AS THEY LIVE, YOU ARE NOT HUMAN. YOU ARE JUST A CLONE. A NUMBER.
LIKE THEM.

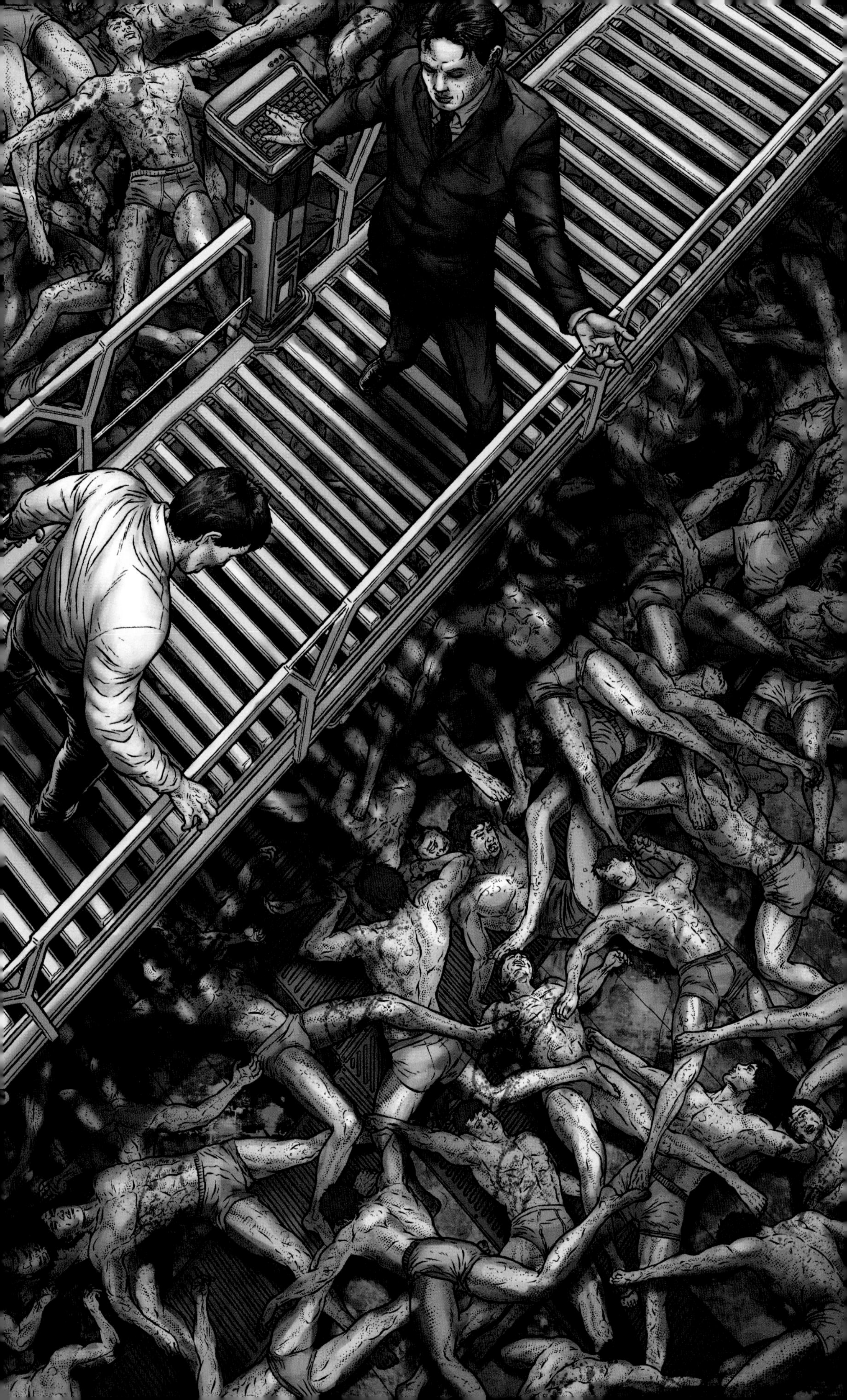

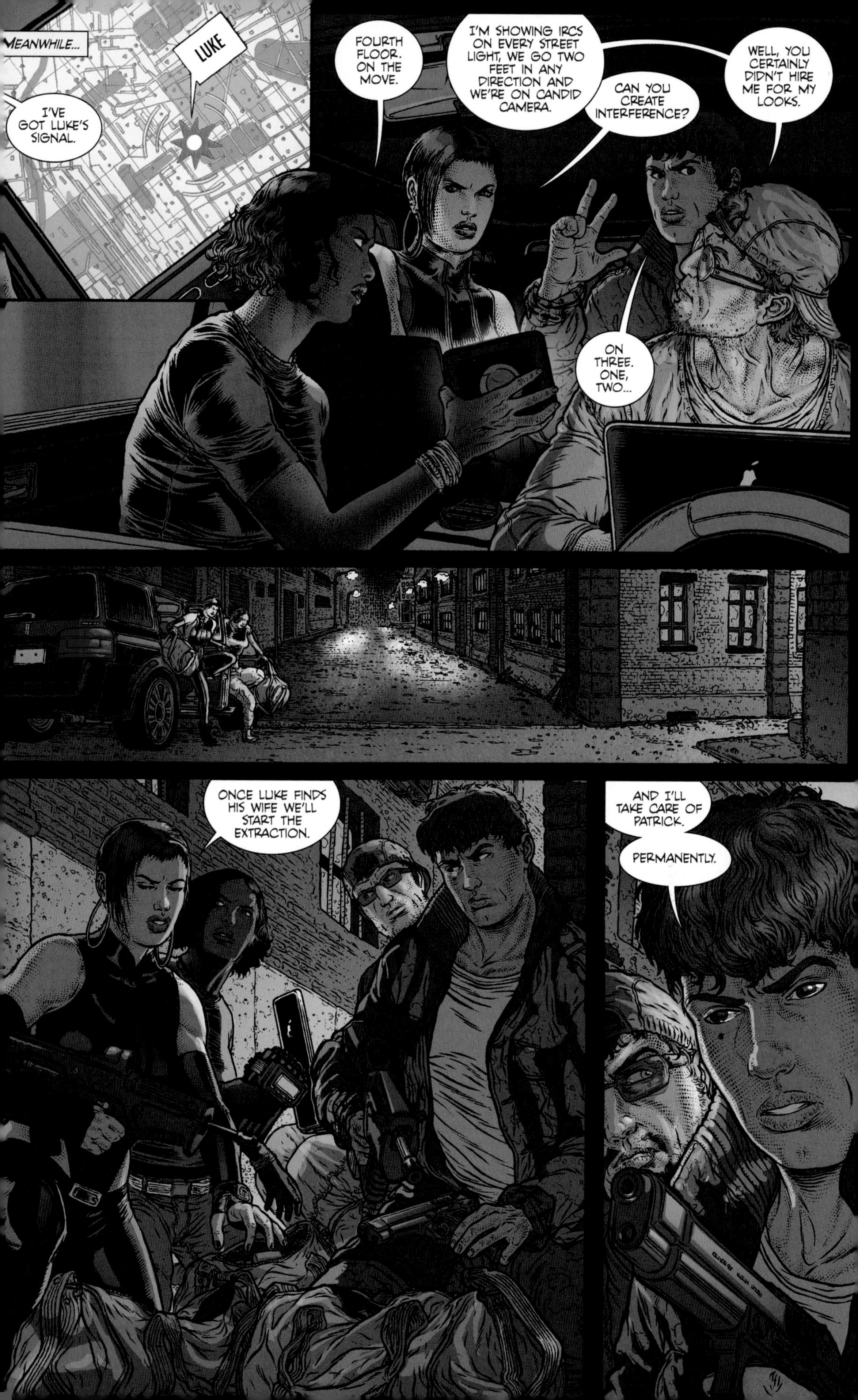
MEANWHILE...
LUKE
I'VE GOT LUKE'S SIGNAL.
FOURTH FLOOR. ON THE MOVE.
I'M SHOWING IRCS ON EVERY STREET LIGHT, WE GO TWO FEET IN ANY DIRECTION AND WE'RE ON CANDID CAMERA.
CAN YOU CREATE INTERFERENCE?
WELL, YOU CERTAINLY DIDN'T HIRE ME FOR MY LOOKS.
ON THREE. ONE, TWO...
ONCE LUKE FINDS HIS WIFE WE'LL START THE EXTRACTION.
AND I'LL TAKE CARE OF PATRICK.
PERMANENTLY.

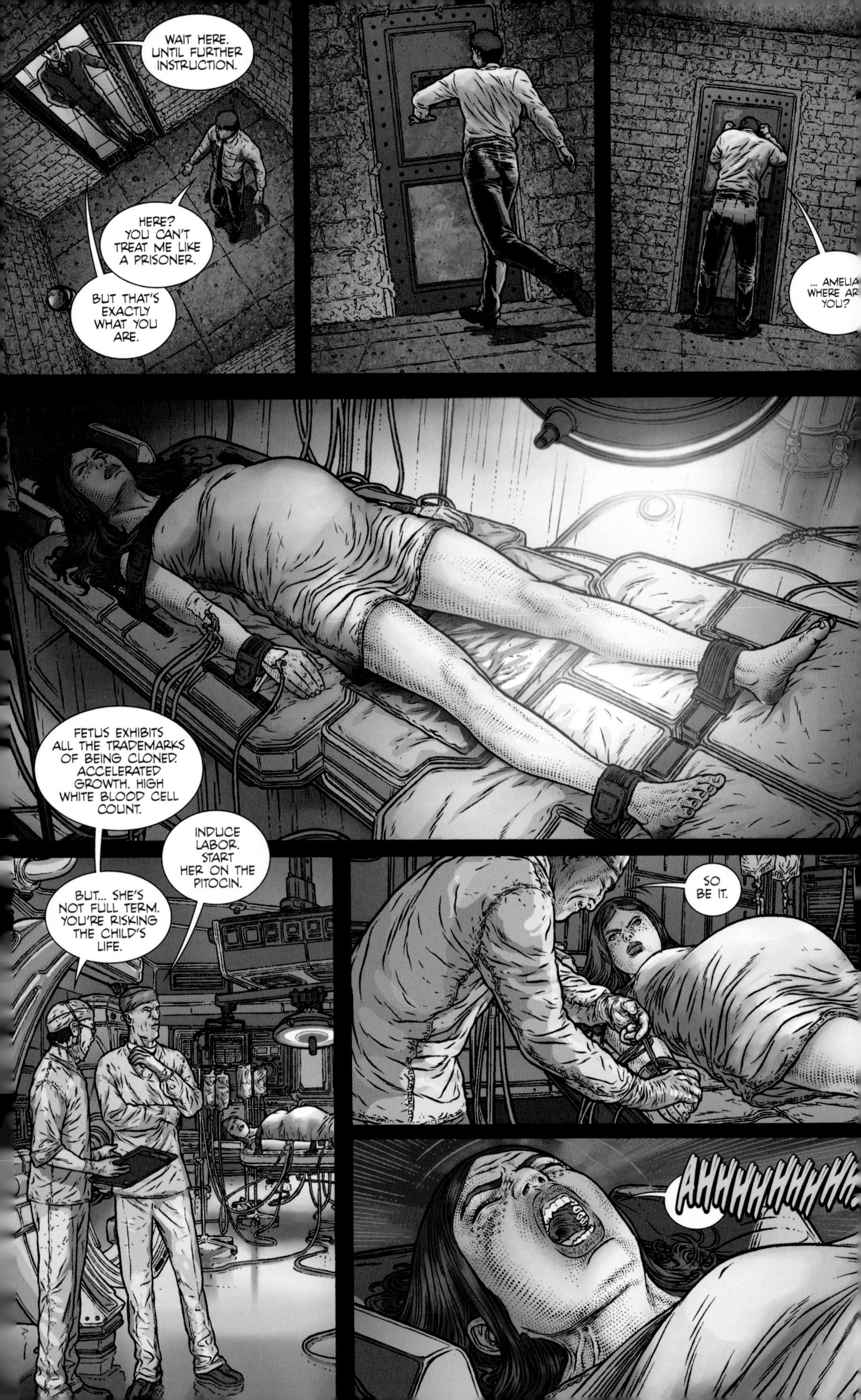
WAIT HERE. UNTIL FURTHER INSTRUCTION.
HERE? YOU CAN'T TREAT ME LIKE A PRISONER.
BUT THAT'S EXACTLY WHAT YOU ARE.
... AMELIA WHERE AR YOU?
FETUS EXHIBITS ALL THE TRADEMARKS OF BEING CLONED. ACCELERATED GROWTH. HIGH WHITE BLOOD CELL COUNT.
INDUCE LABOR. START HER ON THE PITOCIN.
BUT... SHE'S NOT FULL TERM. YOU'RE RISKING THE CHILD'S LIFE.
SO BE IT.
AHHHHHHHHH

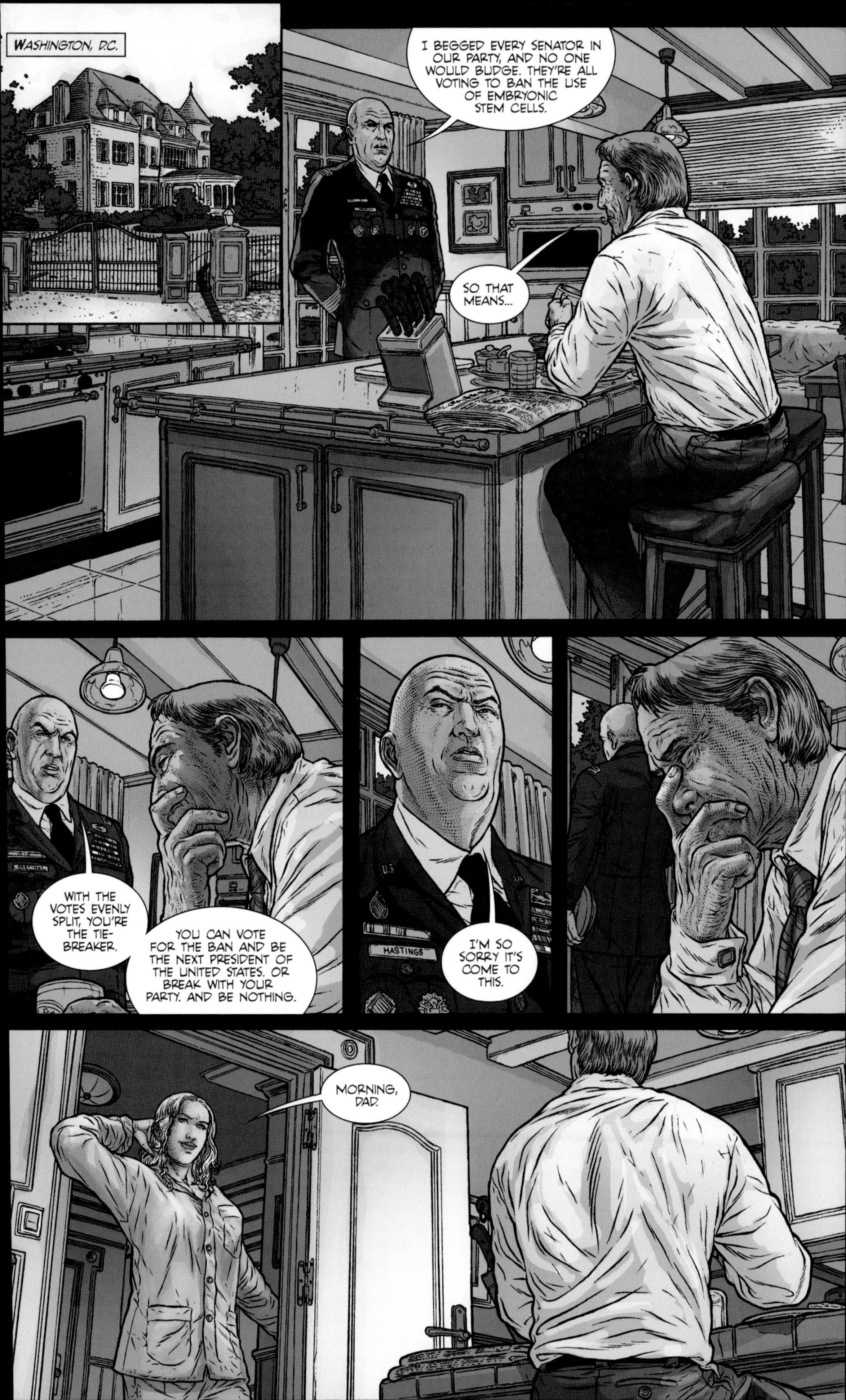
WASHINGTON, D.C.
I BEGGED EVERY SENATOR IN OUR PARTY, AND NO ONE WOULD BUDGE. THEY'RE ALL VOTING TO BAN THE USE OF EMBRYONIC STEM CELLS.
SO THAT MEANS...
WITH THE VOTES EVENLY SPLIT, YOU'RE THE TIE-BREAKER.
YOU CAN VOTE FOR THE BAN AND BE THE NEXT PRESIDENT OF THE UNITED STATES. OR BREAK WITH YOUR PARTY. AND BE NOTHING.
HASTINGS
I'M SO SORRY IT'S COME TO THIS.
MORNING, DAD.

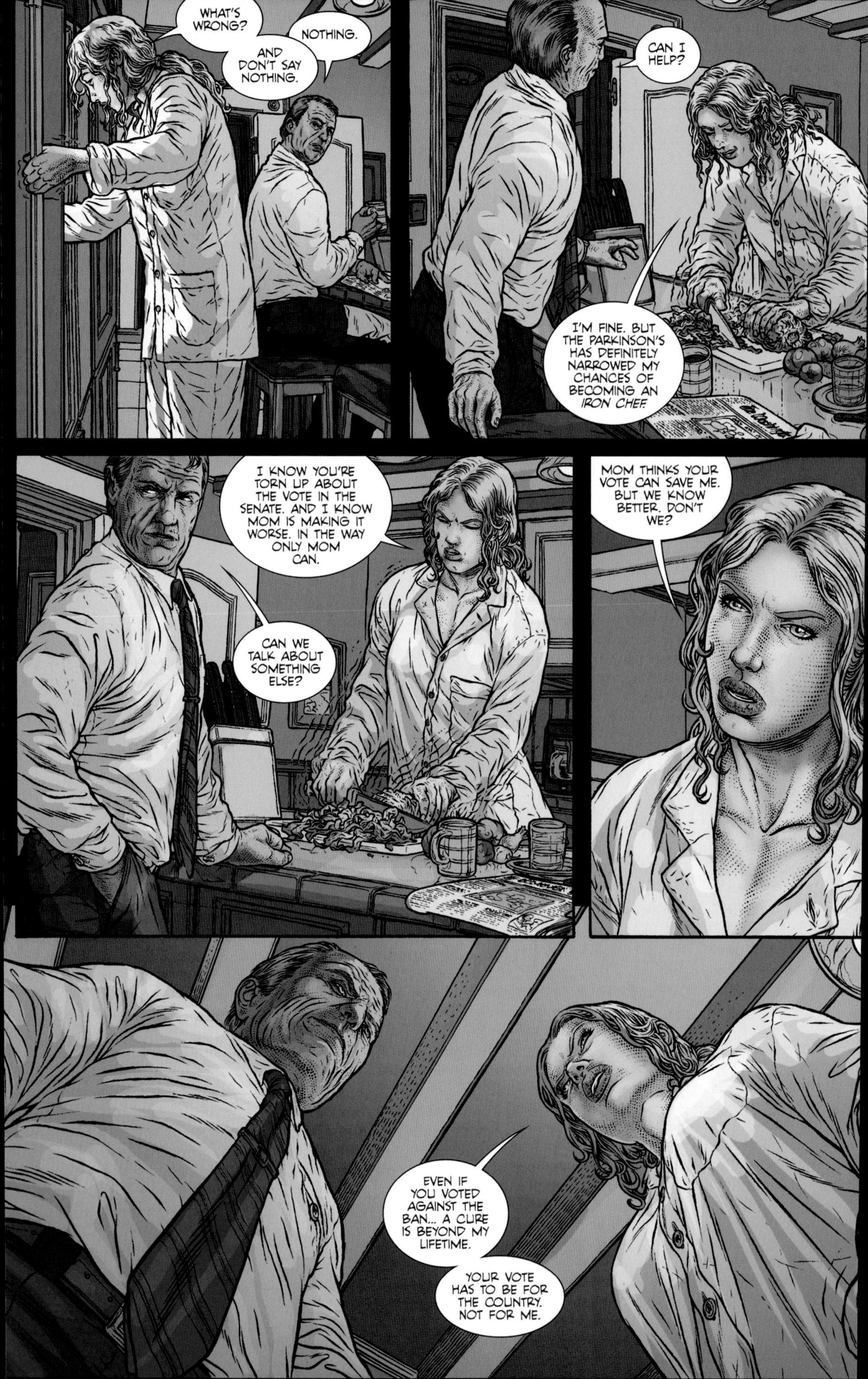
WHAT'S WRONG?
NOTHING.
AND DON'T SAY NOTHING.
CAN I HELP?
I'M FINE. BUT THE PARKINSON'S HAS DEFINITELY NARROWED MY CHANCES OF BECOMING AN *IRON CHEF*.
I KNOW YOU'RE TORN UP ABOUT THE VOTE IN THE SENATE. AND I KNOW MOM IS MAKING IT WORSE. IN THE WAY ONLY MOM CAN.
CAN WE TALK ABOUT SOMETHING ELSE?
MOM THINKS YOUR VOTE CAN SAVE ME. BUT WE KNOW BETTER. DON'T WE?
EVEN IF YOU VOTED AGAINST THE BAN... A CURE IS BEYOND MY LIFETIME.
YOUR VOTE HAS TO BE FOR THE COUNTRY. NOT FOR ME.

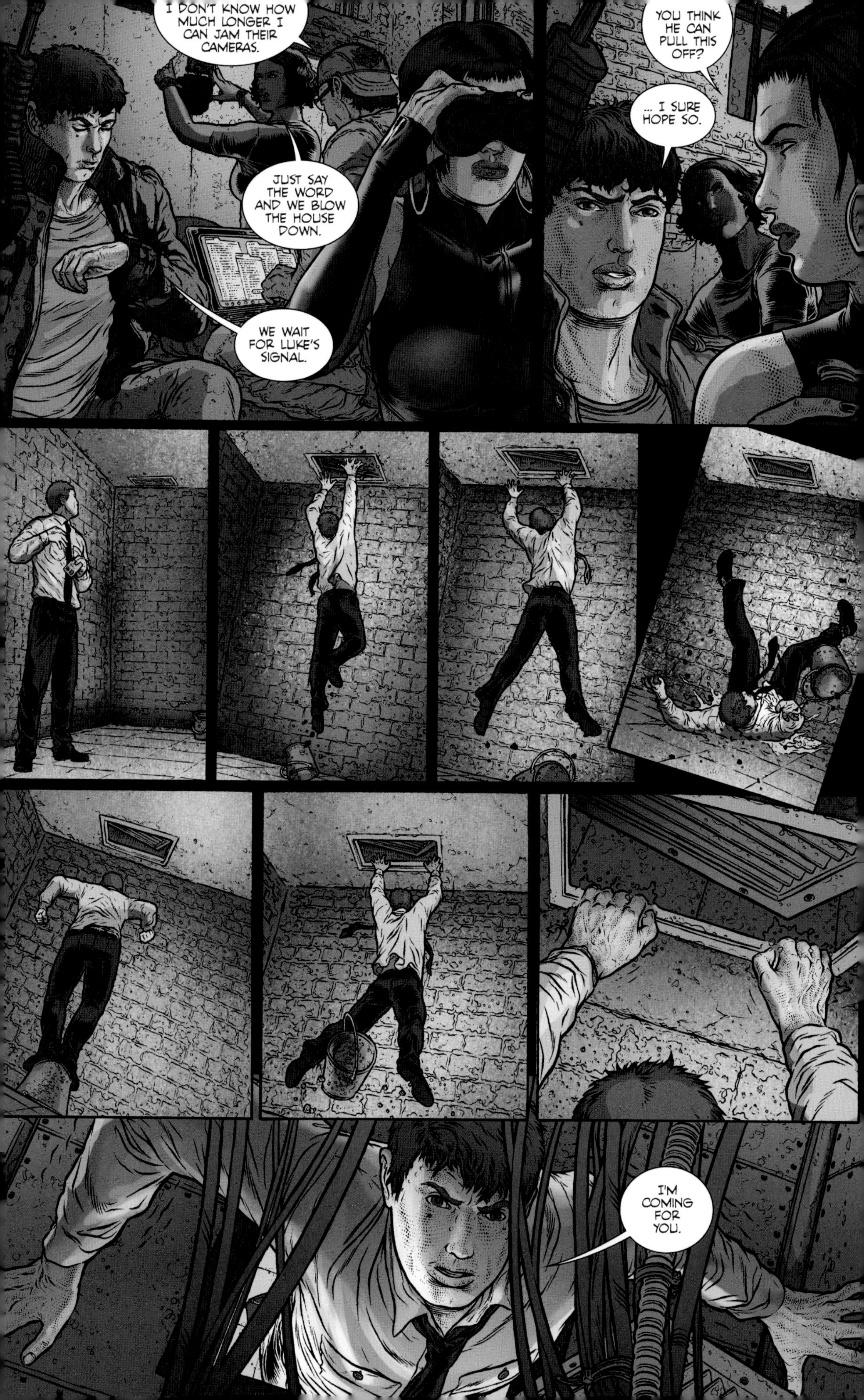
I DON'T KNOW HOW MUCH LONGER I CAN JAM THEIR CAMERAS.
JUST SAY THE WORD AND WE BLOW THE HOUSE DOWN.
WE WAIT FOR LUKE'S SIGNAL.
YOU THINK HE CAN PULL THIS OFF?
... I SURE HOPE SO.
I'M COMING FOR YOU.

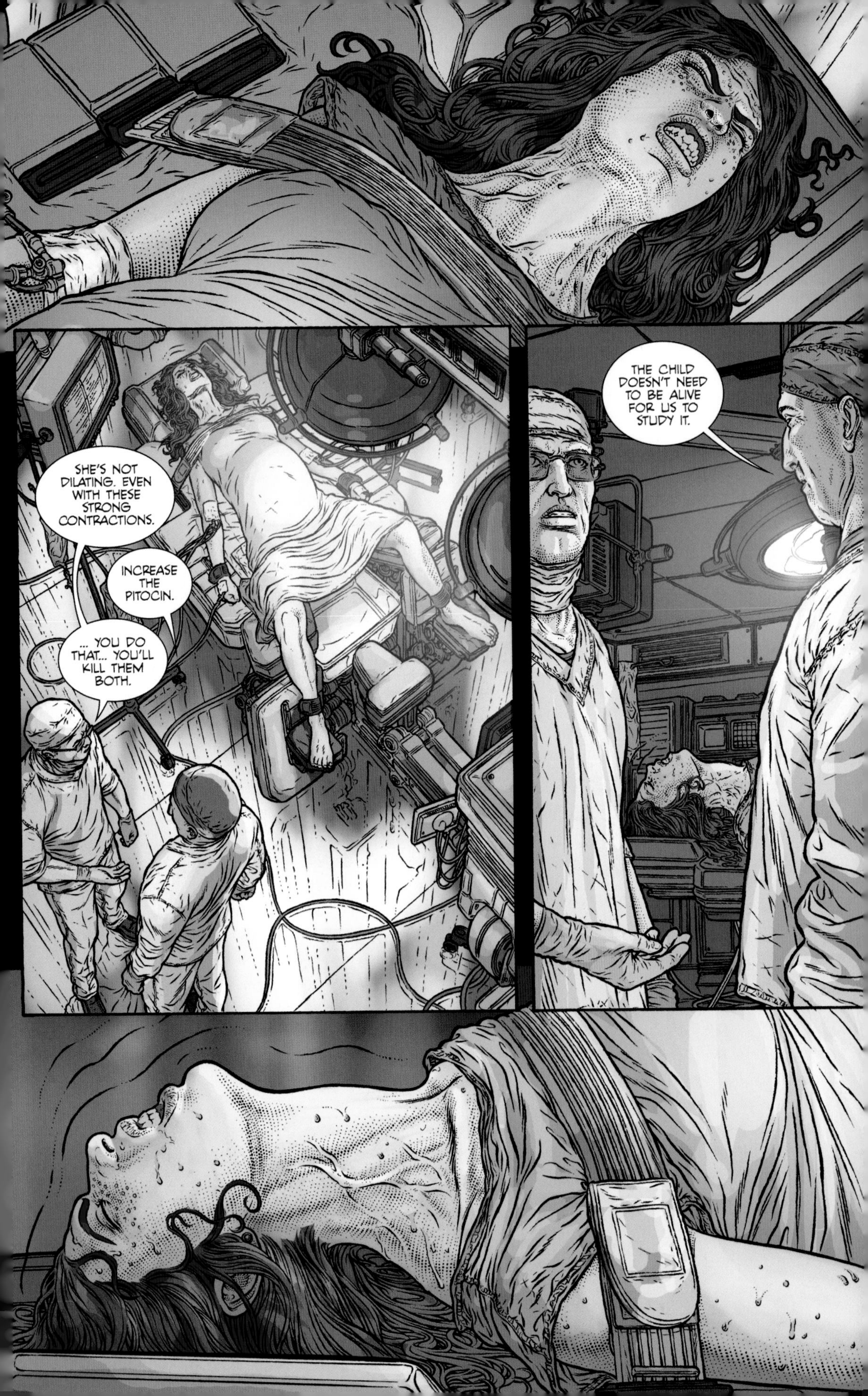
SHE'S NOT DILATING. EVEN WITH THESE STRONG CONTRACTIONS.
INCREASE THE PITOCIN.
... YOU DO THAT... YOU'LL KILL THEM BOTH.
THE CHILD DOESN'T NEED TO BE ALIVE FOR US TO STUDY IT.

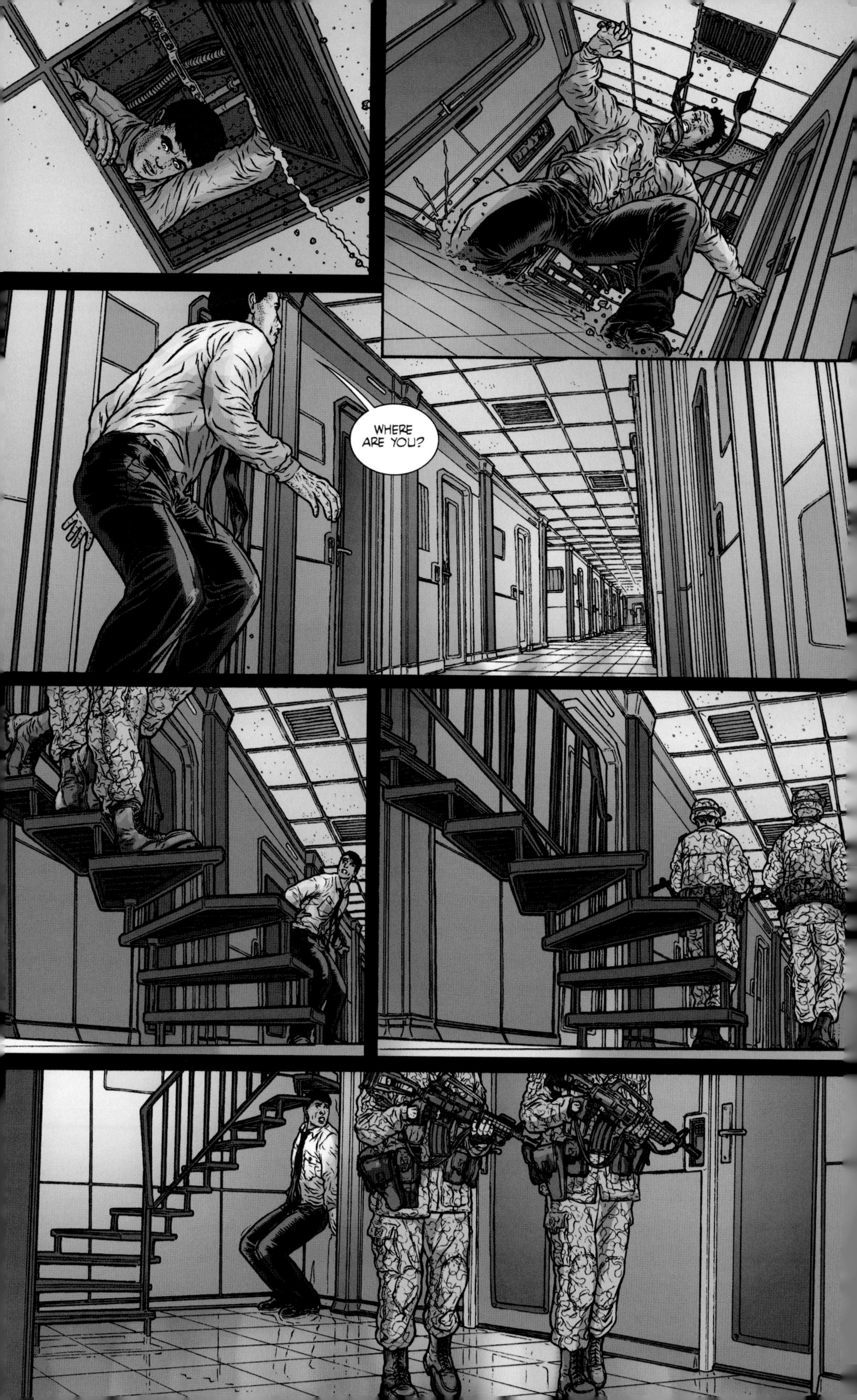
WHERE ARE YOU?

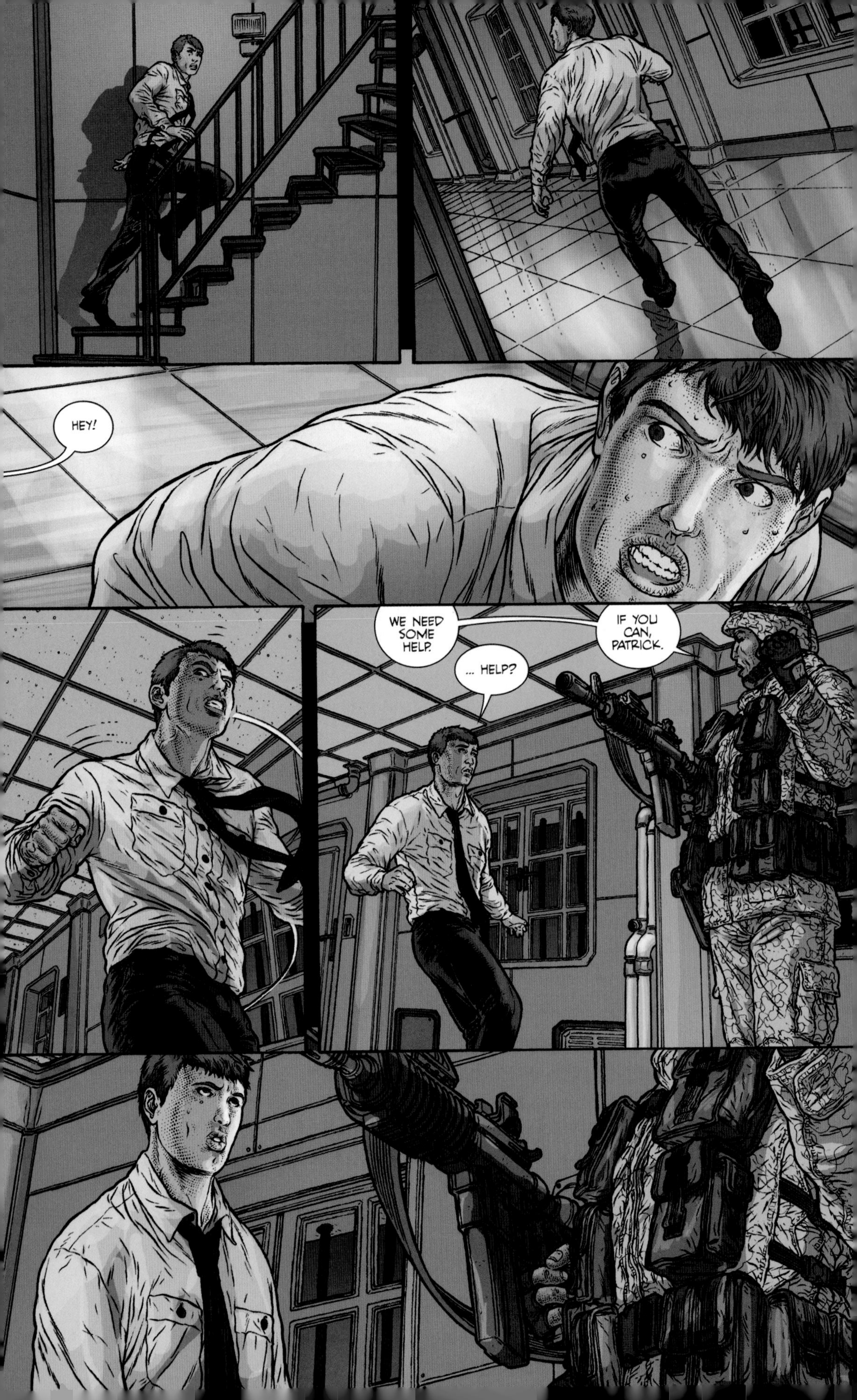
HEY!
WE NEED SOME HELP.
IF YOU CAN, PATRICK.
... HELP?

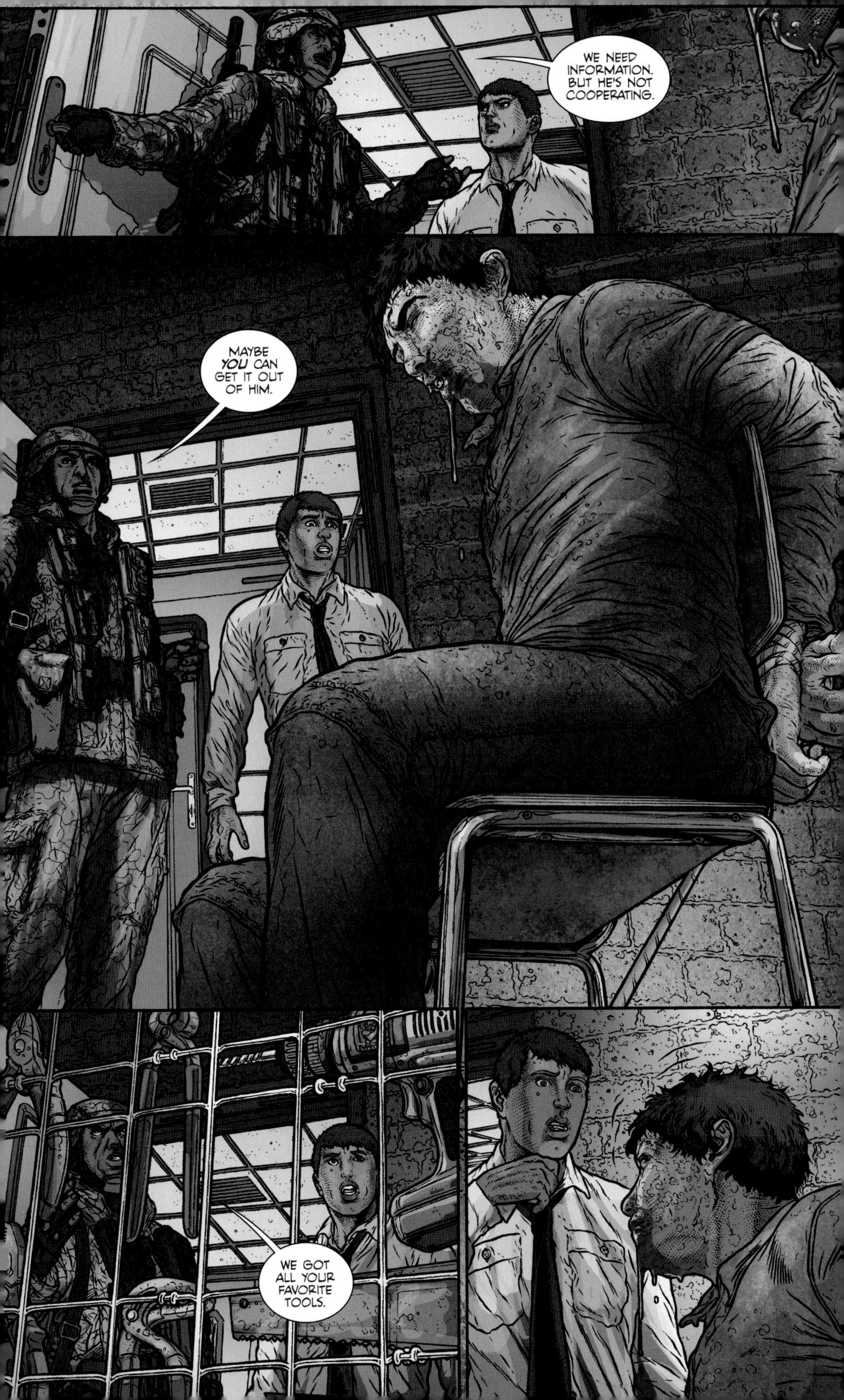
WE NEED INFORMATION. BUT HE'S NOT COOPERATING.
MAYBE YOU CAN GET IT OUT OF HIM.
WE GOT ALL YOUR FAVORITE TOOLS.

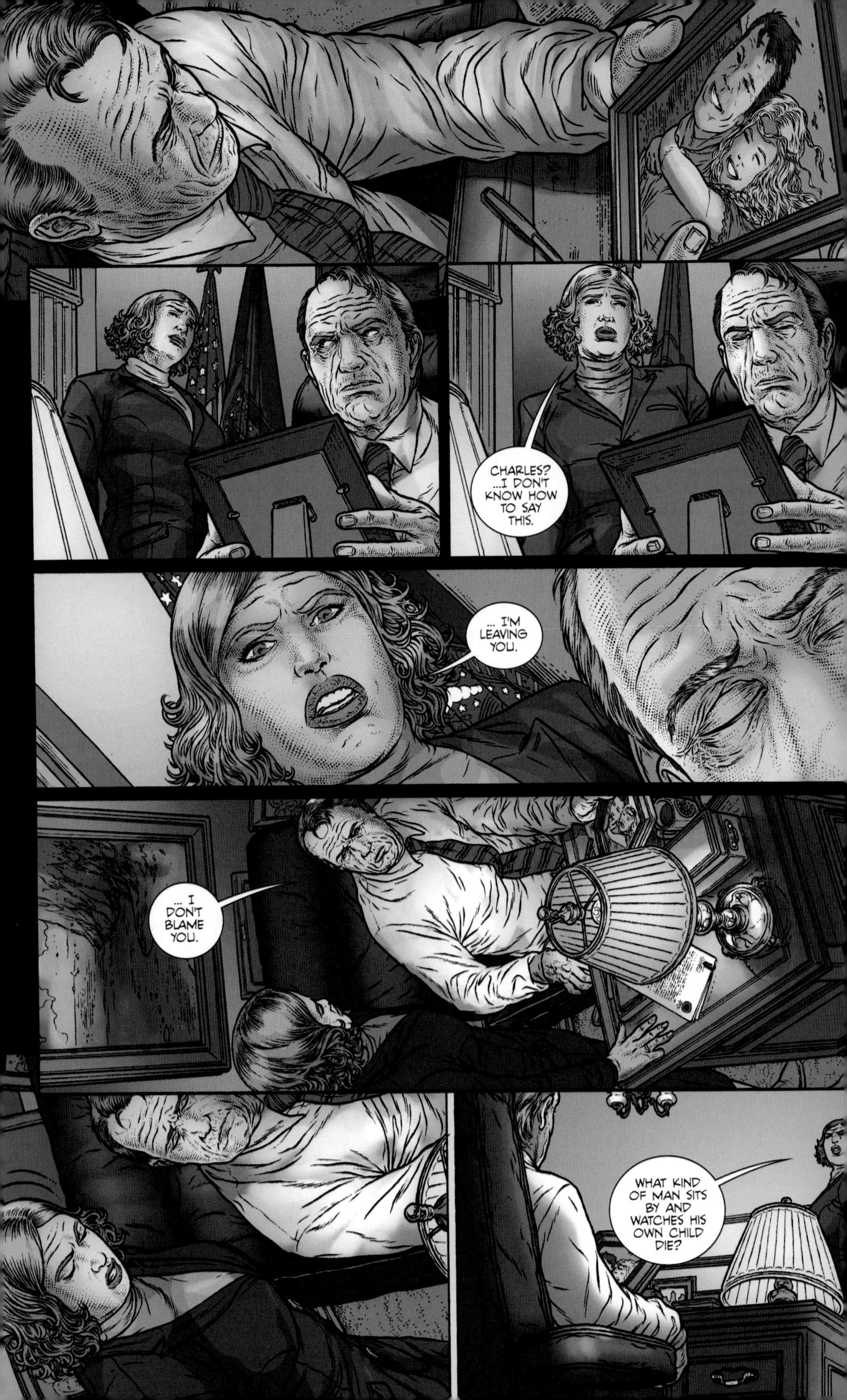
CHARLES? ...I DON'T KNOW HOW TO SAY THIS.
... I'M LEAVING YOU.
... I DON'T BLAME YOU.
WHAT KIND OF MAN SITS BY AND WATCHES HIS OWN CHILD DIE?

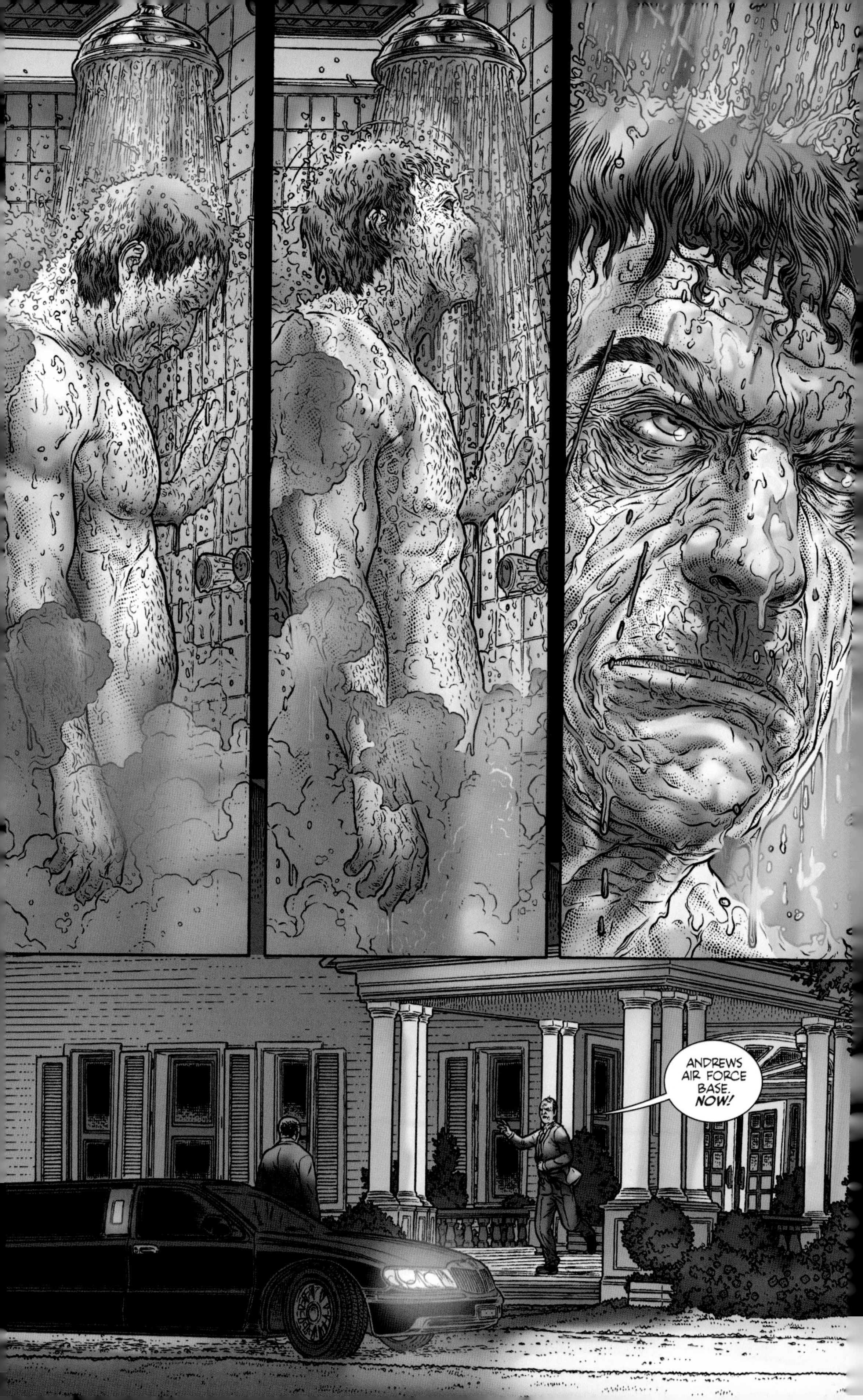
ANDREWS AIR FORCE BASE. NOW!

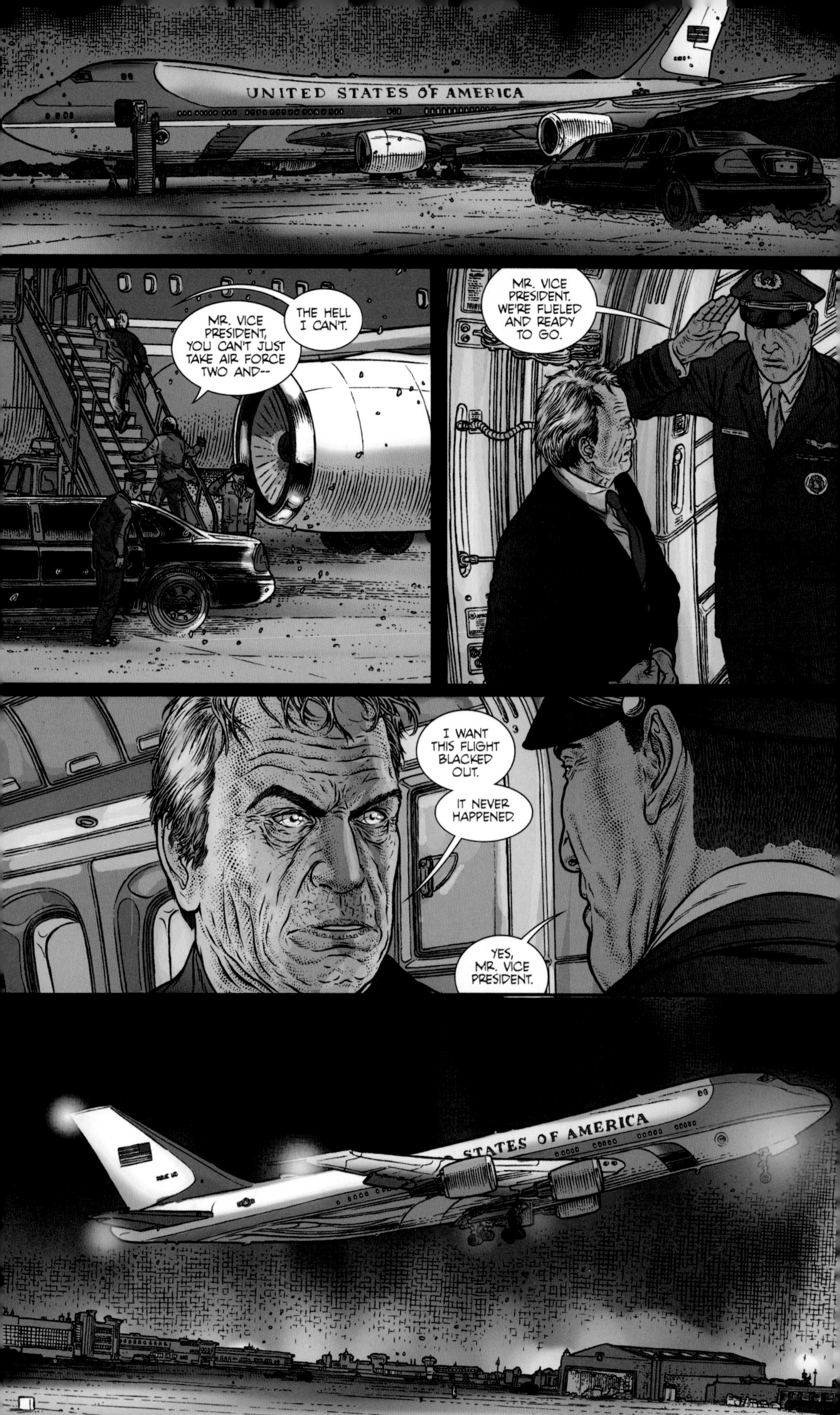
UNITED STATES OF AMERICA
MR. VICE PRESIDENT, YOU CAN'T JUST TAKE AIR FORCE TWO AND--
THE HELL I CAN'T.
MR. VICE PRESIDENT. WE'RE FUELED AND READY TO GO.
I WANT THIS FLIGHT BLACKED OUT.
IT NEVER HAPPENED.
YES, MR. VICE PRESIDENT.
STATES OF AMERICA

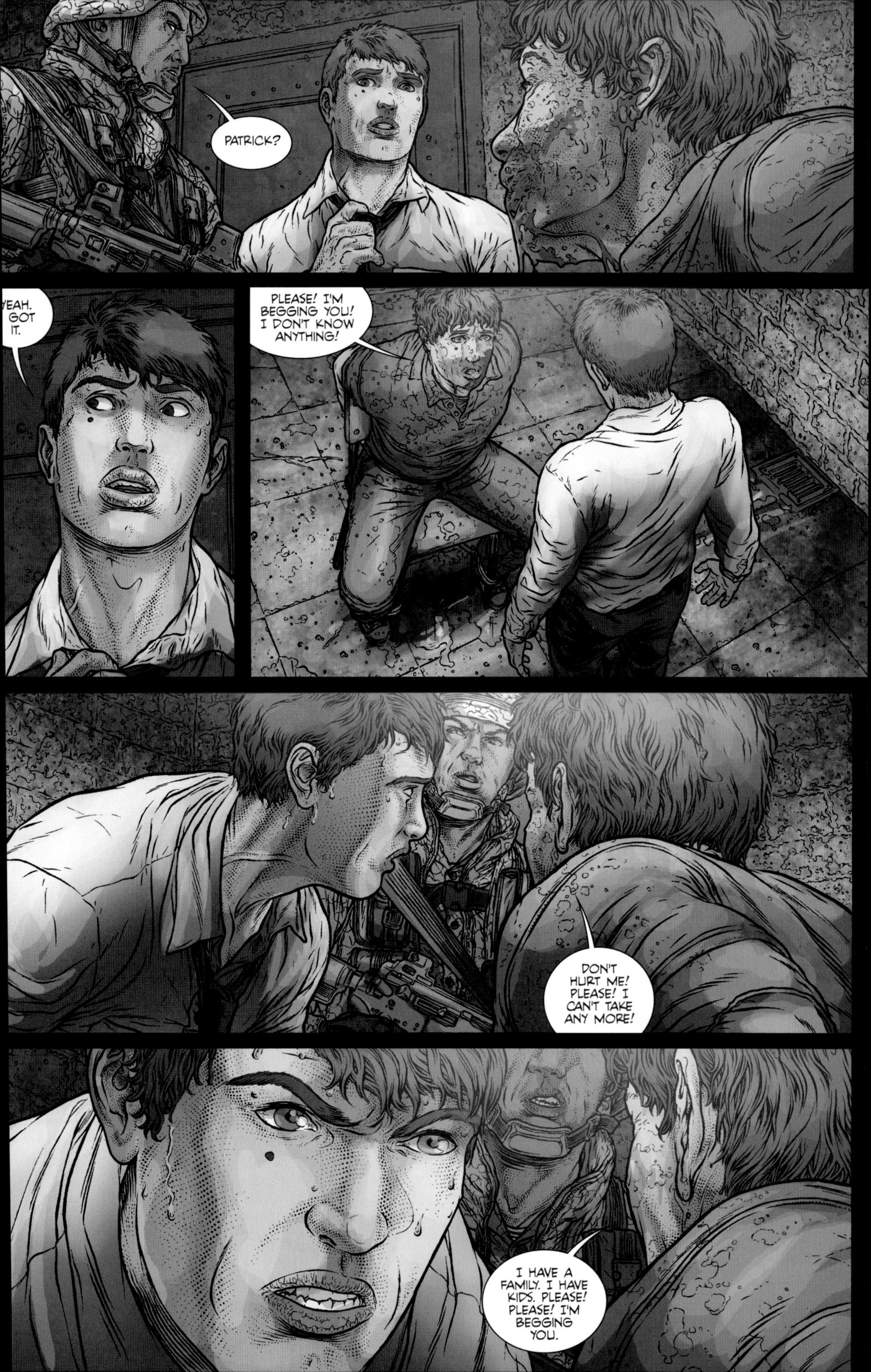
PATRICK?
YEAH. GOT IT.
PLEASE! I'M BEGGING YOU! I DON'T KNOW ANYTHING!
DON'T HURT ME! PLEASE! I CAN'T TAKE ANY MORE!
I HAVE A FAMILY. I HAVE KIDS. PLEASE! PLEASE! I'M BEGGING YOU.

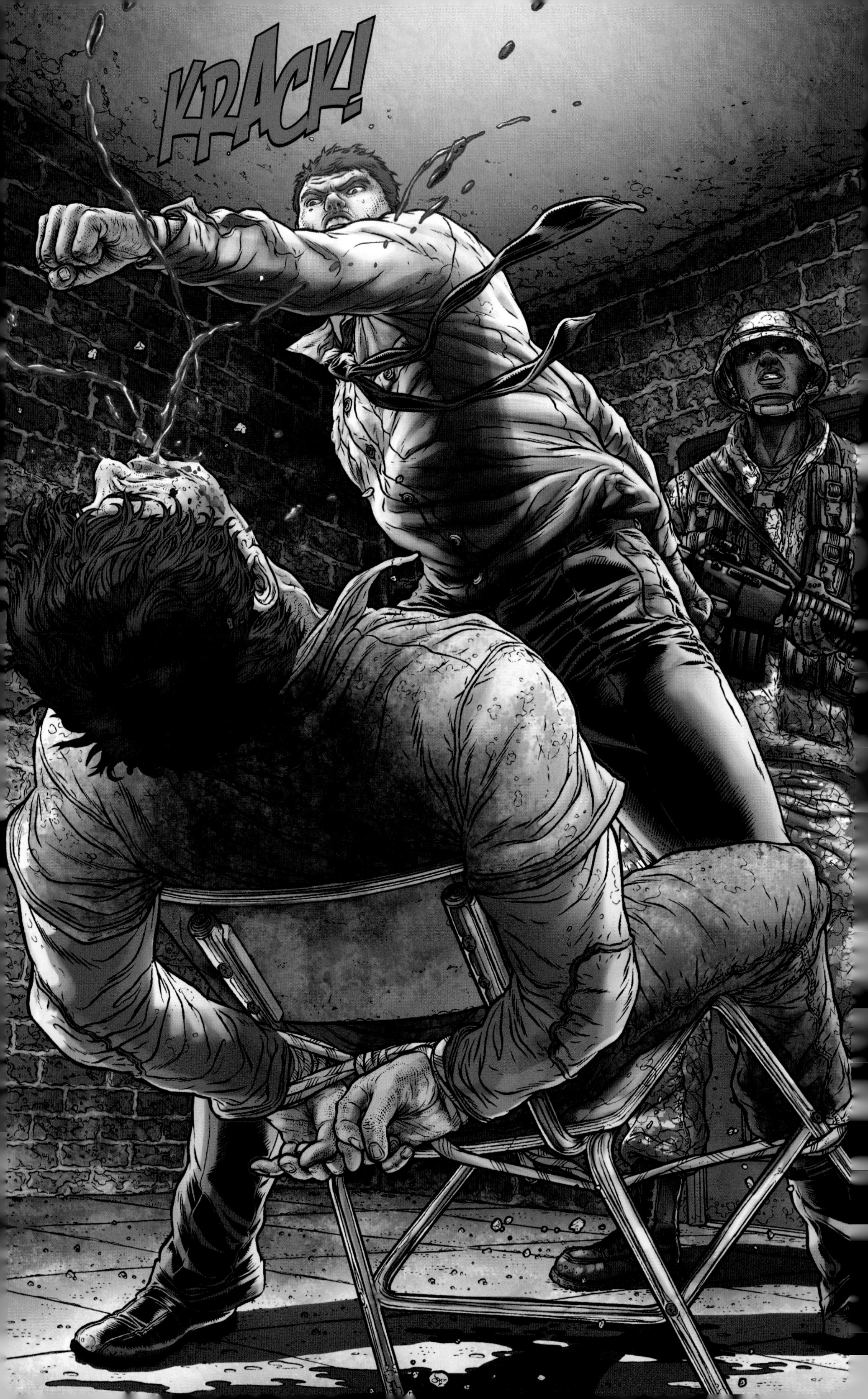
KRACK!

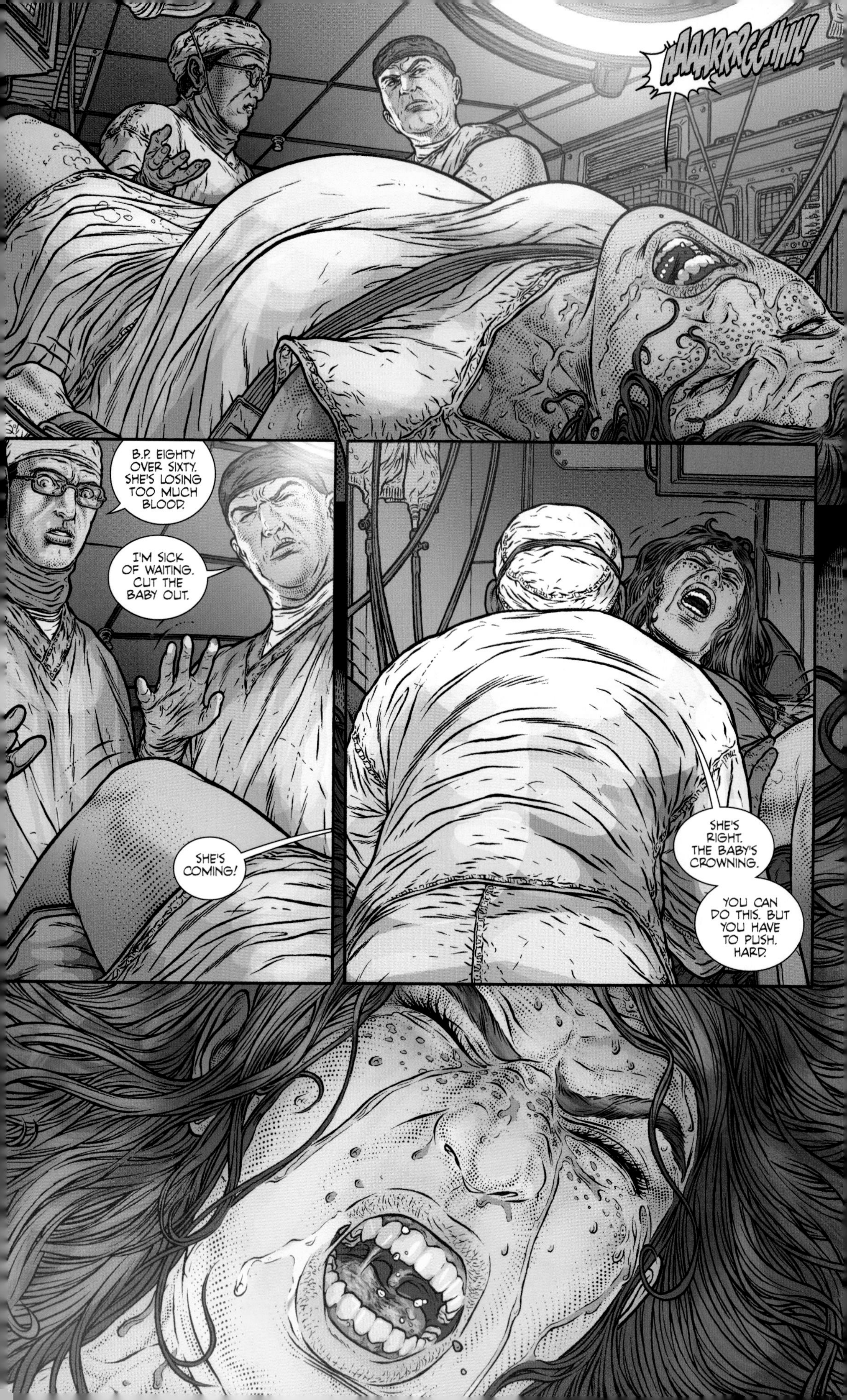
AAAARRRGGHHH!
B.P. EIGHTY OVER SIXTY. SHE'S LOSING TOO MUCH BLOOD.
I'M SICK OF WAITING. CUT THE BABY OUT.
SHE'S COMING!
SHE'S RIGHT. THE BABY'S CROWNING.
YOU CAN DO THIS. BUT YOU HAVE TO PUSH. HARD.

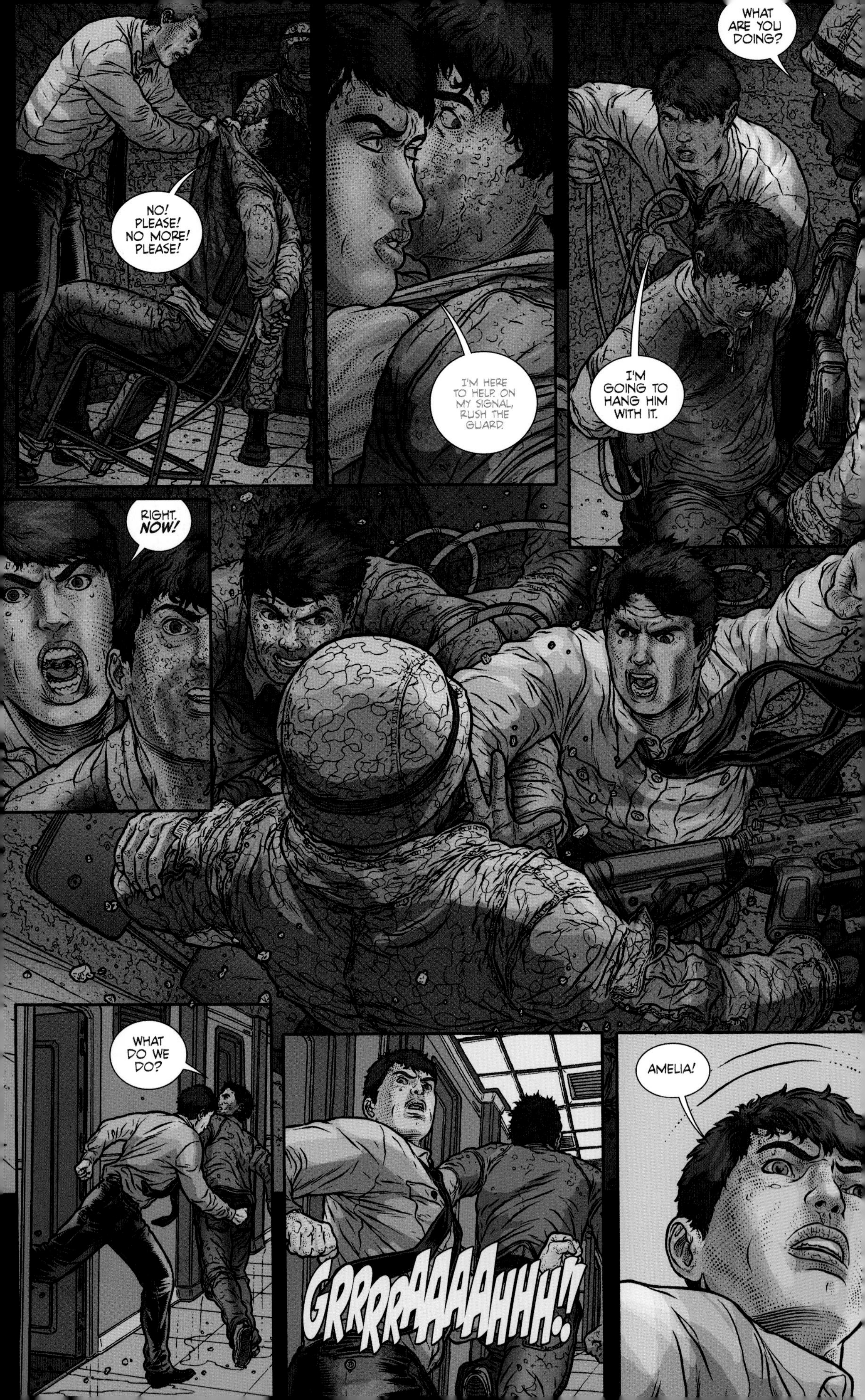
NO! PLEASE! NO MORE! PLEASE!
I'M HERE TO HELP. ON MY SIGNAL, RUSH THE GUARD.
WHAT ARE YOU DOING?
I'M GOING TO HANG HIM WITH IT.
RIGHT. NOW!
WHAT DO WE DO?
GRRRRAAAAAHHH!!
AMELIA!

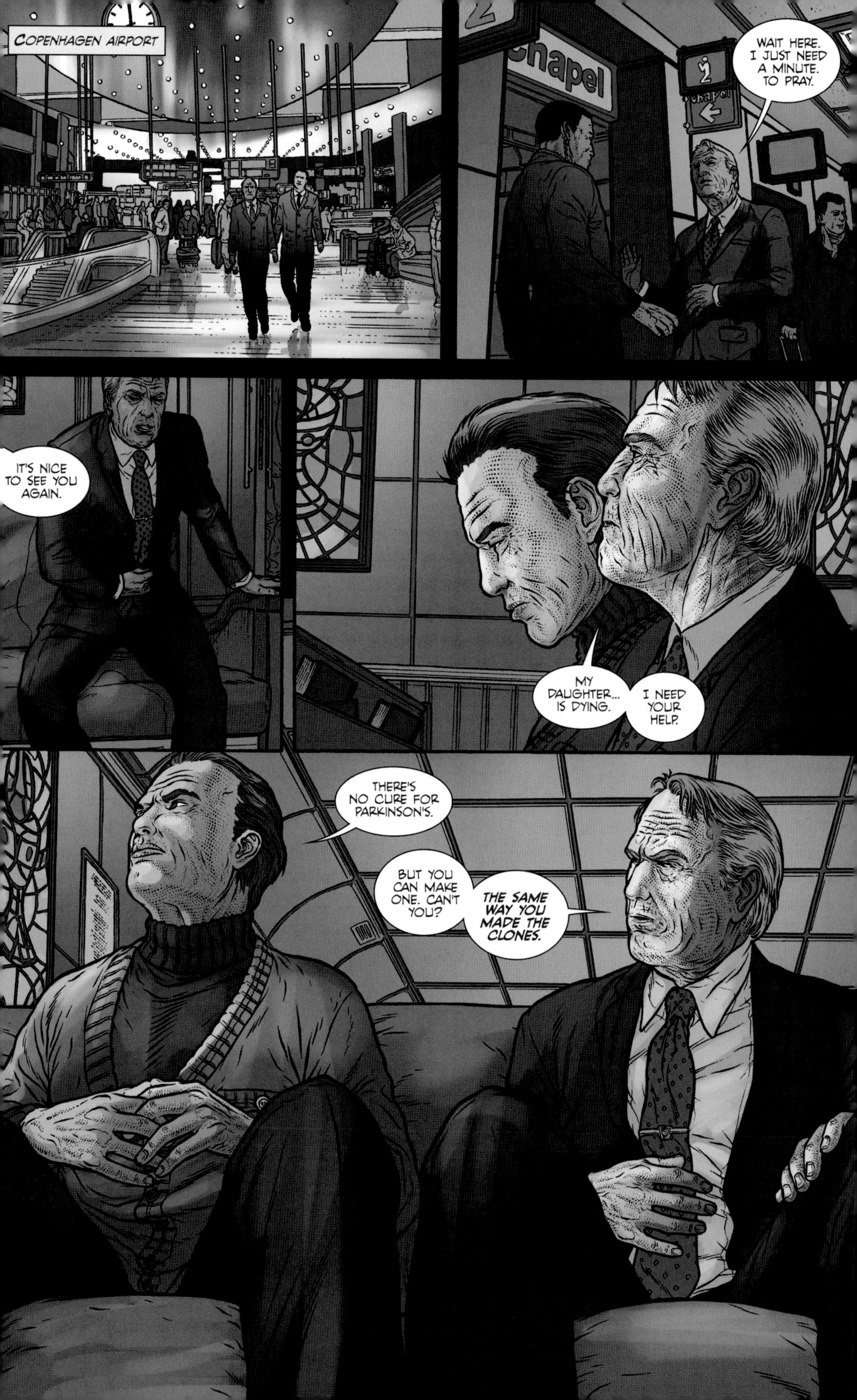
COPENHAGEN AIRPORT
Chapel
chapel
WAIT HERE. I JUST NEED A MINUTE. TO PRAY.
IT'S NICE TO SEE YOU AGAIN.
MY DAUGHTER... IS DYING.
I NEED YOUR HELP.
THERE'S NO CURE FOR PARKINSON'S.
BUT YOU CAN MAKE ONE. CAN'T YOU?
THE SAME WAY YOU MADE THE CLONES.

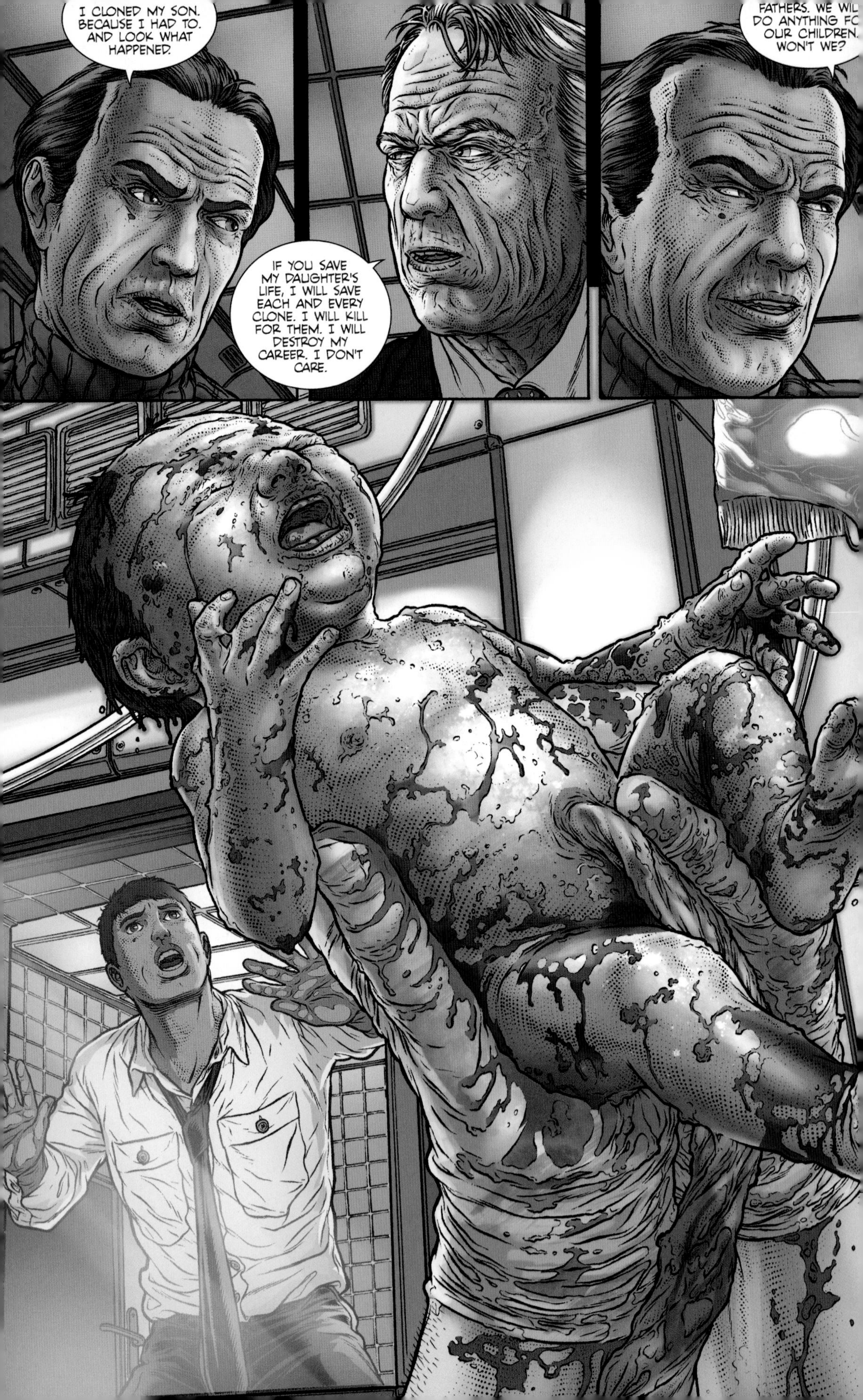
I CLONED MY SON. BECAUSE I HAD TO. AND LOOK WHAT HAPPENED.
IF YOU SAVE MY DAUGHTER'S LIFE, I WILL SAVE EACH AND EVERY CLONE. I WILL KILL FOR THEM. I WILL DESTROY MY CAREER. I DON'T CARE.
FATHERS. WE WIL DO ANYTHING FC OUR CHILDREN. WON'T WE?

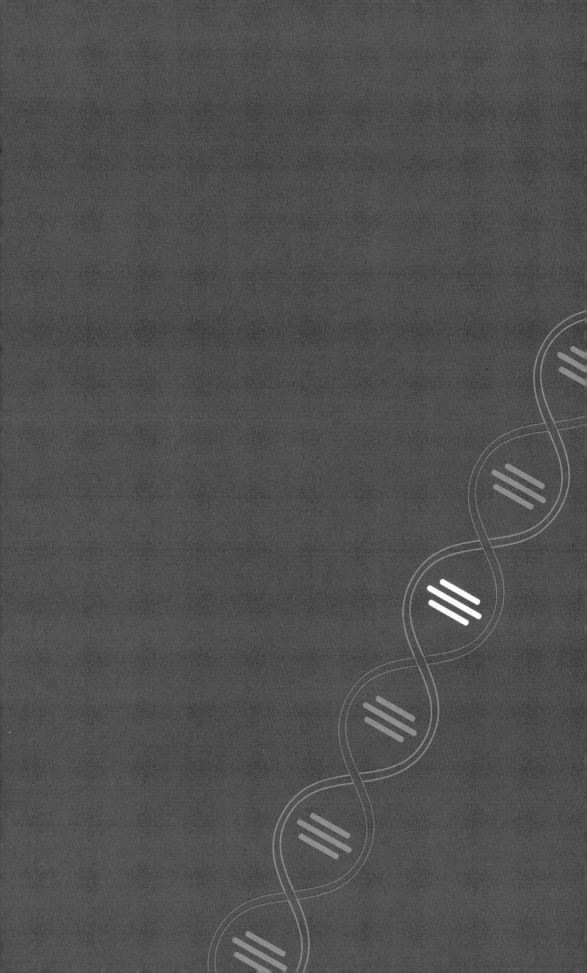

CHAPTER 4

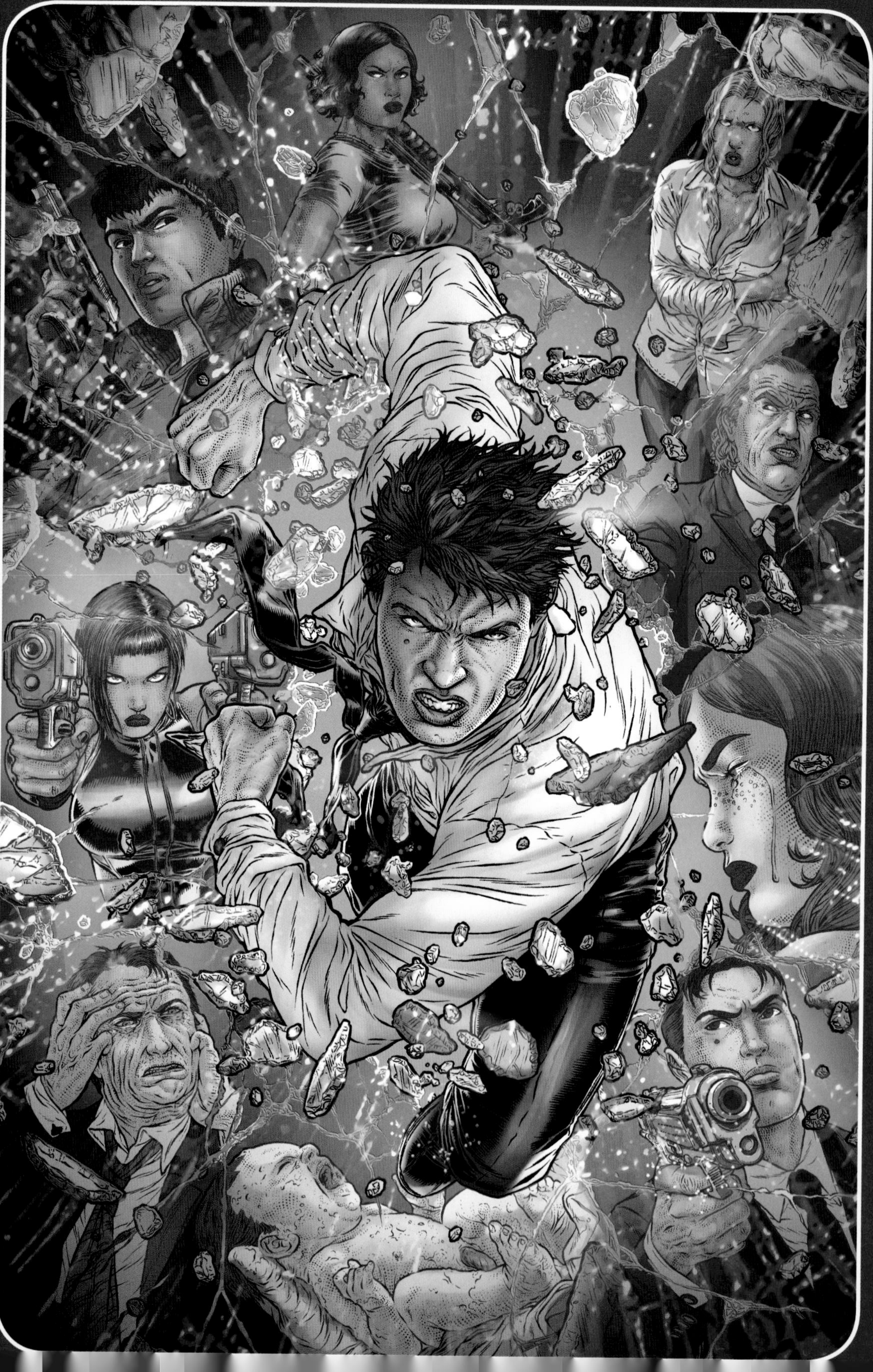

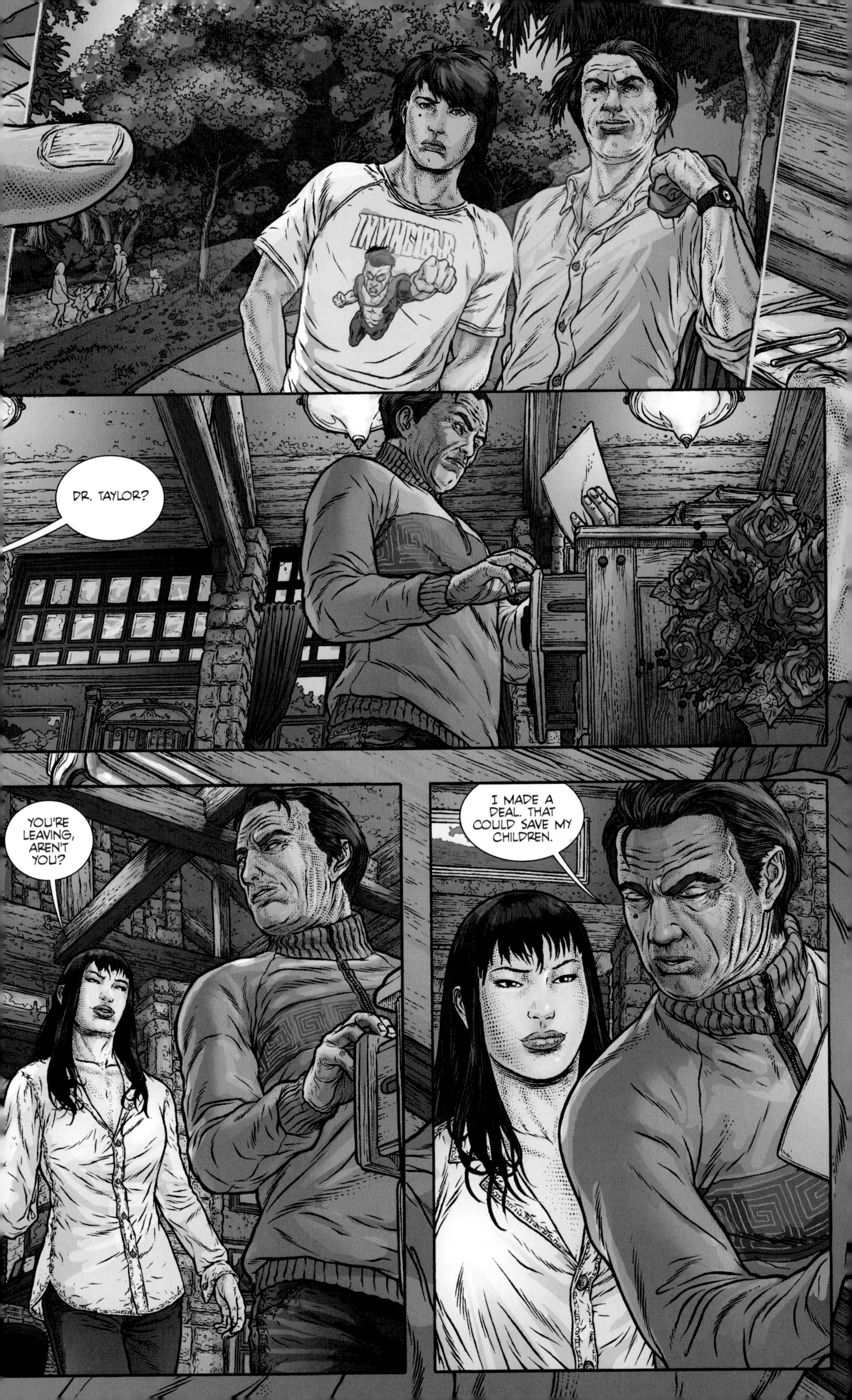
INVINCIBLE
DR. TAYLOR?
YOU'RE LEAVING, AREN'T YOU?
I MADE A DEAL. THAT COULD SAVE MY CHILDREN.

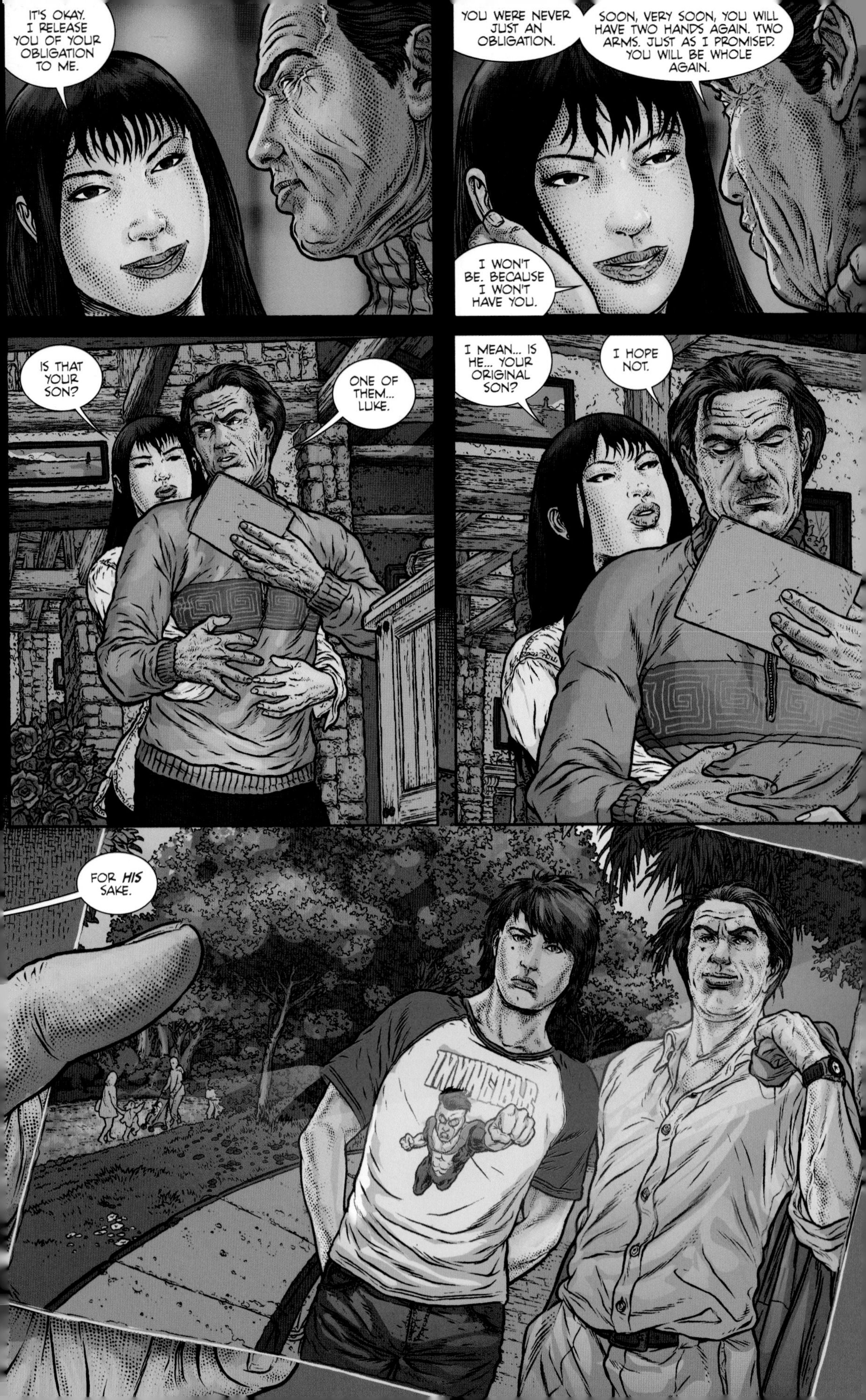
IT'S OKAY. I RELEASE YOU OF YOUR OBLIGATION TO ME.
YOU WERE NEVER JUST AN OBLIGATION.
SOON, VERY SOON, YOU WILL HAVE TWO HANDS AGAIN. TWO ARMS. JUST AS I PROMISED. YOU WILL BE WHOLE AGAIN.
I WON'T BE. BECAUSE I WON'T HAVE YOU.
IS THAT YOUR SON?
ONE OF THEM... LUKE.
I MEAN... IS HE... YOUR ORIGINAL SON?
I HOPE NOT.
FOR HIS SAKE.
INVINCIBLE

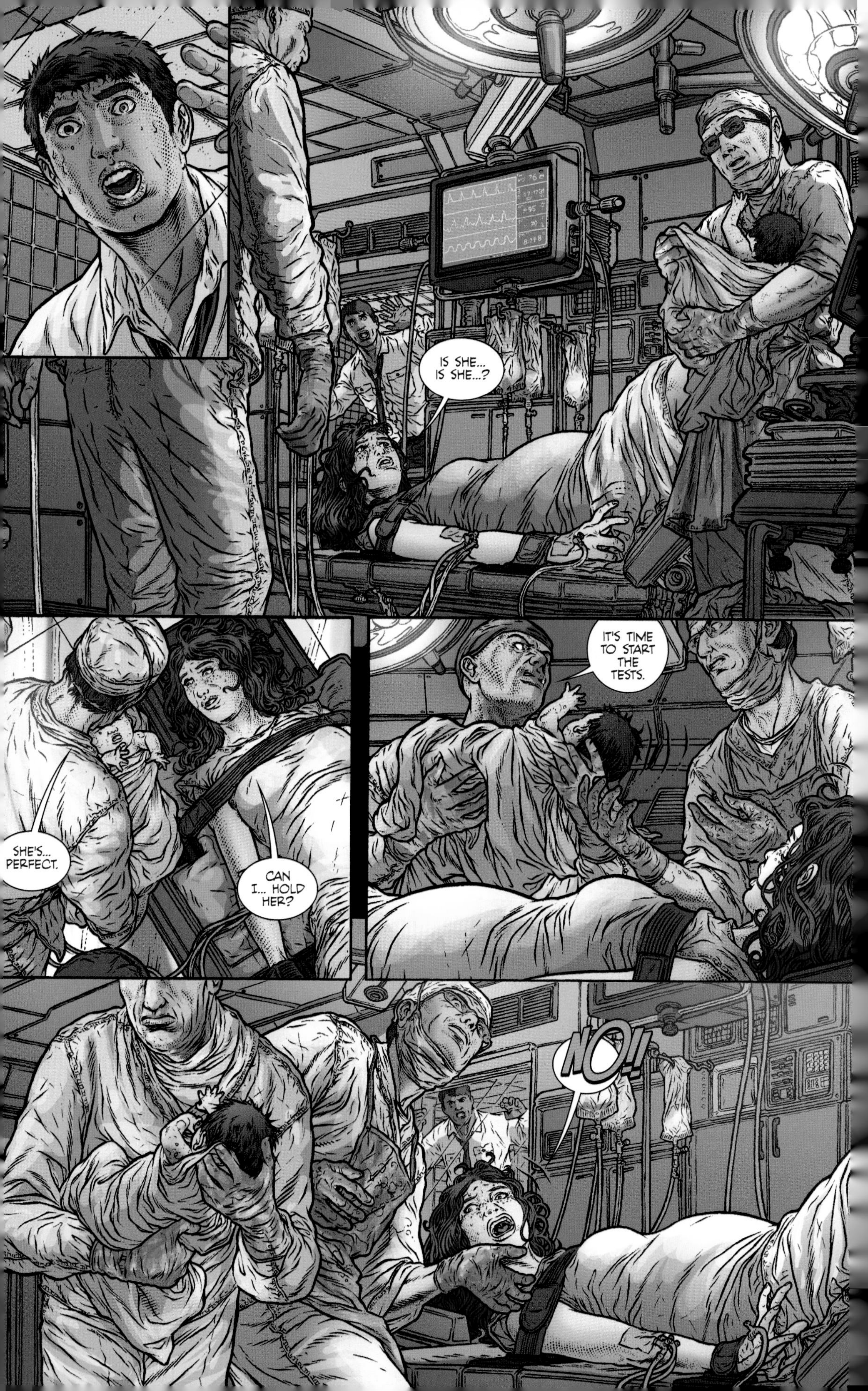
IS SHE... IS SHE...?
SHE'S... PERFECT.
CAN I... HOLD HER?
IT'S TIME TO START THE TESTS.
NO!!

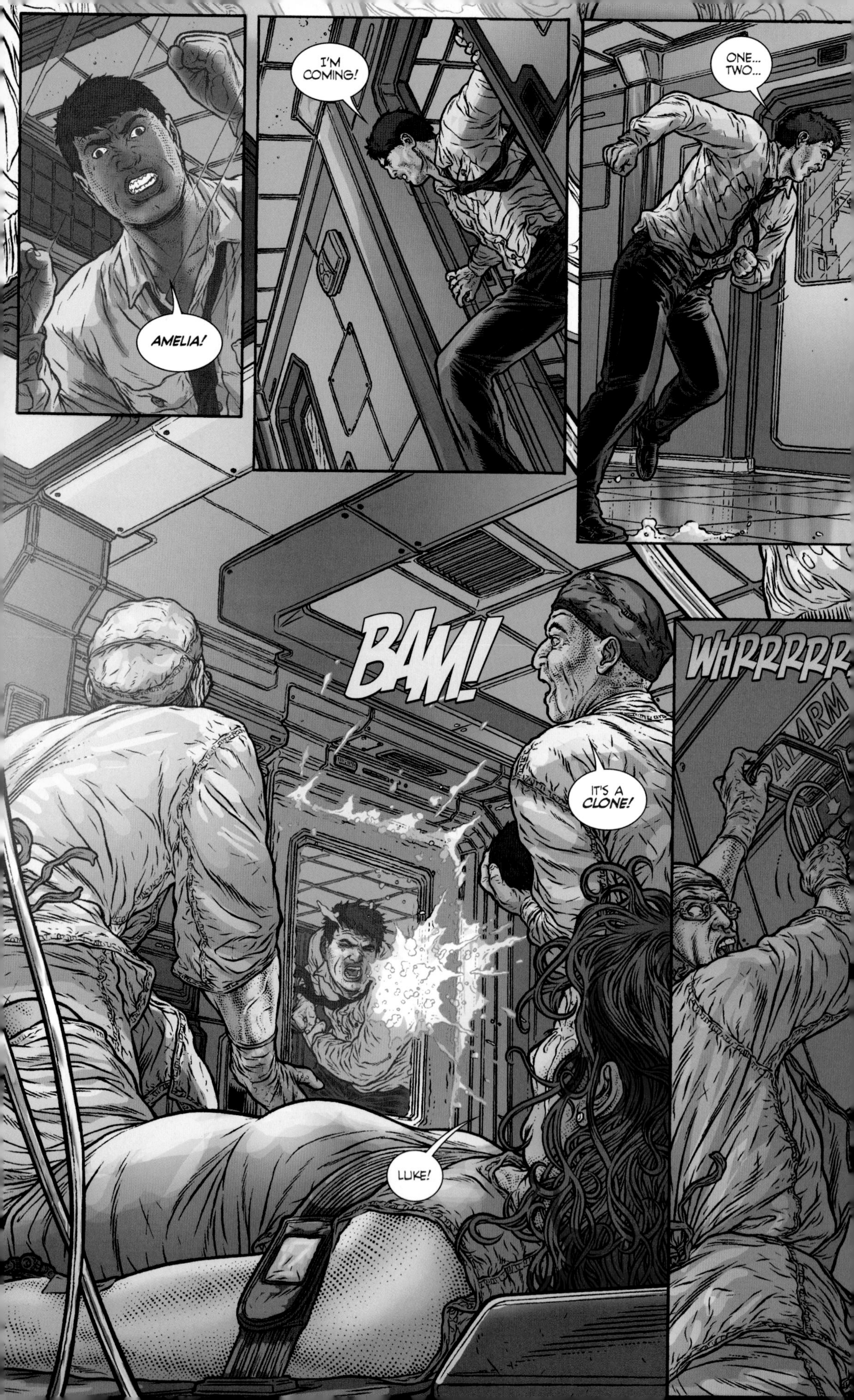
AMELIA!
I'M COMING!
ONE... TWO...
BAM!
IT'S A CLONE!
LUKE!
WHRRRRR
ALARM

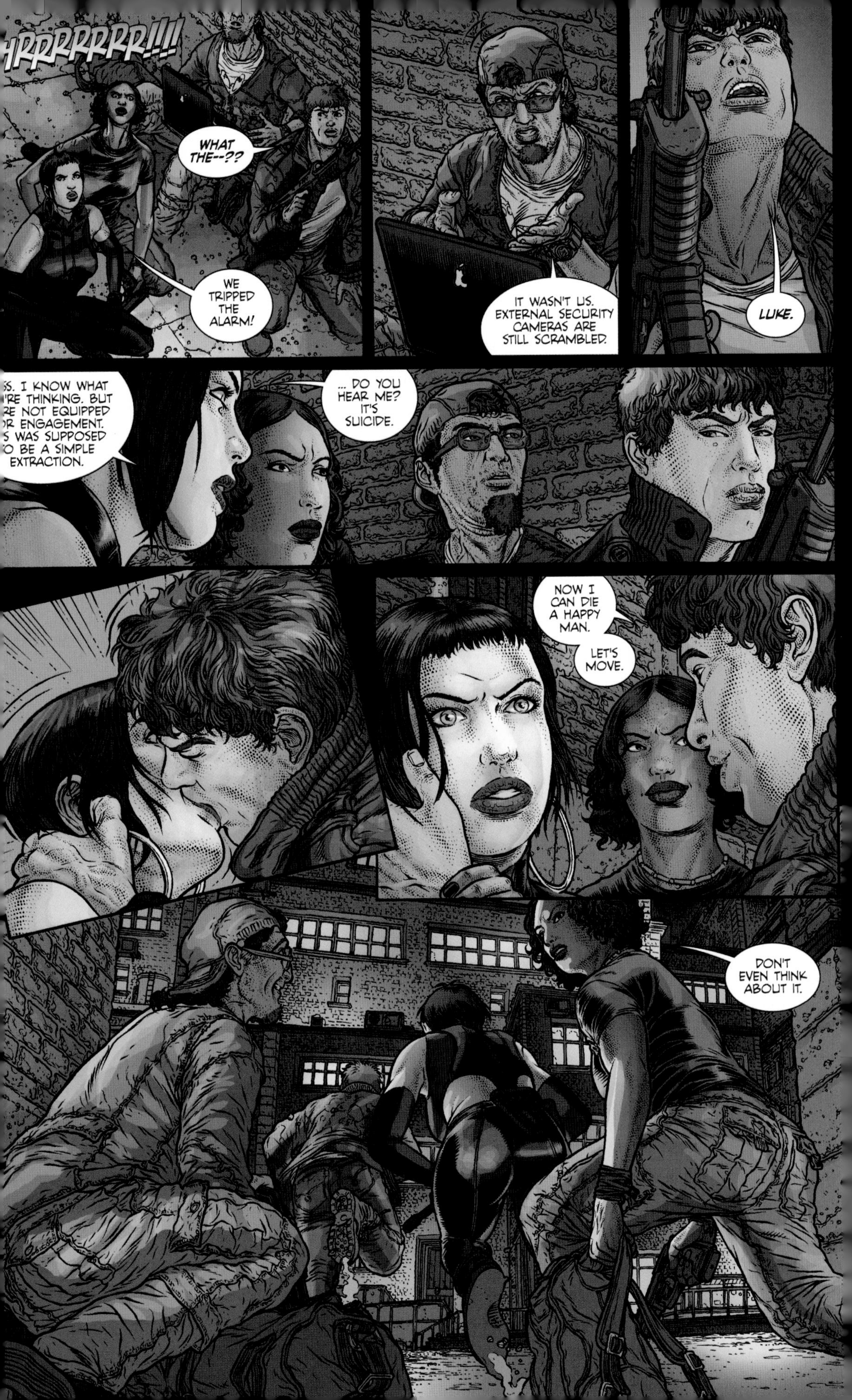
HRRRRRRR!!!!
WHAT THE--??
WE TRIPPED THE ALARM!
IT WASN'T US. EXTERNAL SECURITY CAMERAS ARE STILL SCRAMBLED.
LUKE.
...S. I KNOW WHAT ...'RE THINKING. BUT ...RE NOT EQUIPPED ...R ENGAGEMENT. ...S WAS SUPPOSED ...O BE A SIMPLE EXTRACTION.
... DO YOU HEAR ME? IT'S SUICIDE.
NOW I CAN DIE A HAPPY MAN.
LET'S MOVE.
DON'T EVEN THINK ABOUT IT.

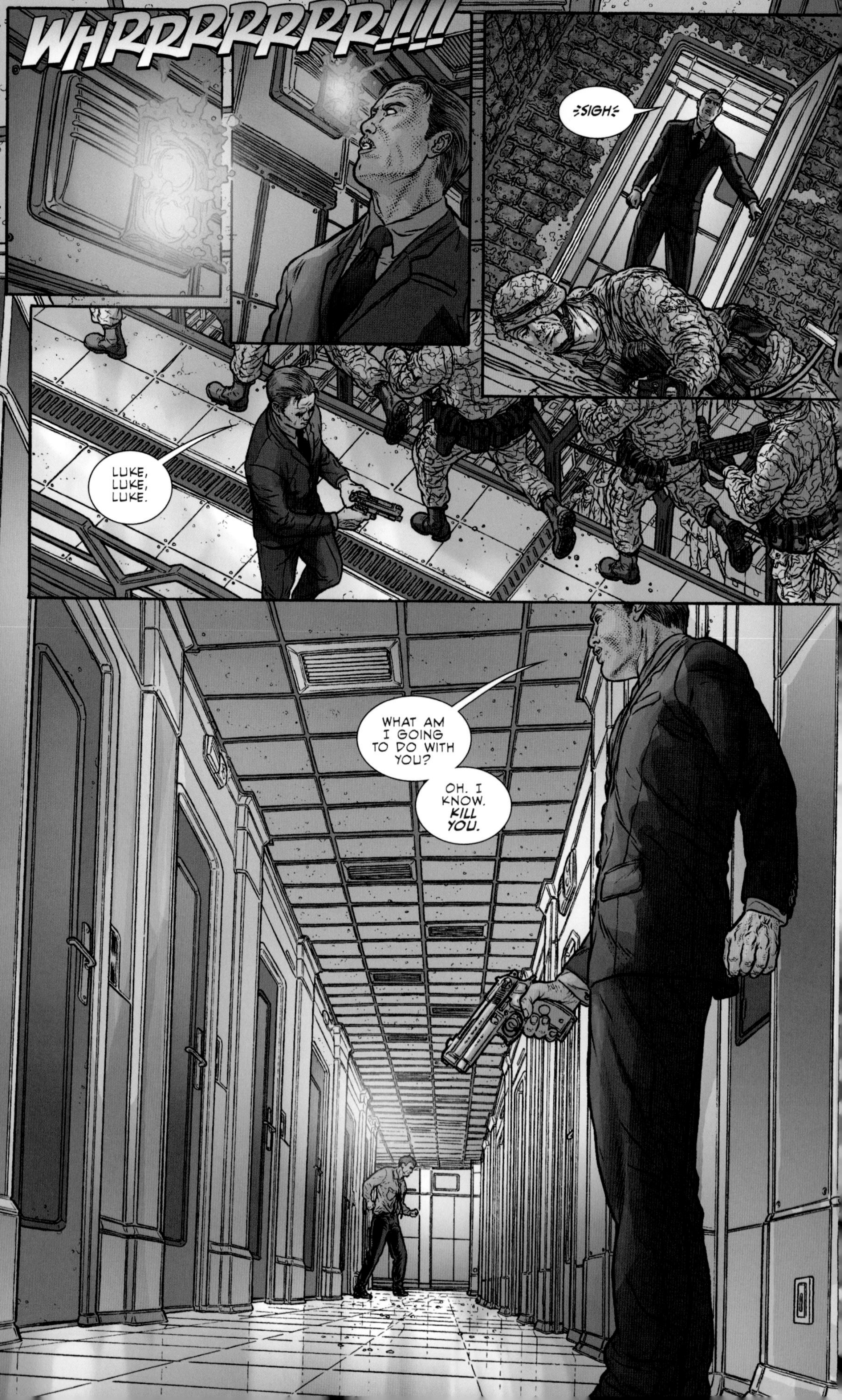
WHRRRRRRRR!!!!
SIGH
LUKE, LUKE, LUKE.
WHAT AM I GOING TO DO WITH YOU?
OH. I KNOW. KILL YOU.

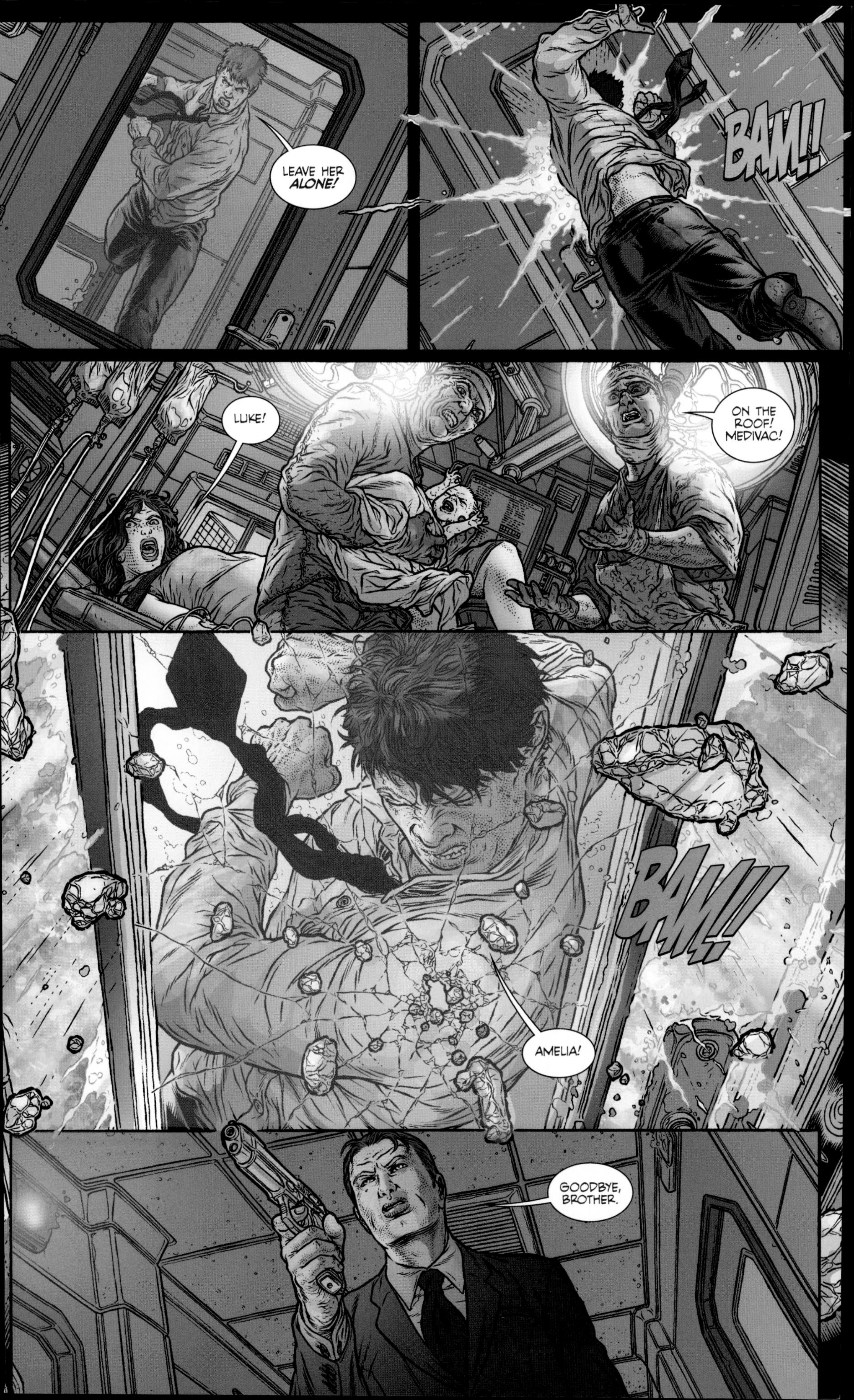
LEAVE HER ALONE!
BAM!!
LUKE!
ON THE ROOF! MEDIVAC!
BAM!!
AMELIA!
GOODBYE, BROTHER.

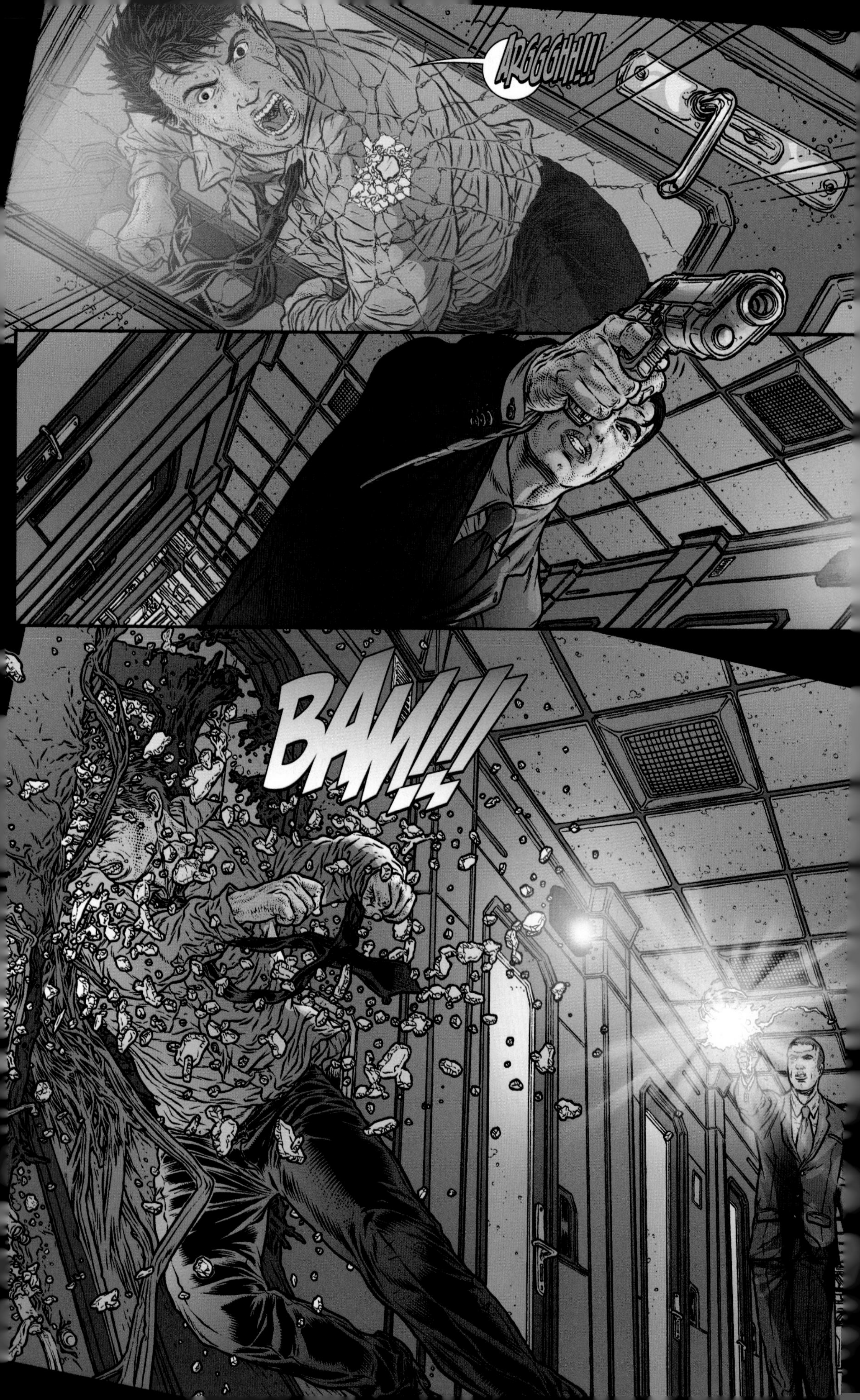
ARGGGHH!!!
BAM!!!

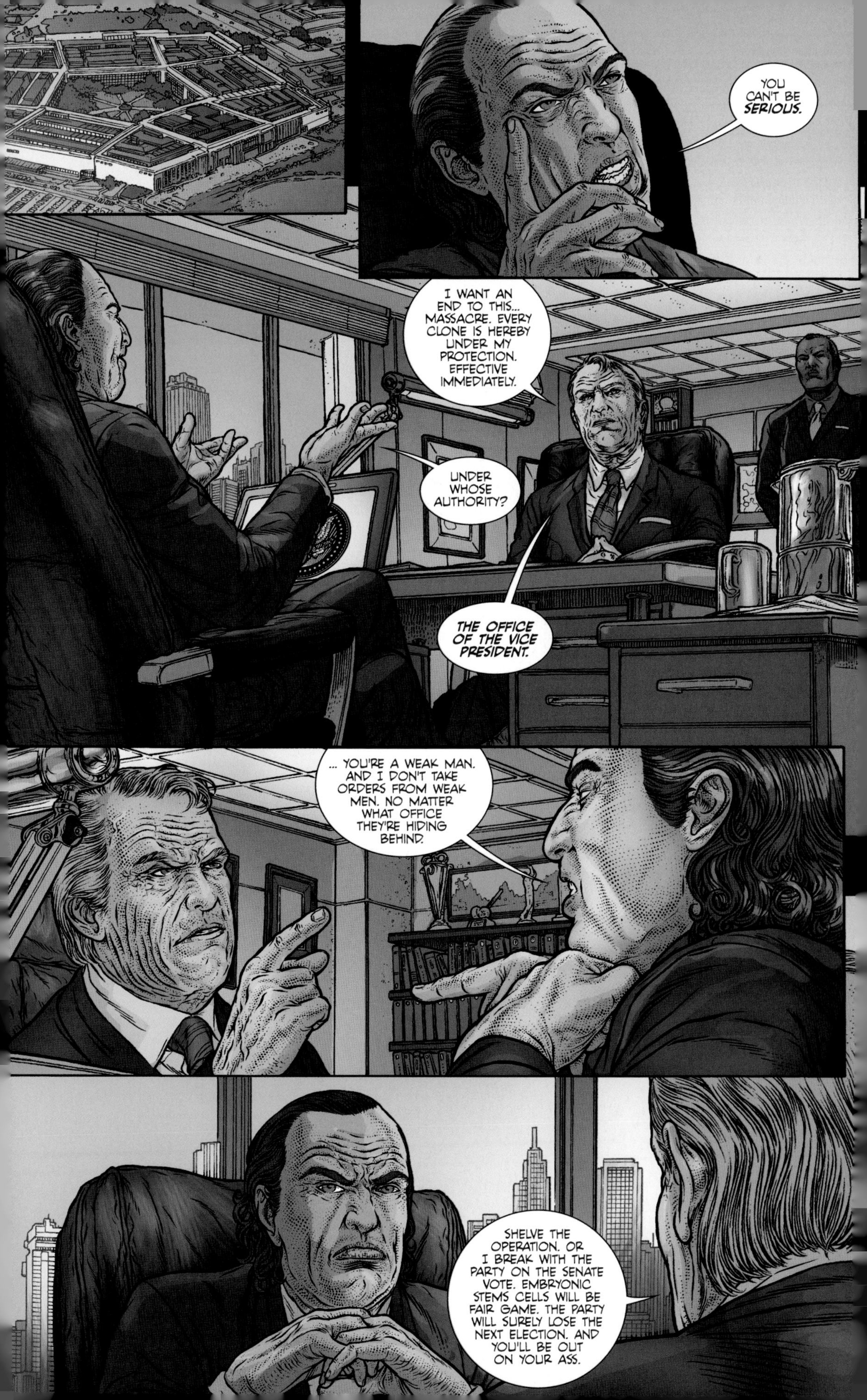
YOU CAN'T BE SERIOUS.
I WANT AN END TO THIS... MASSACRE. EVERY CLONE IS HEREBY UNDER MY PROTECTION. EFFECTIVE IMMEDIATELY.
UNDER WHOSE AUTHORITY?
THE OFFICE OF THE VICE PRESIDENT.
... YOU'RE A WEAK MAN. AND I DON'T TAKE ORDERS FROM WEAK MEN. NO MATTER WHAT OFFICE THEY'RE HIDING BEHIND.
SHELVE THE OPERATION. OR I BREAK WITH THE PARTY ON THE SENATE VOTE. EMBRYONIC STEMS CELLS WILL BE FAIR GAME. THE PARTY WILL SURELY LOSE THE NEXT ELECTION. AND YOU'LL BE OUT ON YOUR ASS.

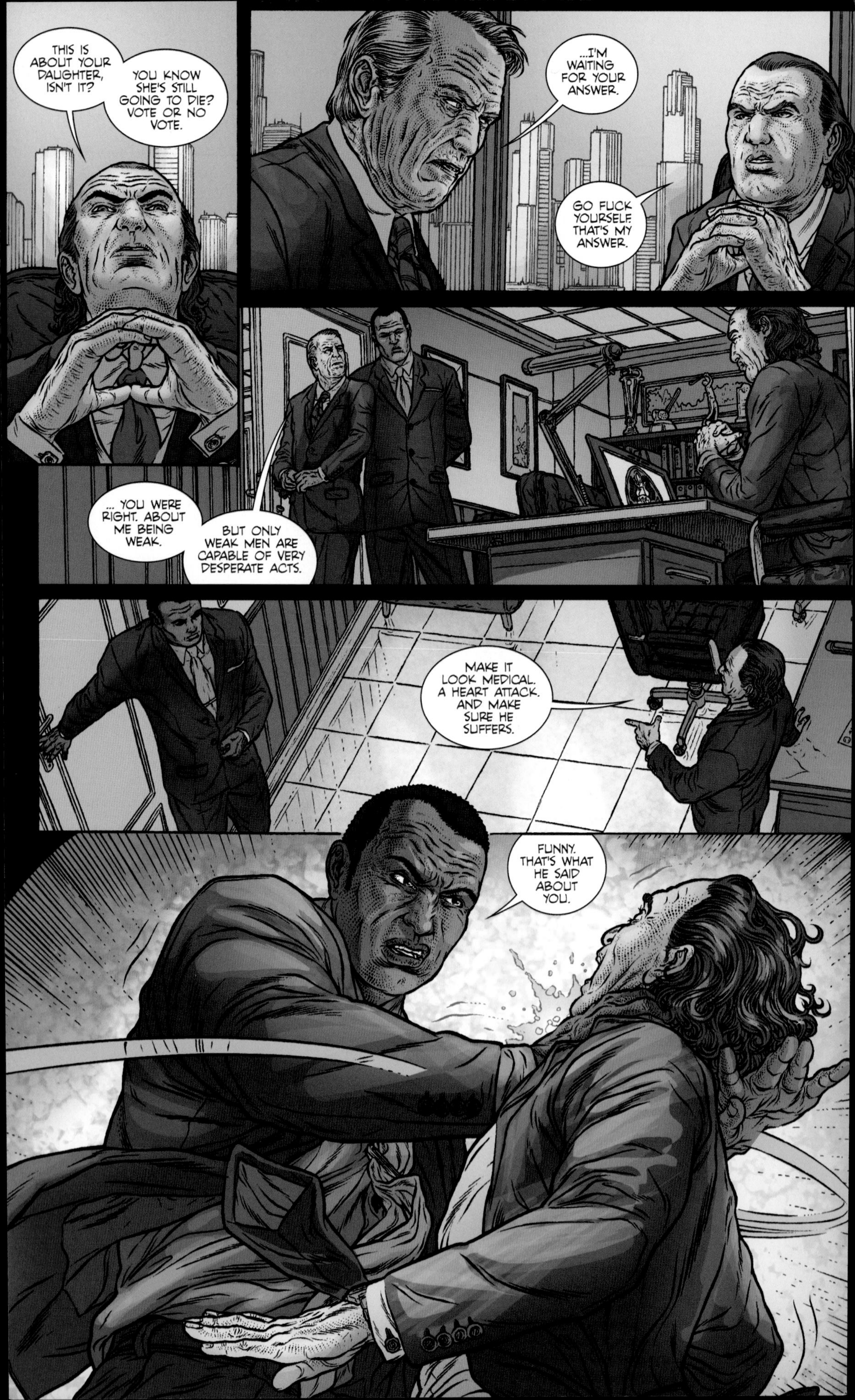
THIS IS ABOUT YOUR DAUGHTER, ISN'T IT?
YOU KNOW SHE'S STILL GOING TO DIE? VOTE OR NO VOTE.
...I'M WAITING FOR YOUR ANSWER.
GO FUCK YOURSELF. THAT'S MY ANSWER.
... YOU WERE RIGHT. ABOUT ME BEING WEAK.
BUT ONLY WEAK MEN ARE CAPABLE OF VERY DESPERATE ACTS.
MAKE IT LOOK MEDICAL. A HEART ATTACK. AND MAKE SURE HE SUFFERS.
FUNNY. THAT'S WHAT HE SAID ABOUT YOU.

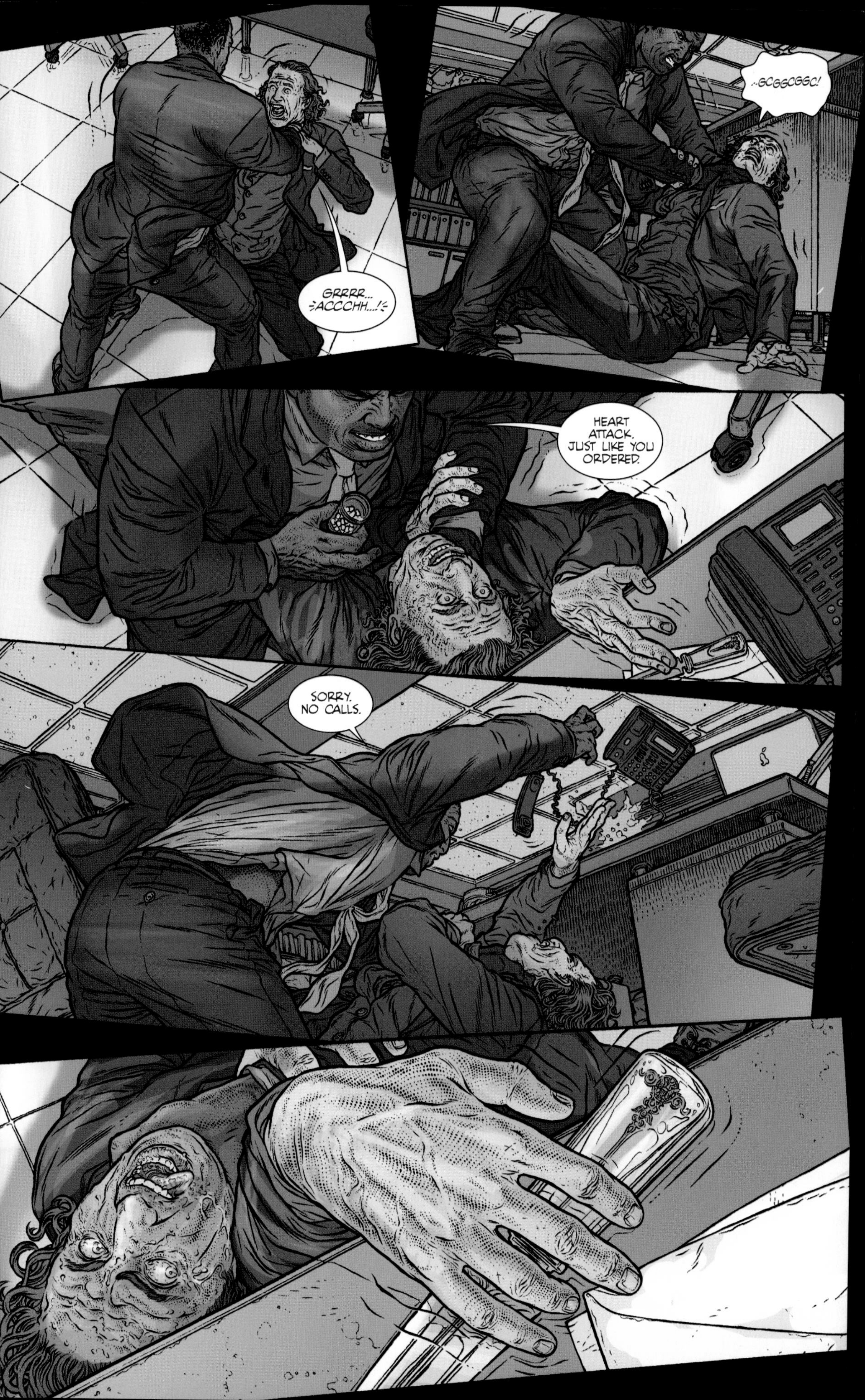
GRRRR... ACCCHH...!
..GCGGCGGC!
HEART ATTACK. JUST LIKE YOU ORDERED.
SORRY. NO CALLS.

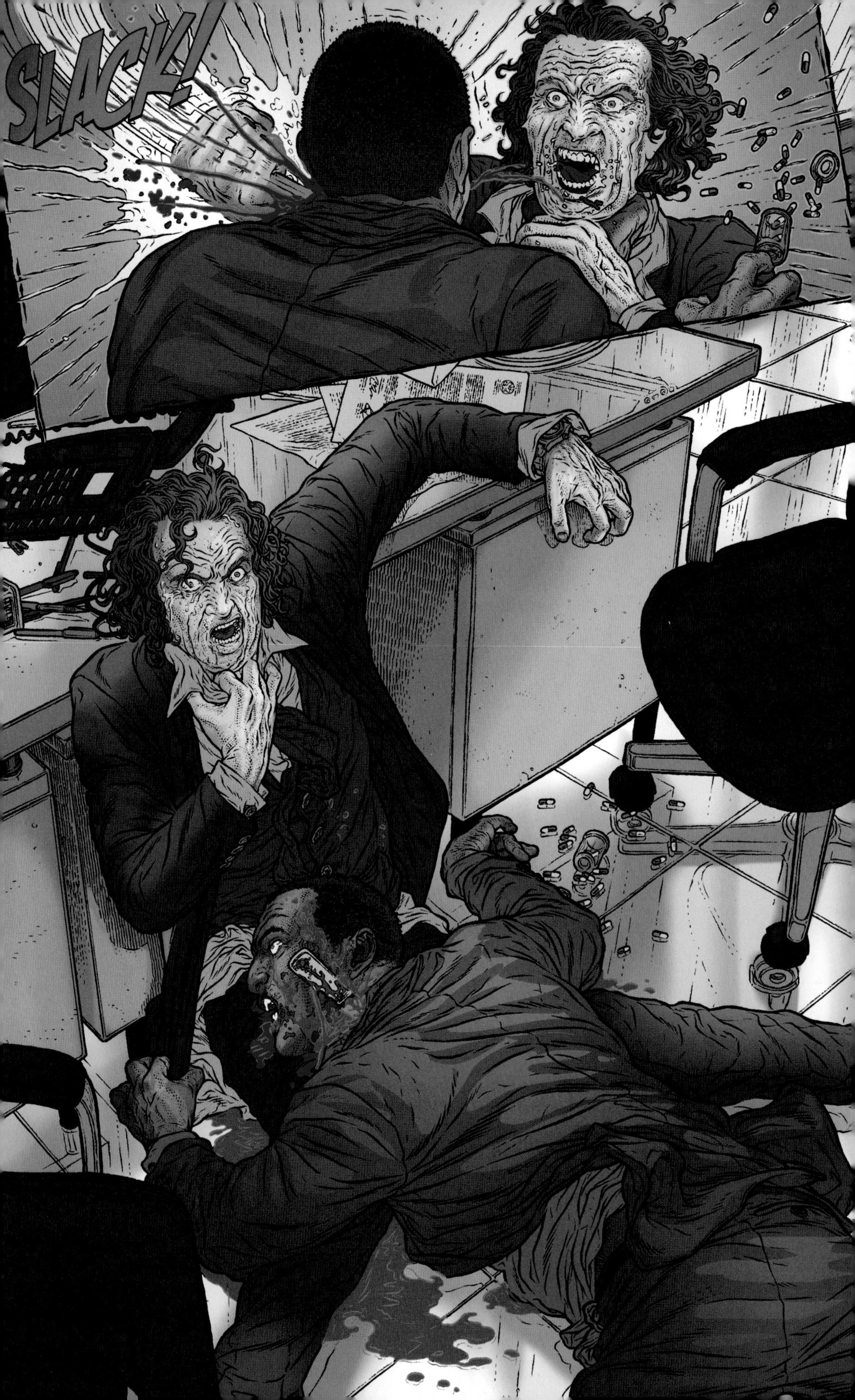
SLACK!

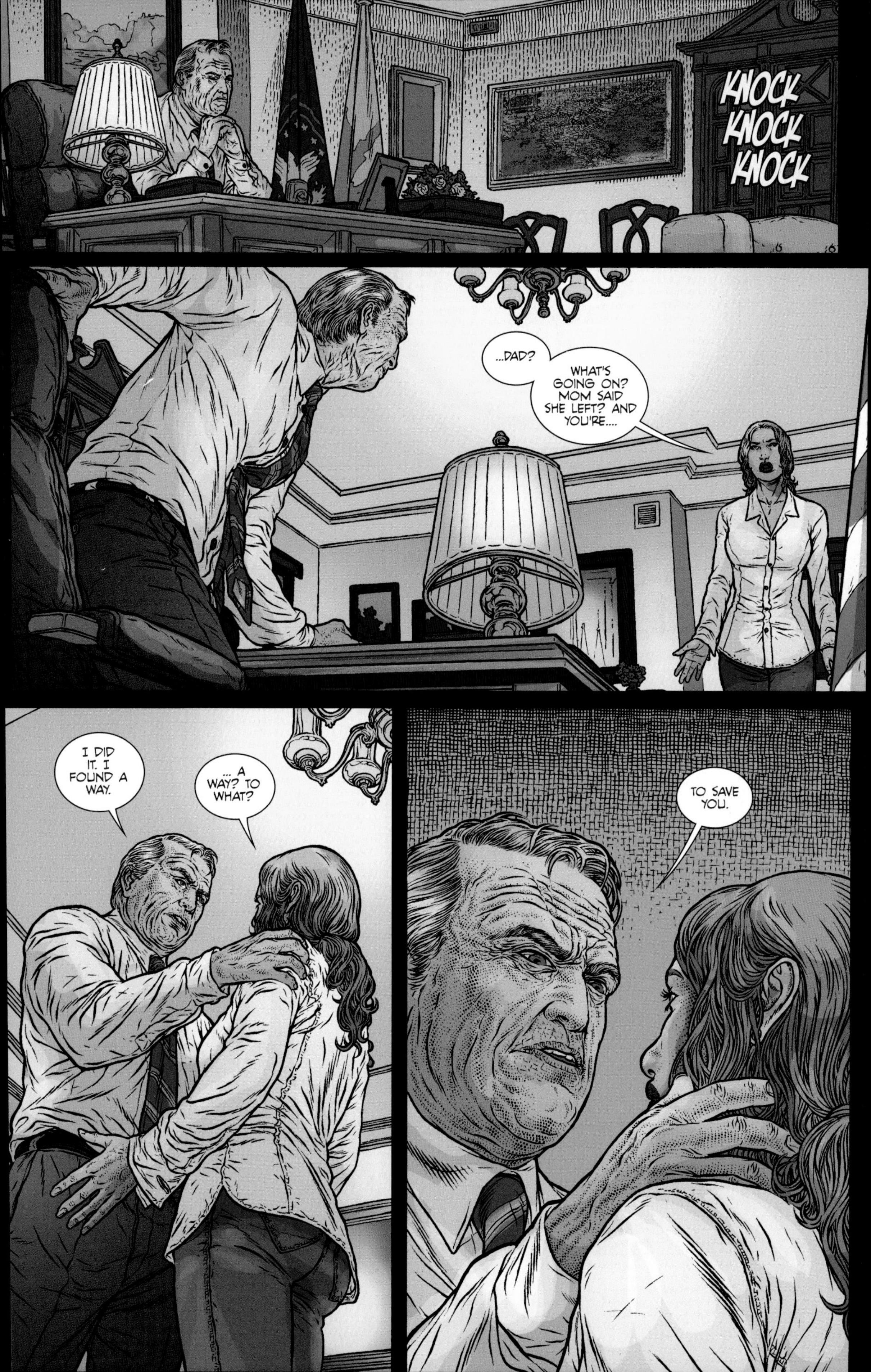
KNOCK KNOCK KNOCK
...DAD?
WHAT'S GOING ON? MOM SAID SHE LEFT? AND YOU'RE....
I DID IT. I FOUND A WAY.
... A WAY? TO WHAT?
TO SAVE YOU.

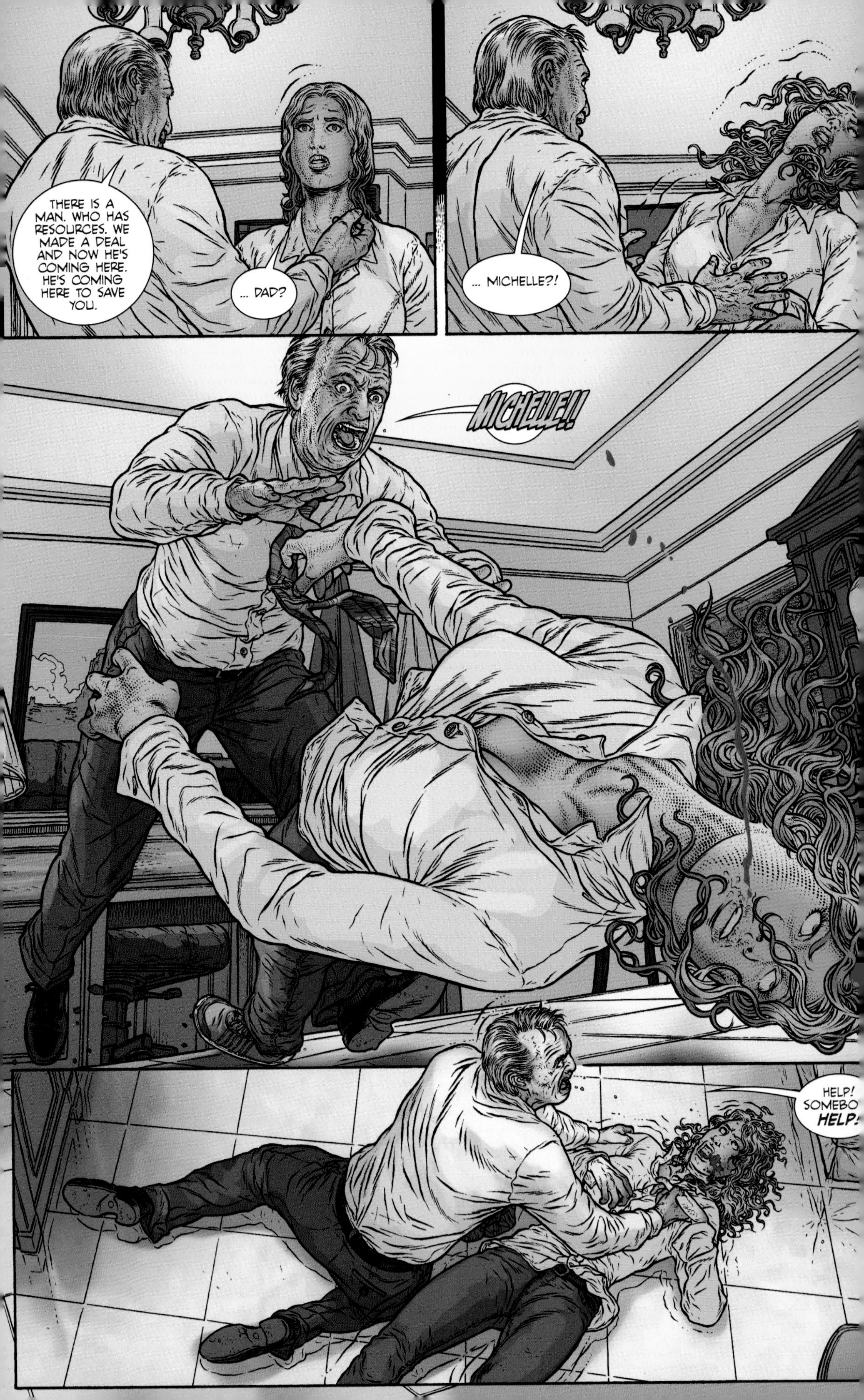
THERE IS A MAN. WHO HAS RESOURCES. WE MADE A DEAL AND NOW HE'S COMING HERE. HE'S COMING HERE TO SAVE YOU.
... DAD?
... MICHELLE?!
MICHELLE!!
HELP! SOMEBO HELP!

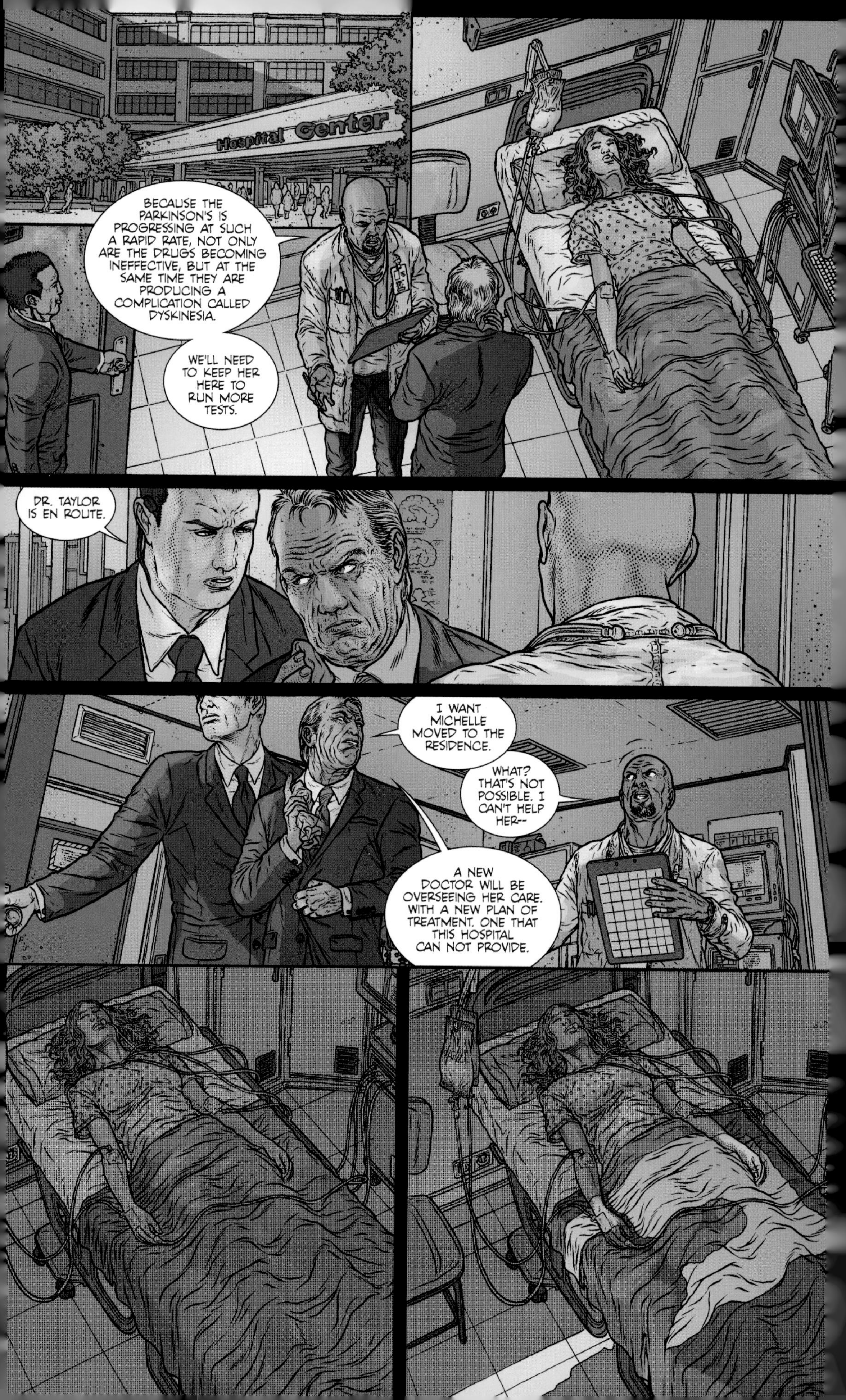
Hospital Center
BECAUSE THE PARKINSON'S IS PROGRESSING AT SUCH A RAPID RATE, NOT ONLY ARE THE DRUGS BECOMING INEFFECTIVE, BUT AT THE SAME TIME THEY ARE PRODUCING A COMPLICATION CALLED DYSKINESIA.
WE'LL NEED TO KEEP HER HERE TO RUN MORE TESTS.
DR. TAYLOR IS EN ROUTE.
I WANT MICHELLE MOVED TO THE RESIDENCE.
WHAT? THAT'S NOT POSSIBLE. I CAN'T HELP HER--
A NEW DOCTOR WILL BE OVERSEEING HER CARE. WITH A NEW PLAN OF TREATMENT. ONE THAT THIS HOSPITAL CAN NOT PROVIDE.

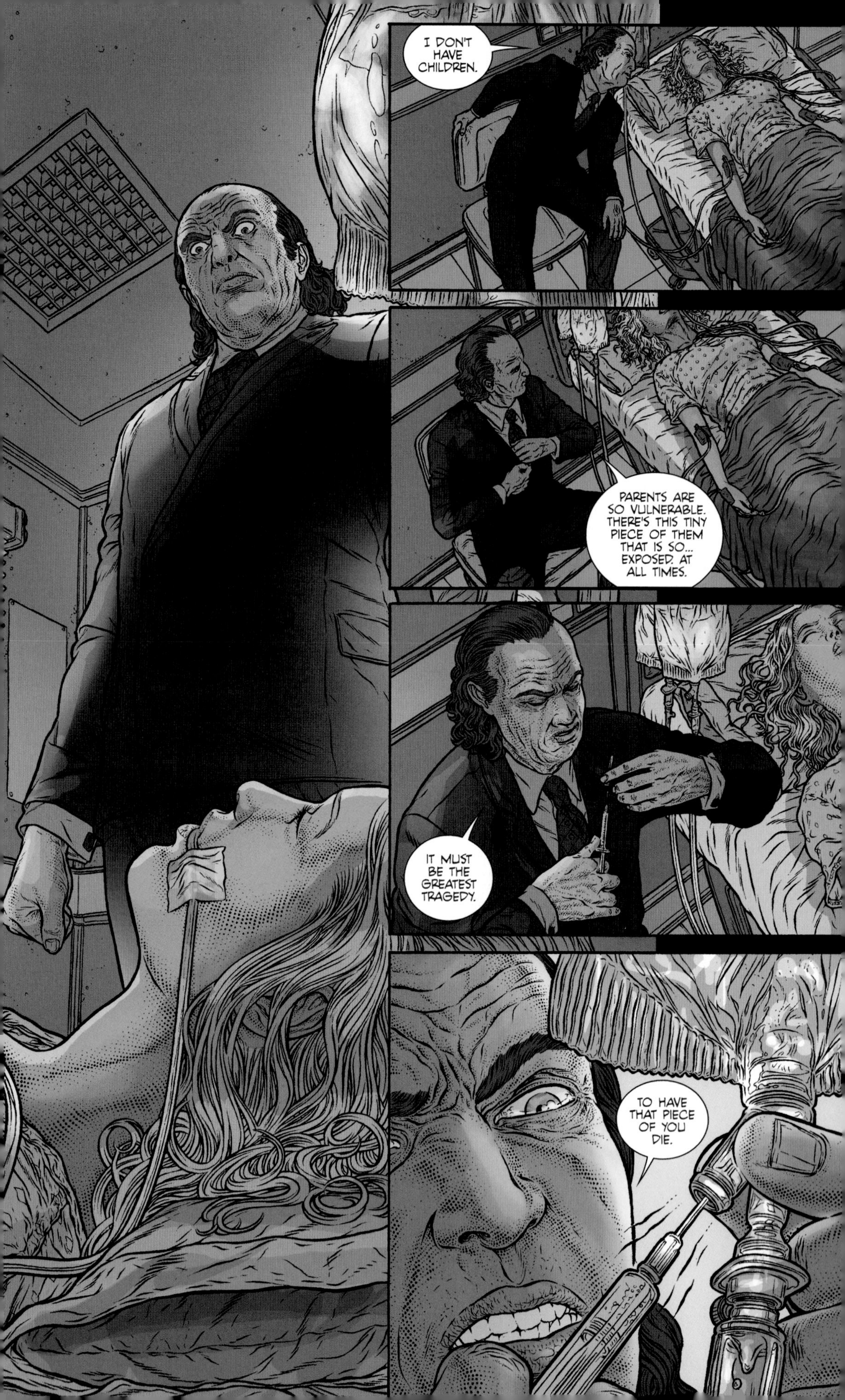
I DON'T HAVE CHILDREN.
PARENTS ARE SO VULNERABLE. THERE'S THIS TINY PIECE OF THEM THAT IS SO... EXPOSED. AT ALL TIMES.
IT MUST BE THE GREATEST TRAGEDY.
TO HAVE THAT PIECE OF YOU DIE.

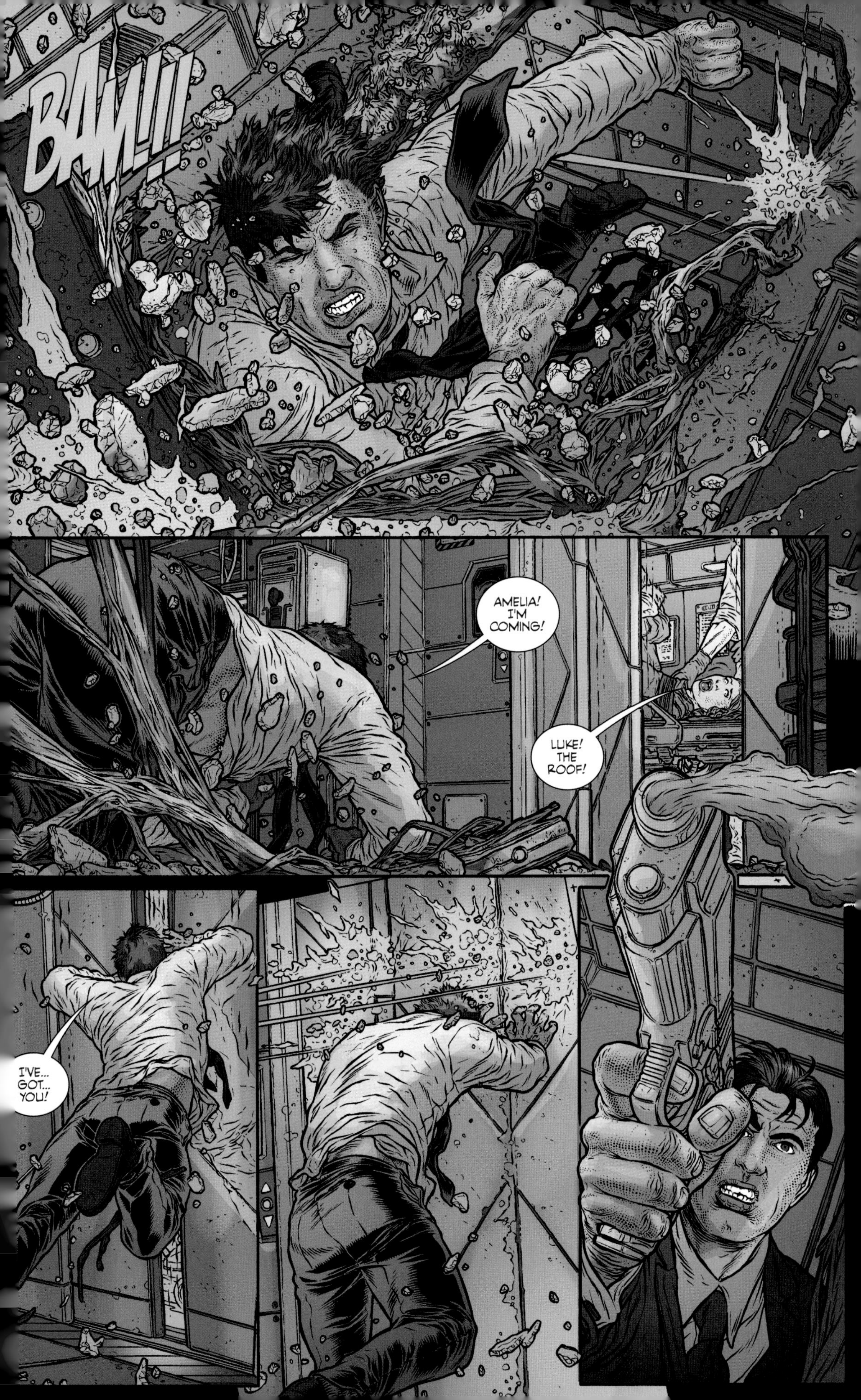
BAM!!!
AMELIA! I'M COMING!
LUKE! THE ROOF!
I'VE... GOT... YOU!

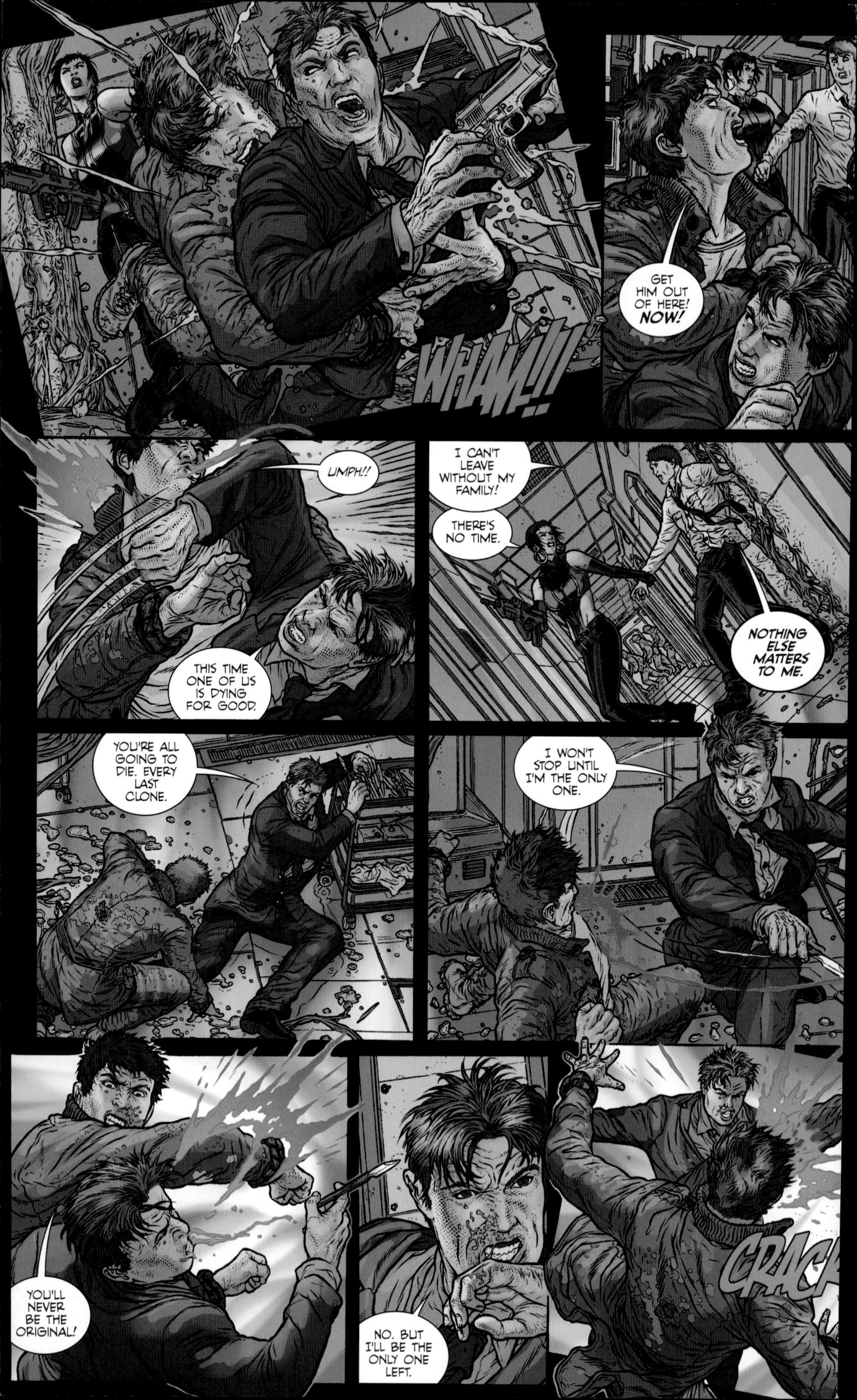
WHAM!!!
GET HIM OUT OF HERE! NOW!
UMPH!!
THIS TIME ONE OF US IS DYING FOR GOOD.
I CAN'T LEAVE WITHOUT MY FAMILY!
THERE'S NO TIME.
NOTHING ELSE MATTERS TO ME.
YOU'RE ALL GOING TO DIE. EVERY LAST CLONE.
I WON'T STOP UNTIL I'M THE ONLY ONE.
YOU'LL NEVER BE THE ORIGINAL!
NO. BUT I'LL BE THE ONLY ONE LEFT.

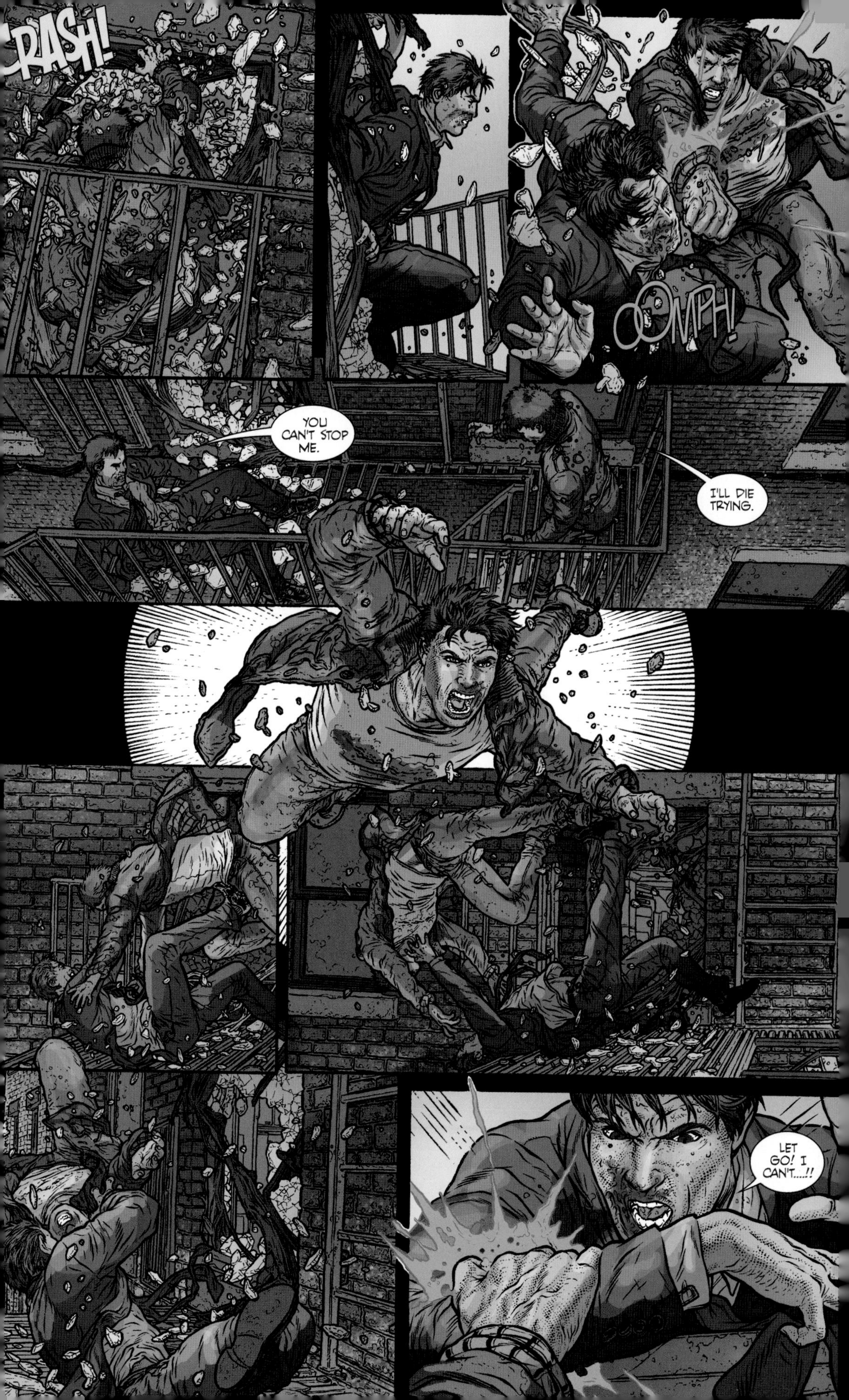

RASH!
OOMPH!
YOU CAN'T STOP ME.
I'LL DIE TRYING.
LET GO! I CAN'T....!!

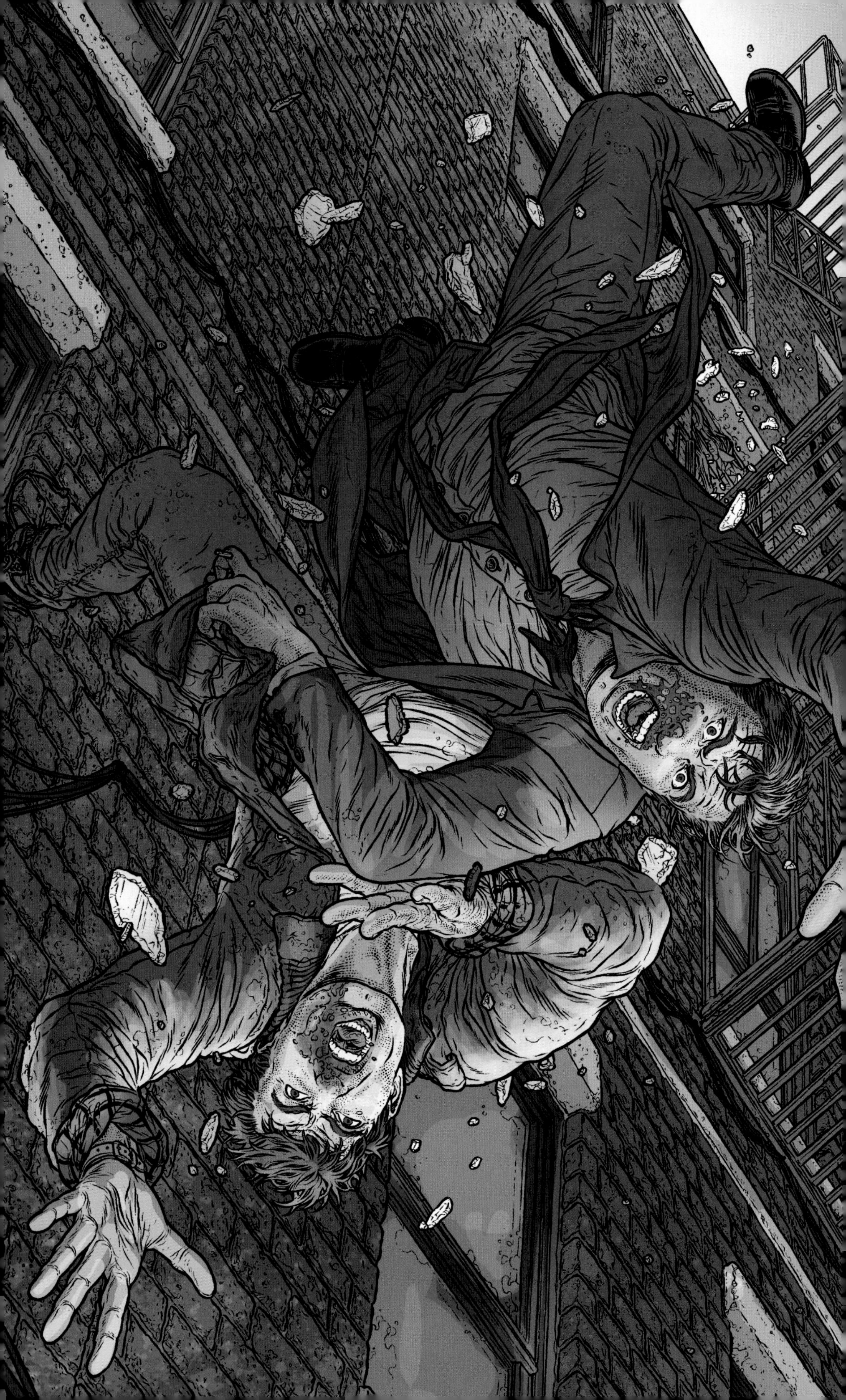

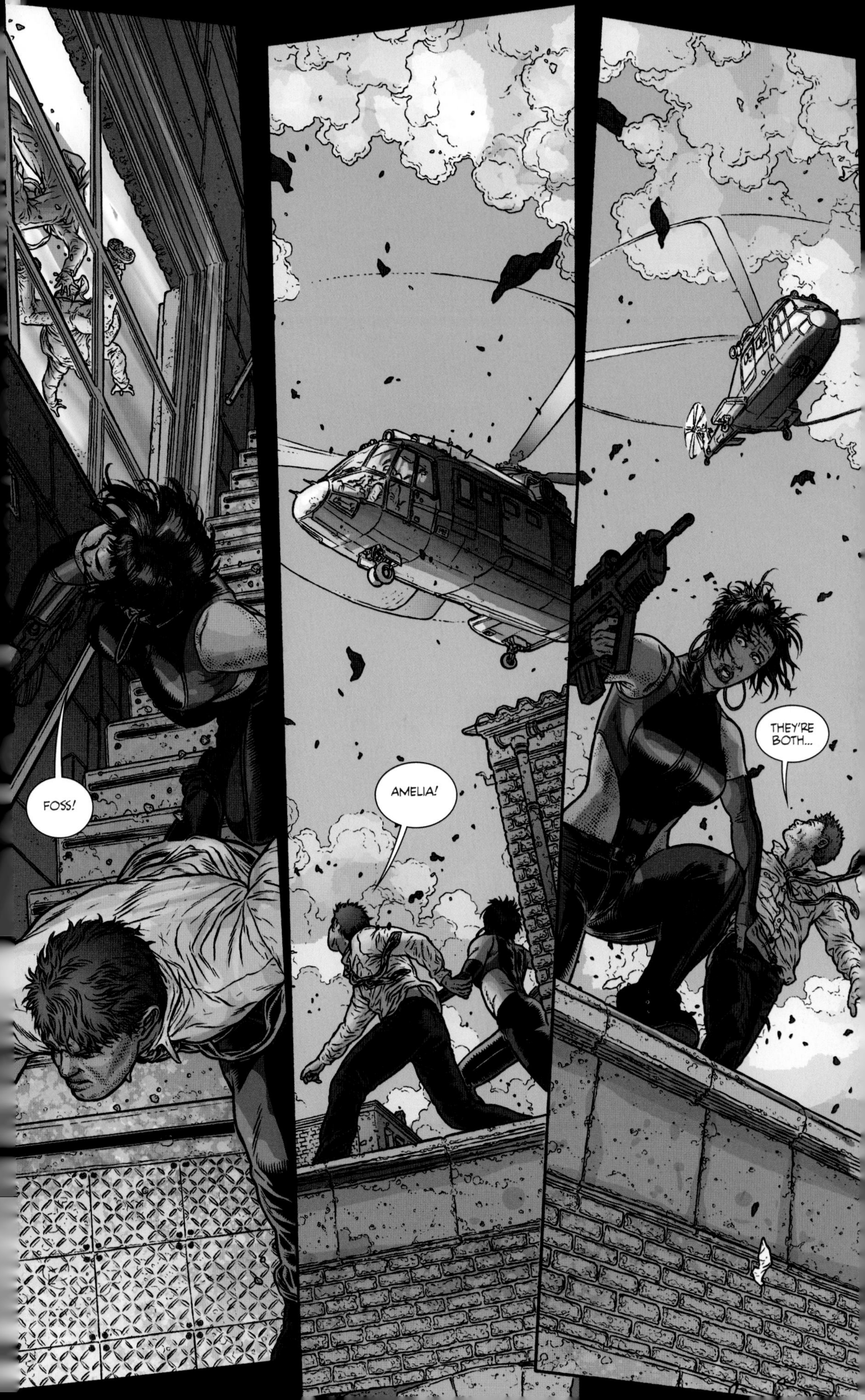
FOSS!
AMELIA!
THEY'RE BOTH...

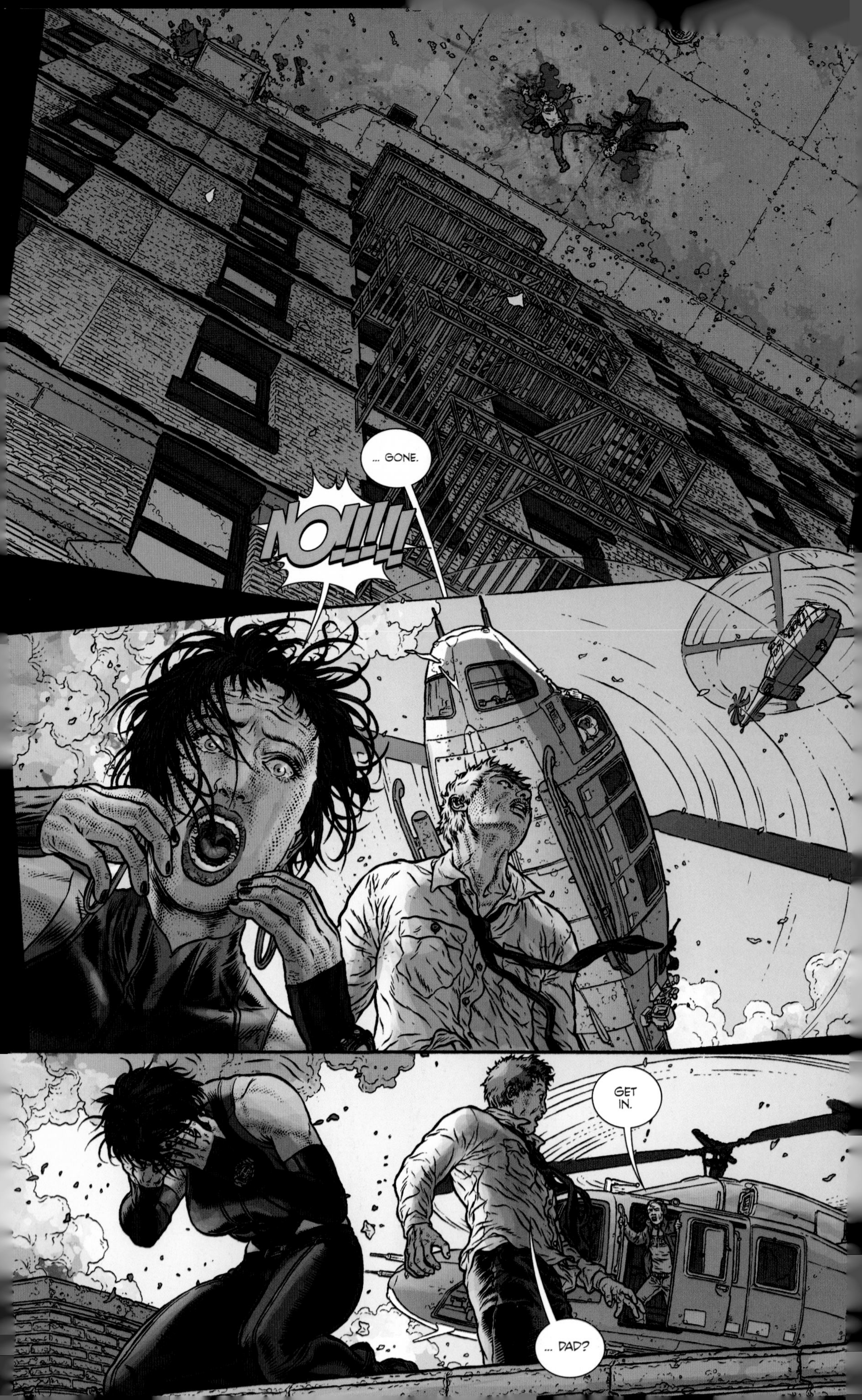
... GONE.
NO!!!!!
GET IN.
... DAD?

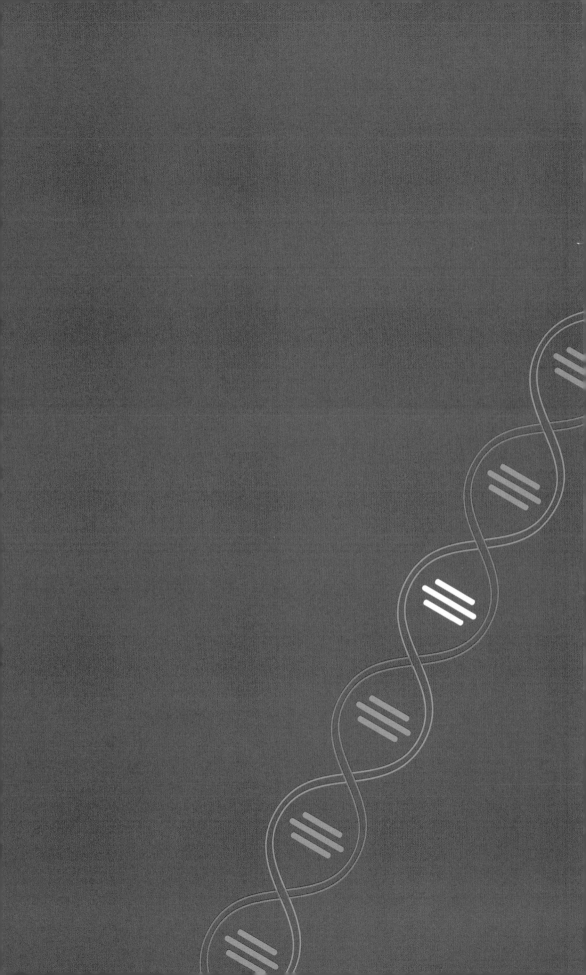

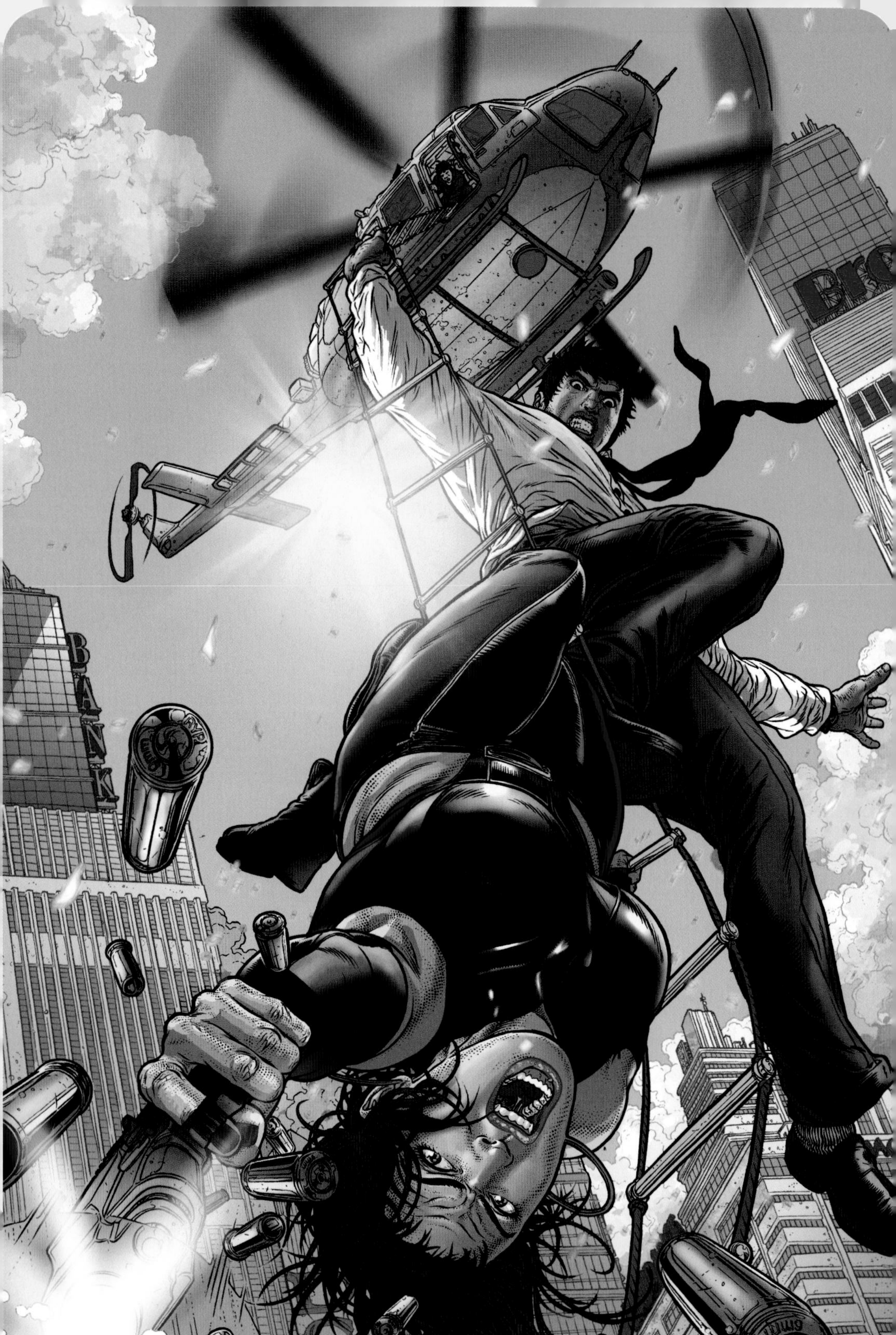
BANK

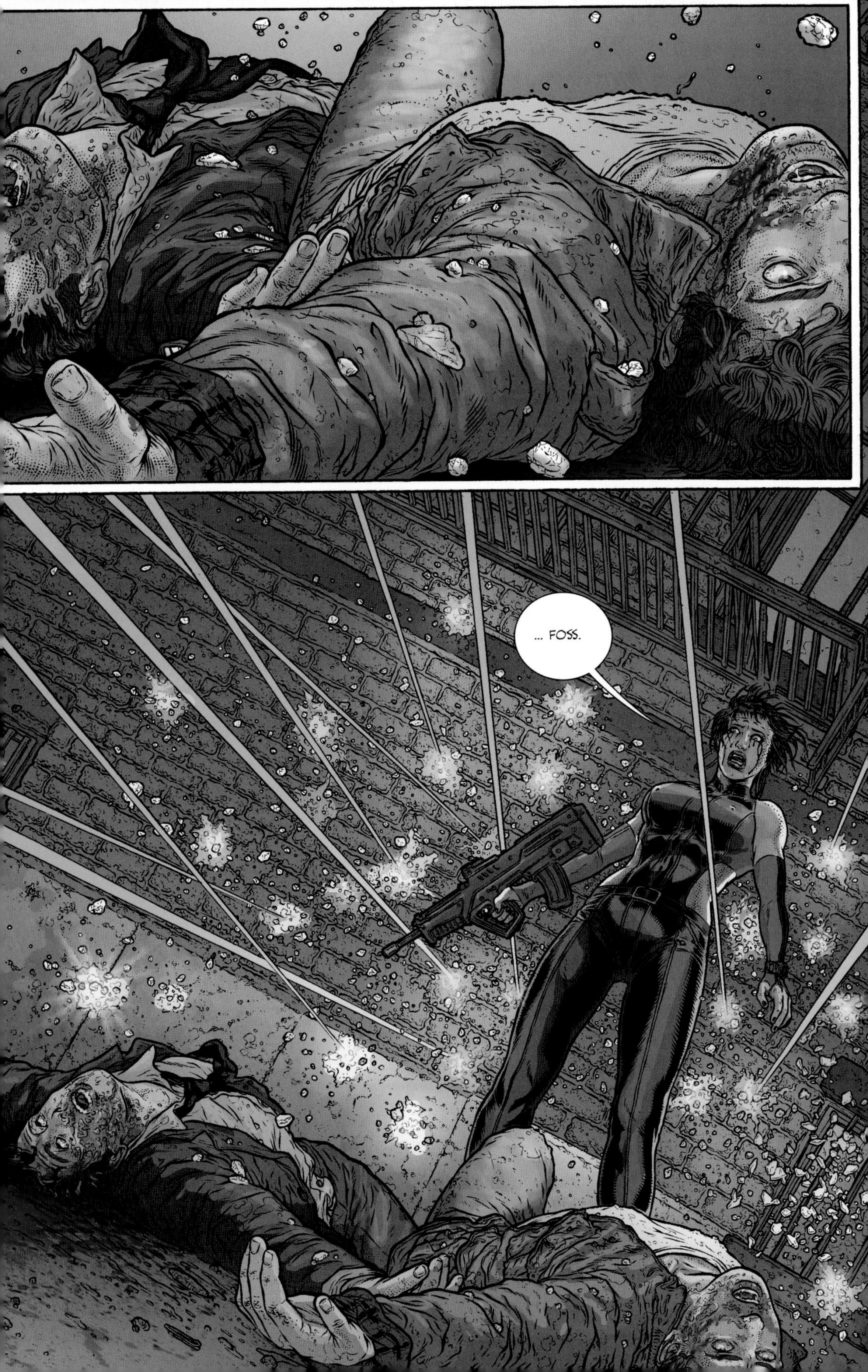
... FOSS.

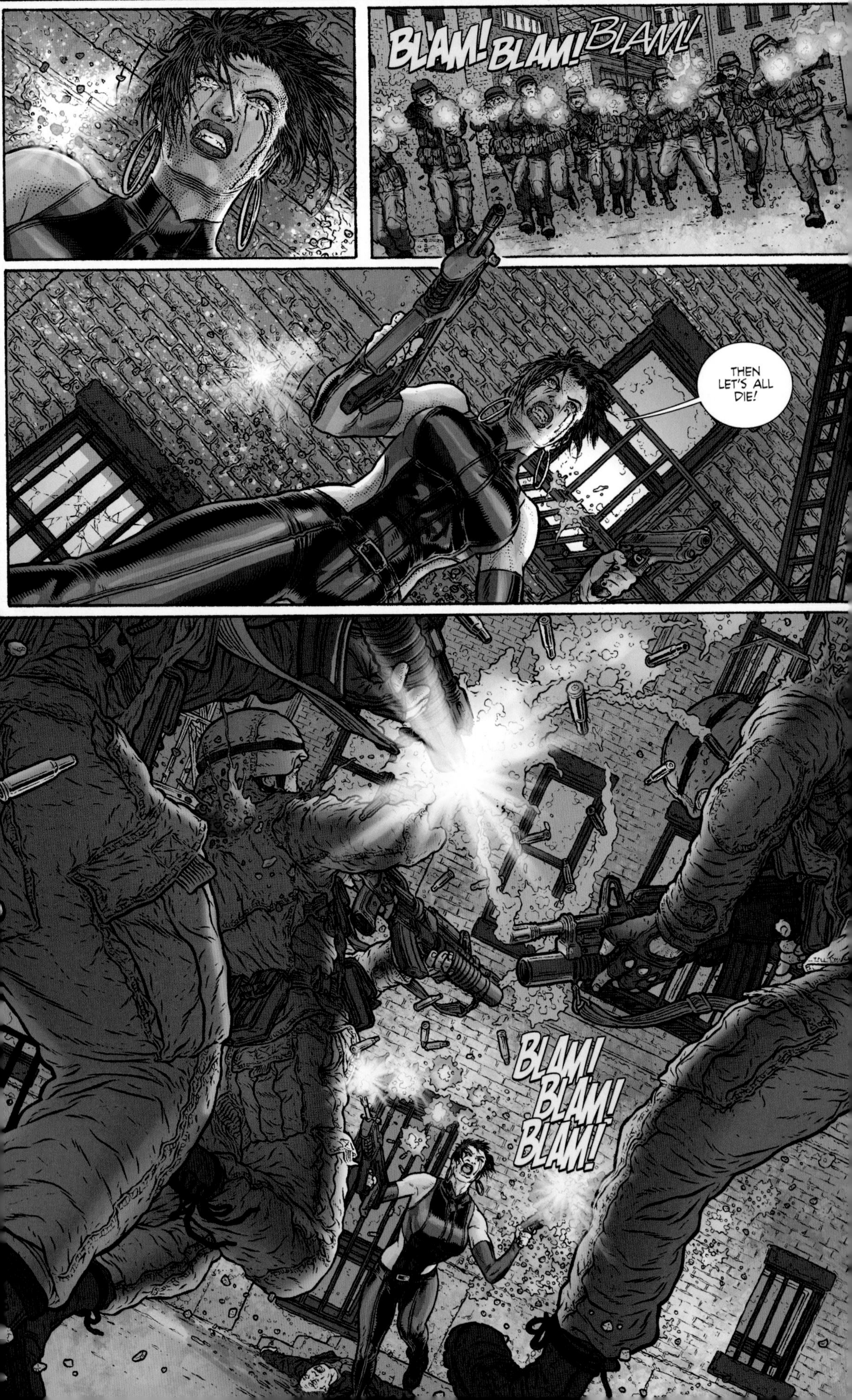
BLAM! BLAM! BLAM!
THEN LET'S ALL DIE!
BLAM! BLAM! BLAM!

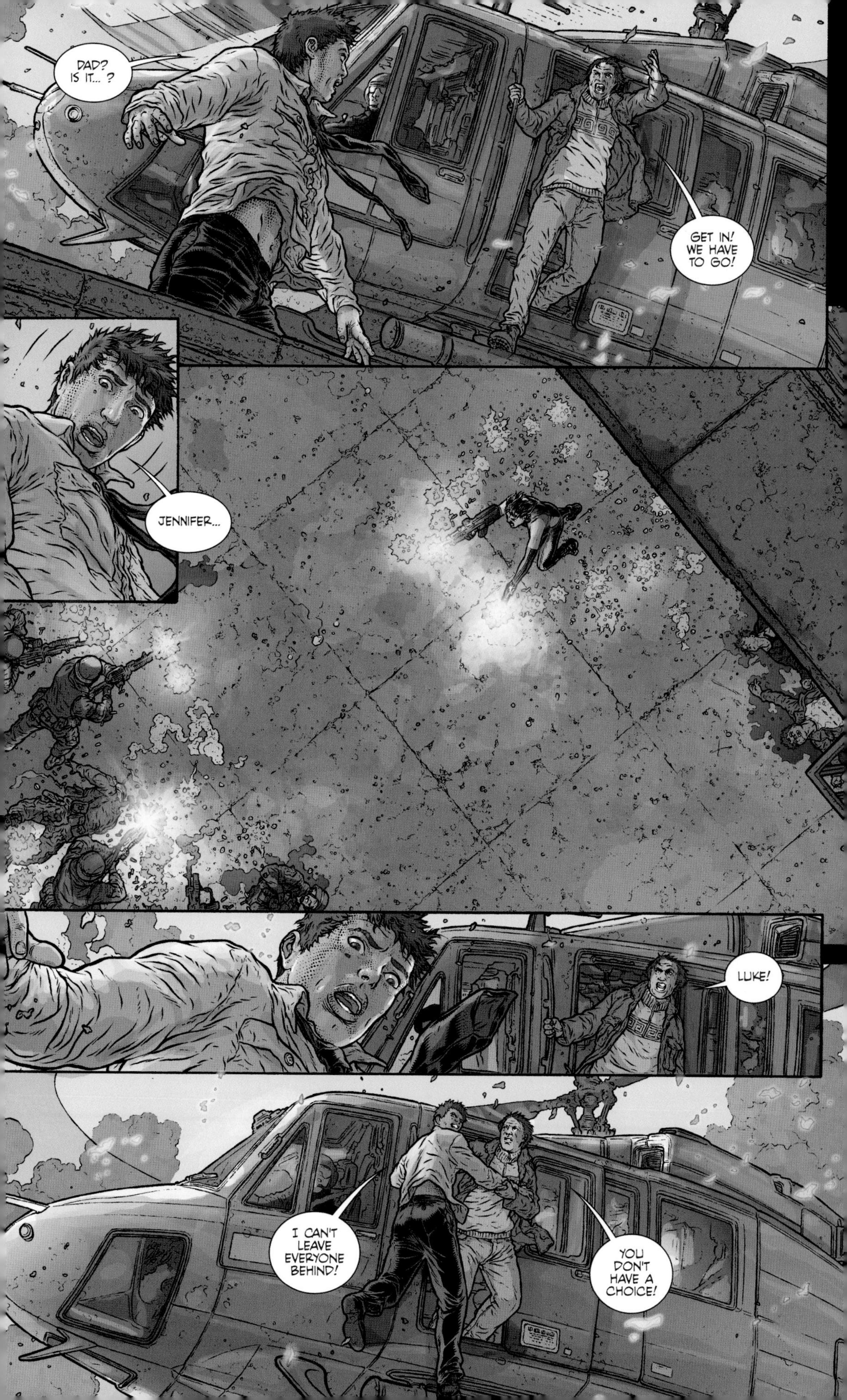
DAD? IS IT... ?
GET IN! WE HAVE TO GO!
JENNIFER...
LUKE!
I CAN'T LEAVE EVERYONE BEHIND!
YOU DON'T HAVE A CHOICE!

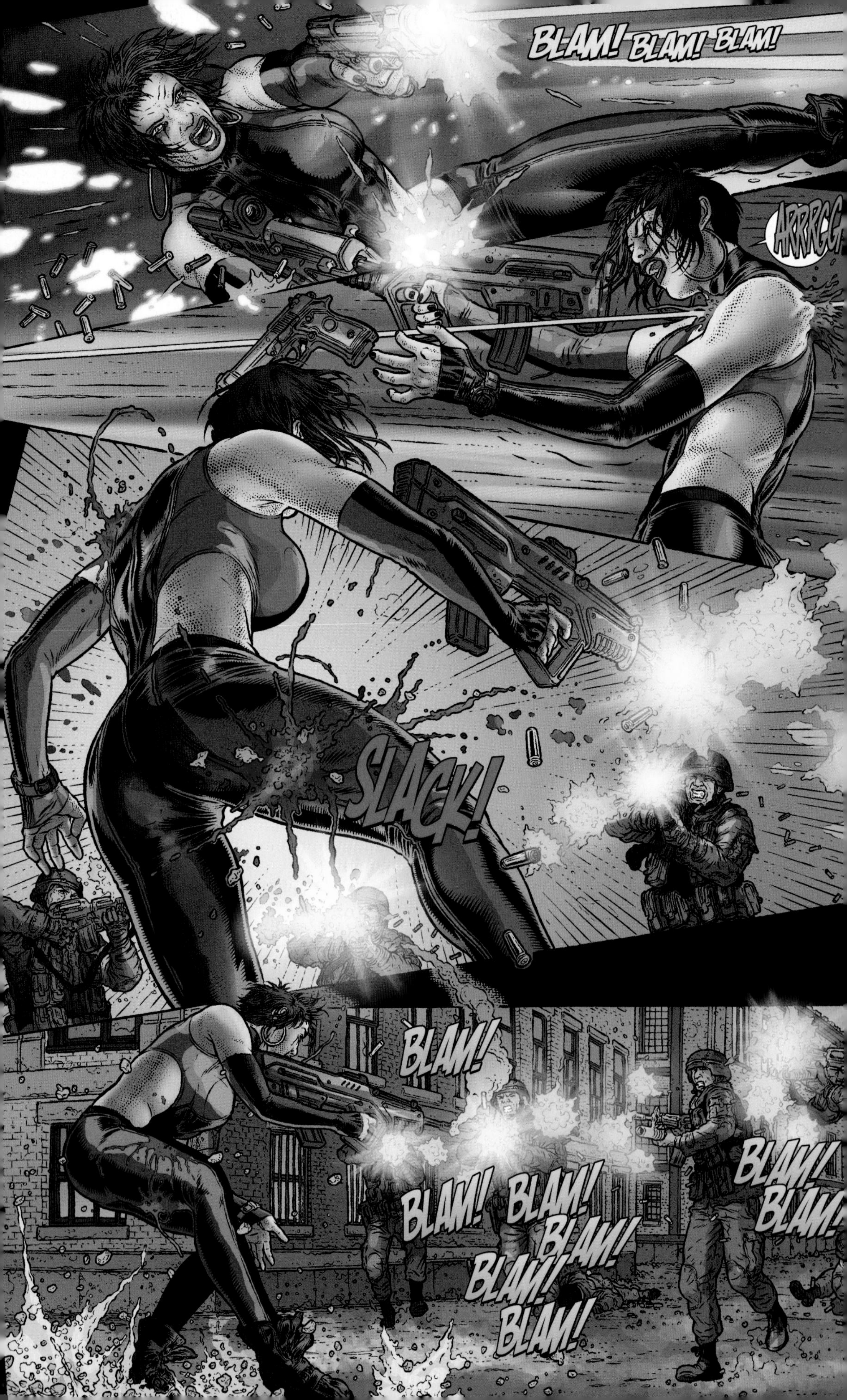
BLAM! BLAM! BLAM!
ARRRGG
SLACK!
BLAM!
BLAM! BLAM! BLAM!
BLAM!
BLAM!
BLAM! BLAM!

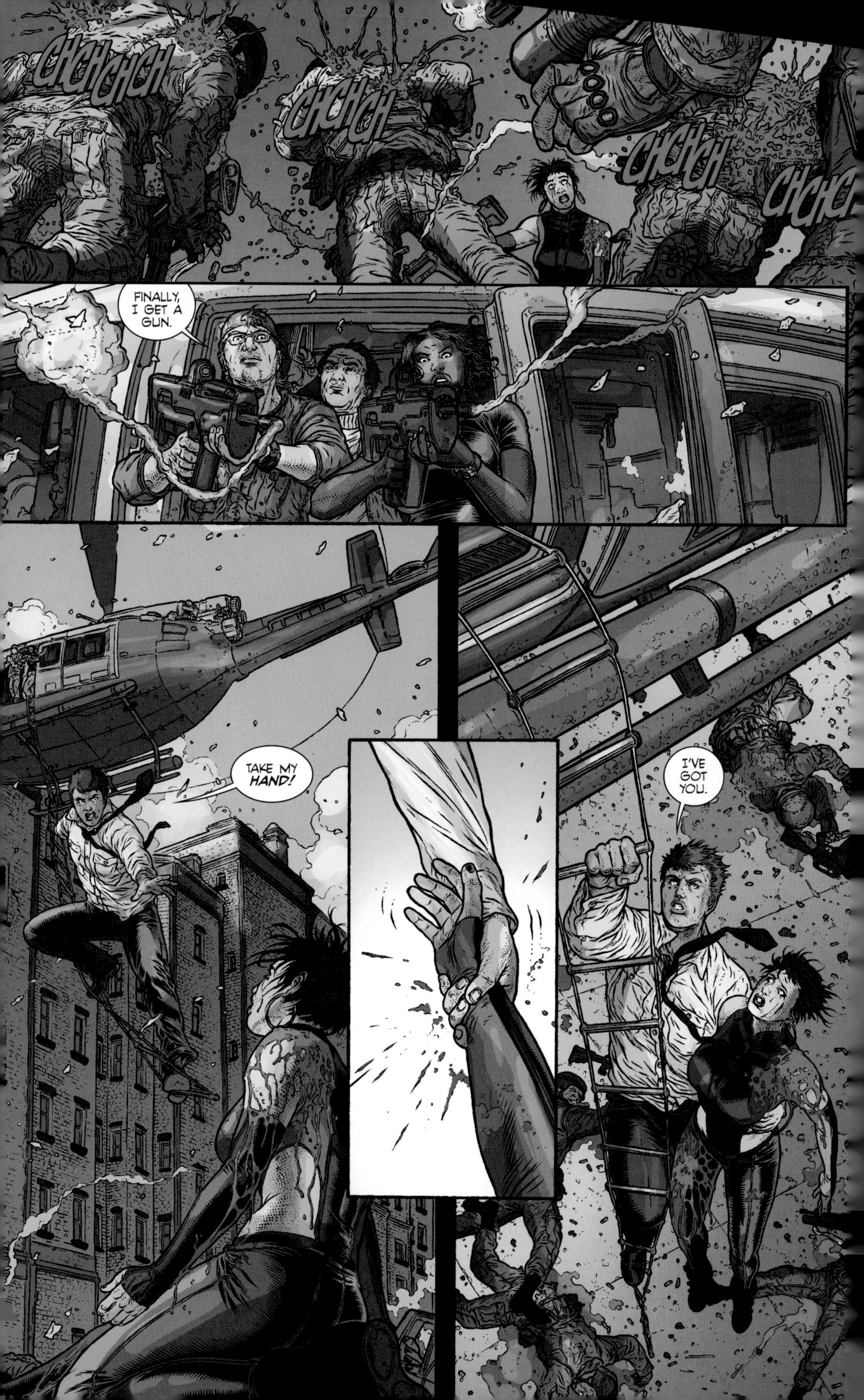
CHCHCHCH
CHCHCH
CHCHCH
CHCHC
FINALLY, I GET A GUN.
TAKE MY HAND!
I'VE GOT YOU.

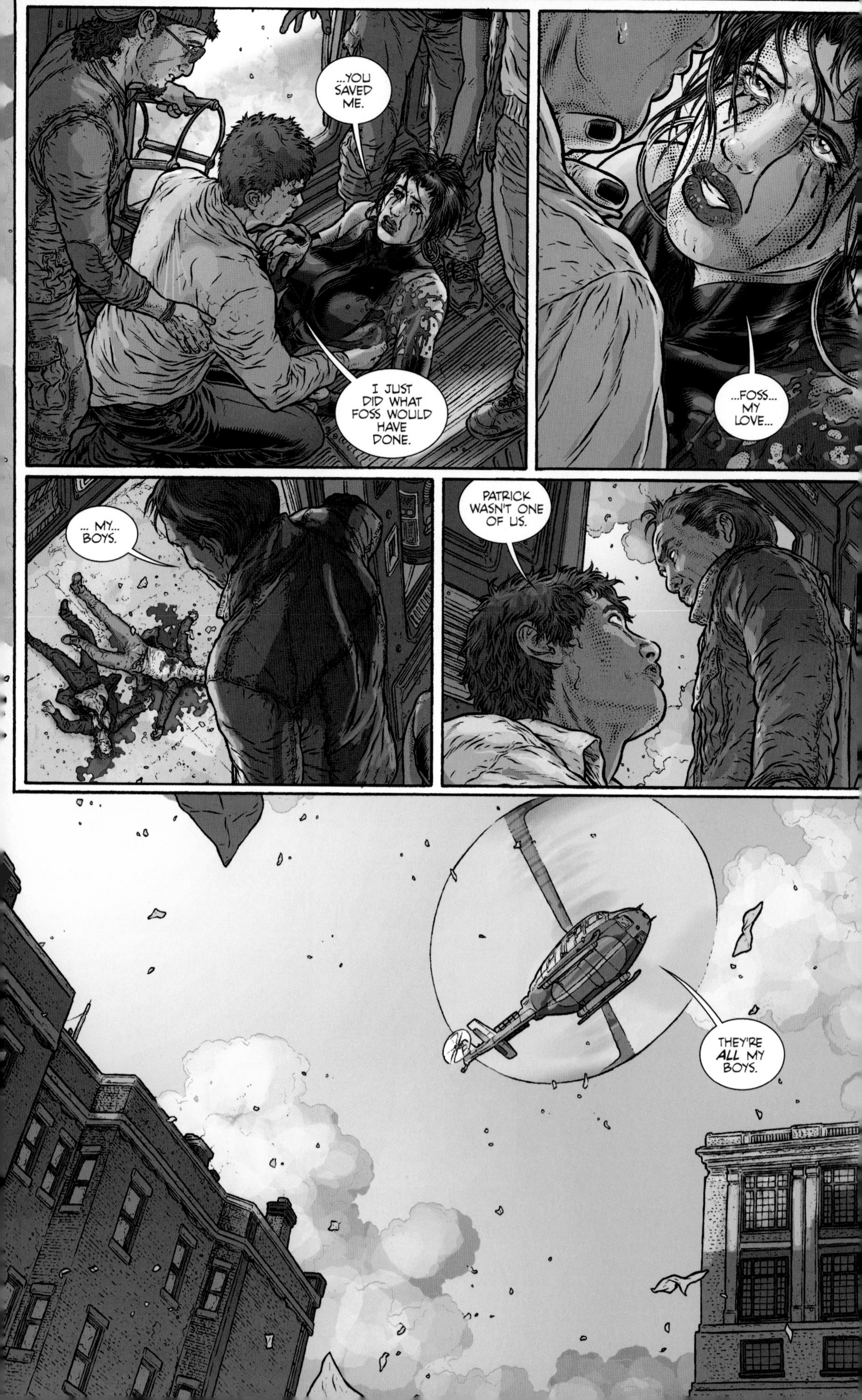

...YOU SAVED ME.
I JUST DID WHAT FOSS WOULD HAVE DONE.
...FOSS... MY LOVE...
... MY... BOYS.
PATRICK WASN'T ONE OF US.
THEY'RE ALL MY BOYS.

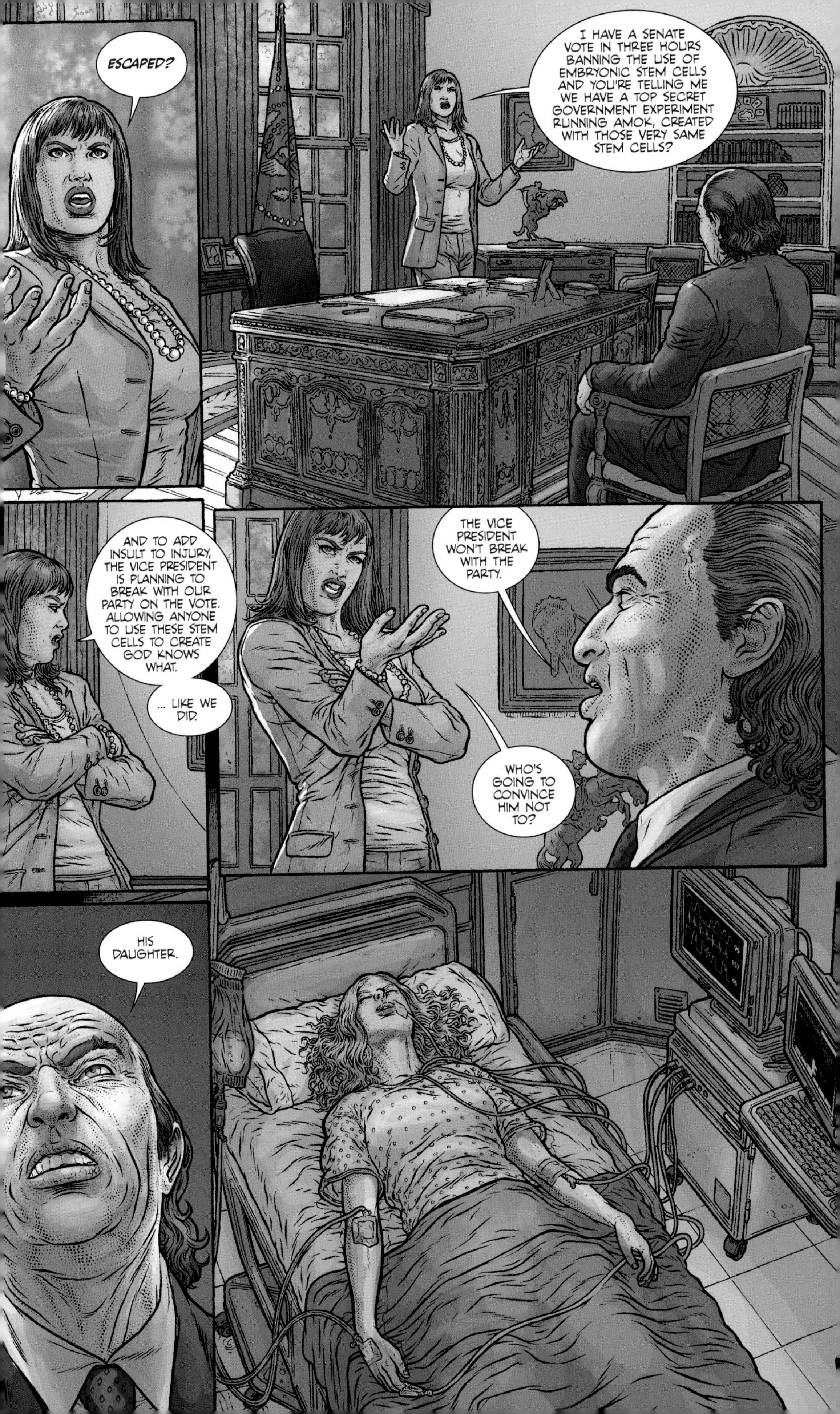
ESCAPED?
I HAVE A SENATE VOTE IN THREE HOURS BANNING THE USE OF EMBRYONIC STEM CELLS AND YOU'RE TELLING ME WE HAVE A TOP SECRET GOVERNMENT EXPERIMENT RUNNING AMOK, CREATED WITH THOSE VERY SAME STEM CELLS?
AND TO ADD INSULT TO INJURY, THE VICE PRESIDENT IS PLANNING TO BREAK WITH OUR PARTY ON THE VOTE. ALLOWING ANYONE TO USE THESE STEM CELLS TO CREATE GOD KNOWS WHAT.
... LIKE WE DID.
THE VICE PRESIDENT WON'T BREAK WITH THE PARTY.
WHO'S GOING TO CONVINCE HIM NOT TO?
HIS DAUGHTER.

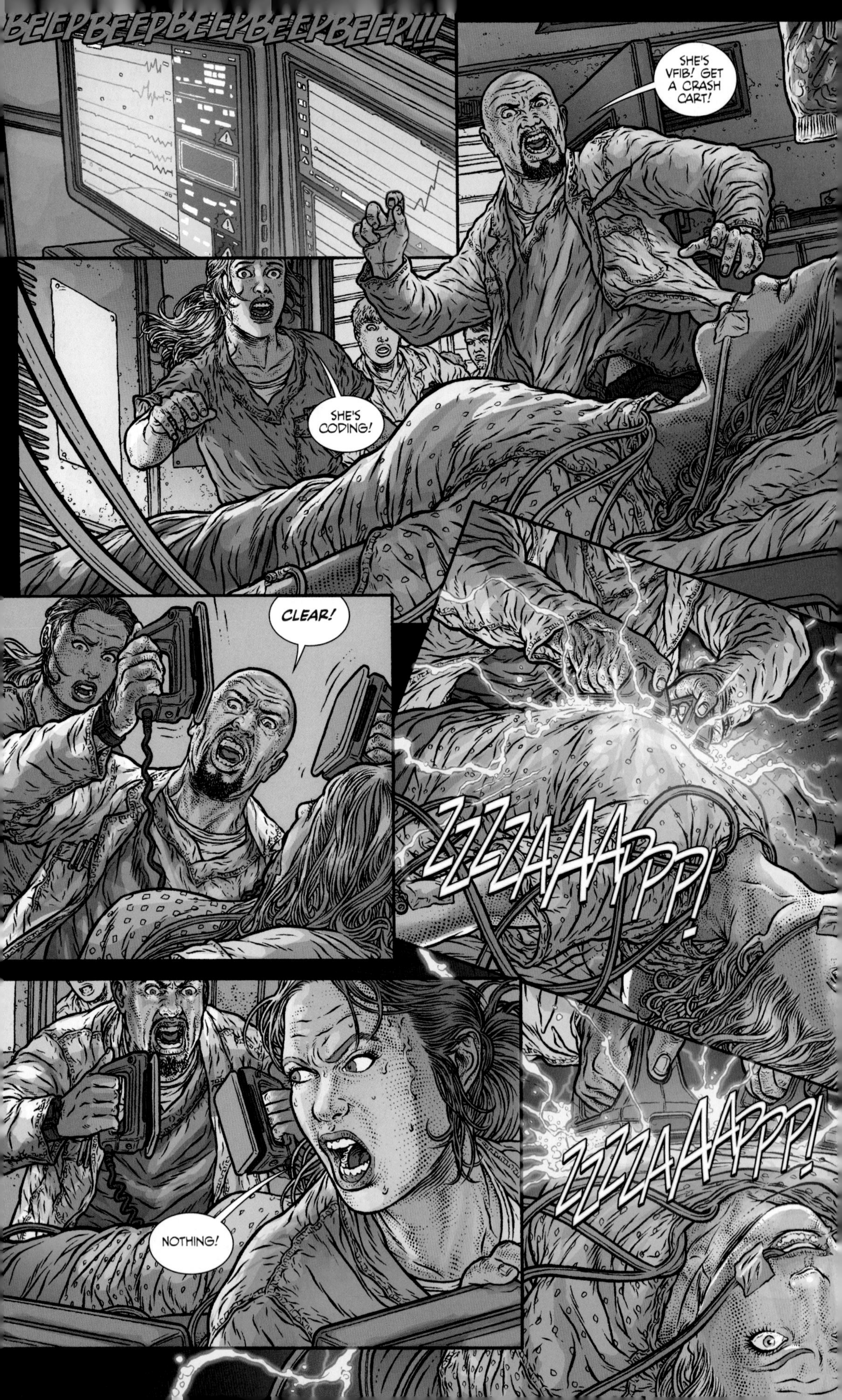
BEEPBEEPBEEPBEEPBEEP!!!
SHE'S VFIB! GET A CRASH CART!
SHE'S CODING!
CLEAR!
ZZZZAAAAPPP!
NOTHING!
ZZZZAAAAPPP!

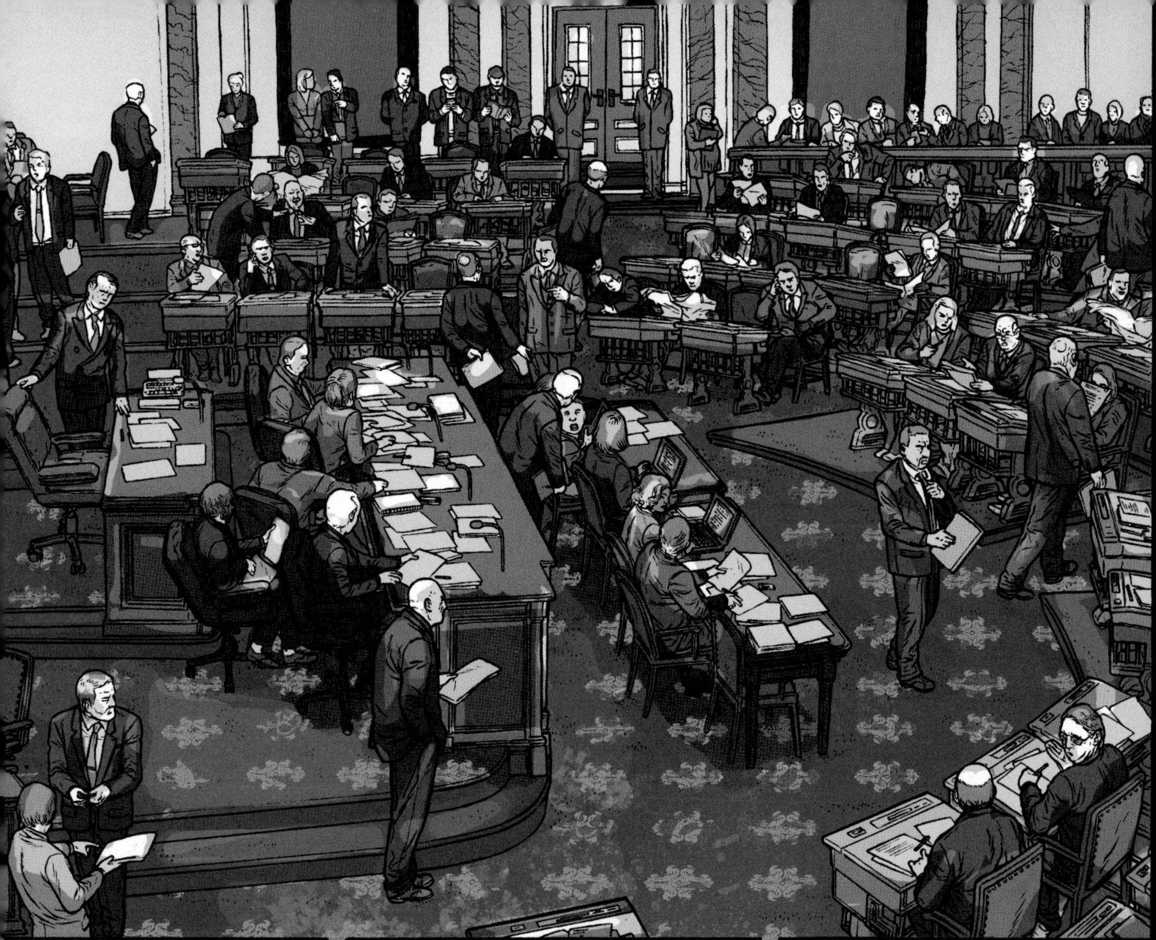

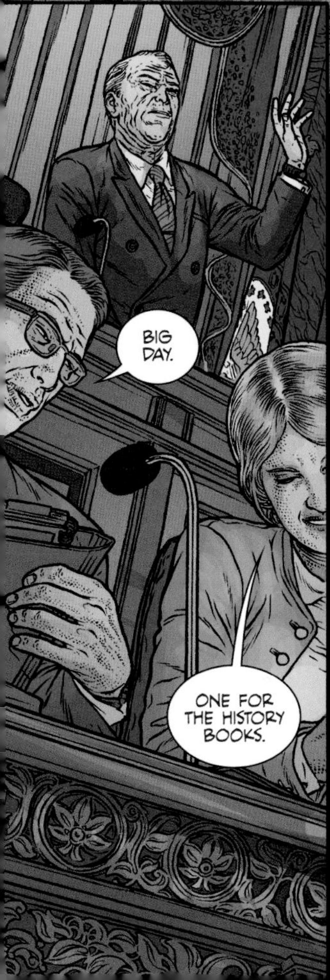
BIG DAY.
ONE FOR THE HISTORY BOOKS.

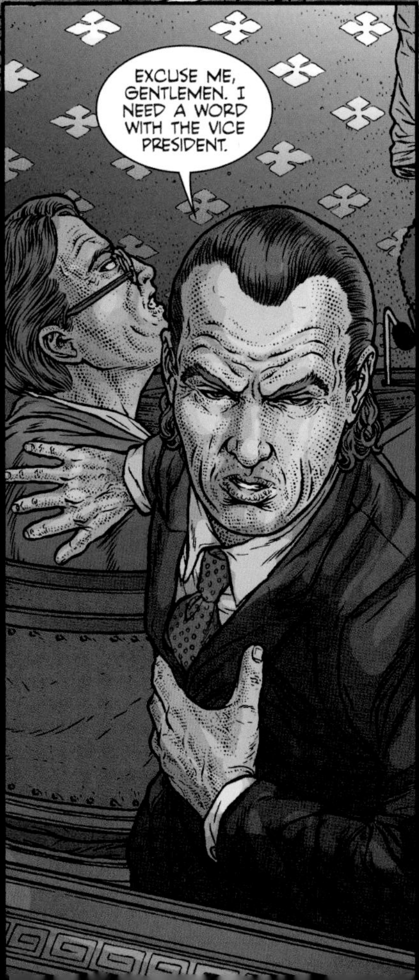
EXCUSE ME, GENTLEMEN. I NEED A WORD WITH THE VICE PRESIDENT.

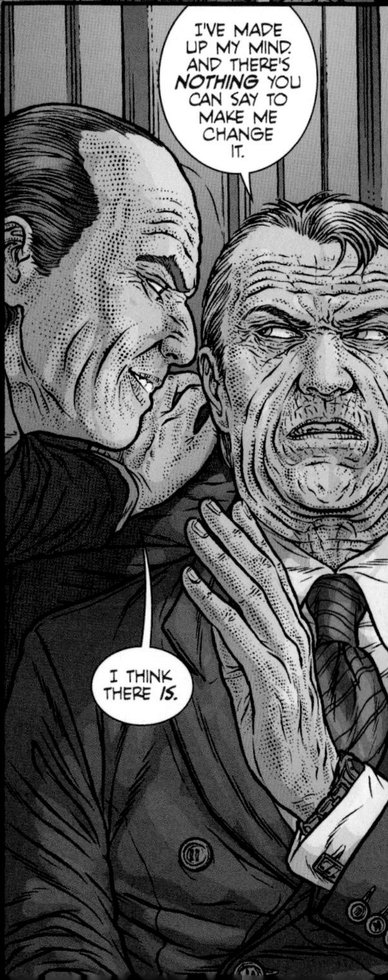
I'VE MADE UP MY MIND. AND THERE'S NOTHING YOU CAN SAY TO MAKE ME CHANGE IT.
I THINK THERE IS.

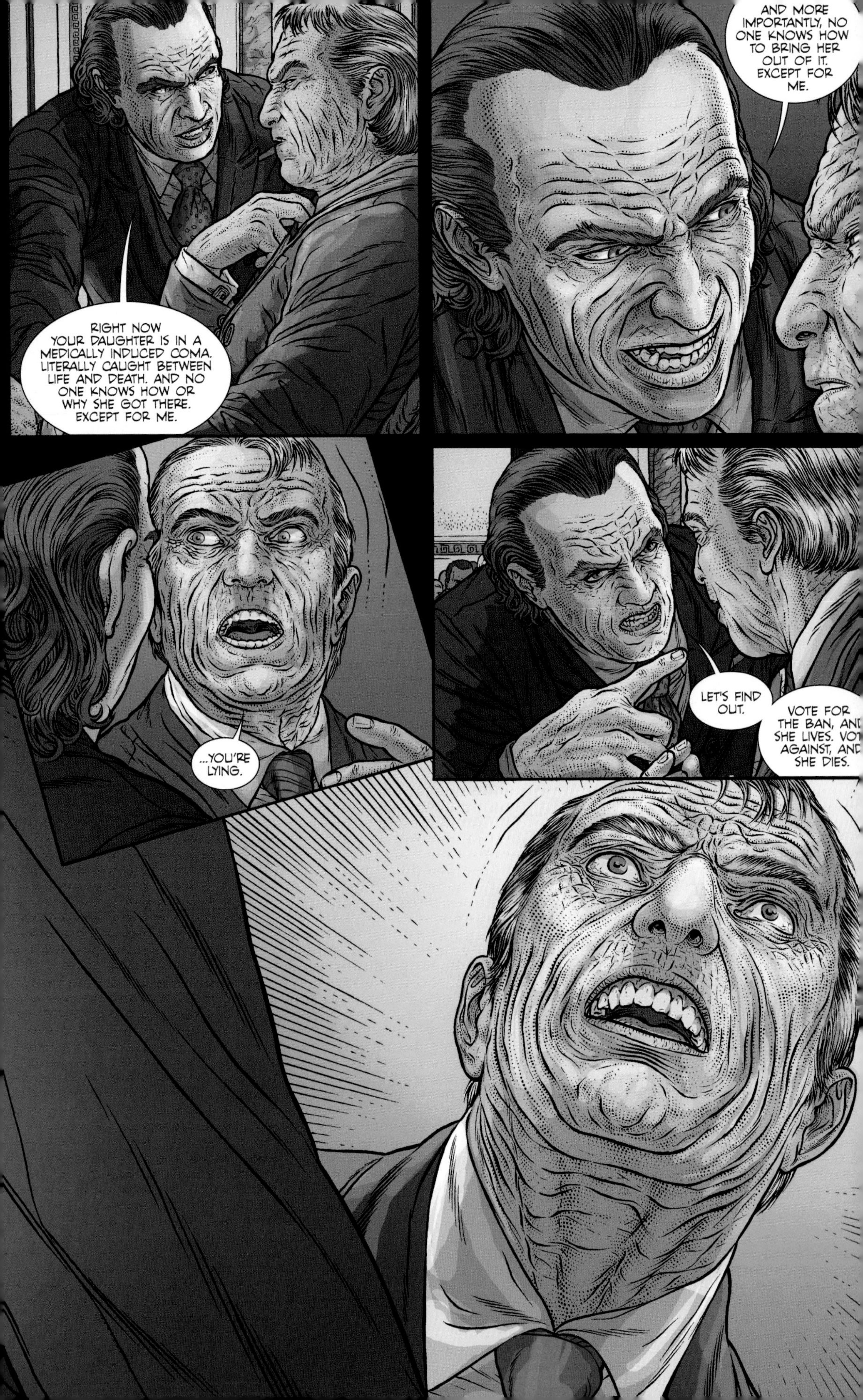
RIGHT NOW YOUR DAUGHTER IS IN A MEDICALLY INDUCED COMA. LITERALLY CAUGHT BETWEEN LIFE AND DEATH. AND NO ONE KNOWS HOW OR WHY SHE GOT THERE. EXCEPT FOR ME.
AND MORE IMPORTANTLY, NO ONE KNOWS HOW TO BRING HER OUT OF IT. EXCEPT FOR ME.
...YOU'RE LYING.
LET'S FIND OUT.
VOTE FOR THE BAN, AND SHE LIVES. VOTE AGAINST, AND SHE DIES.

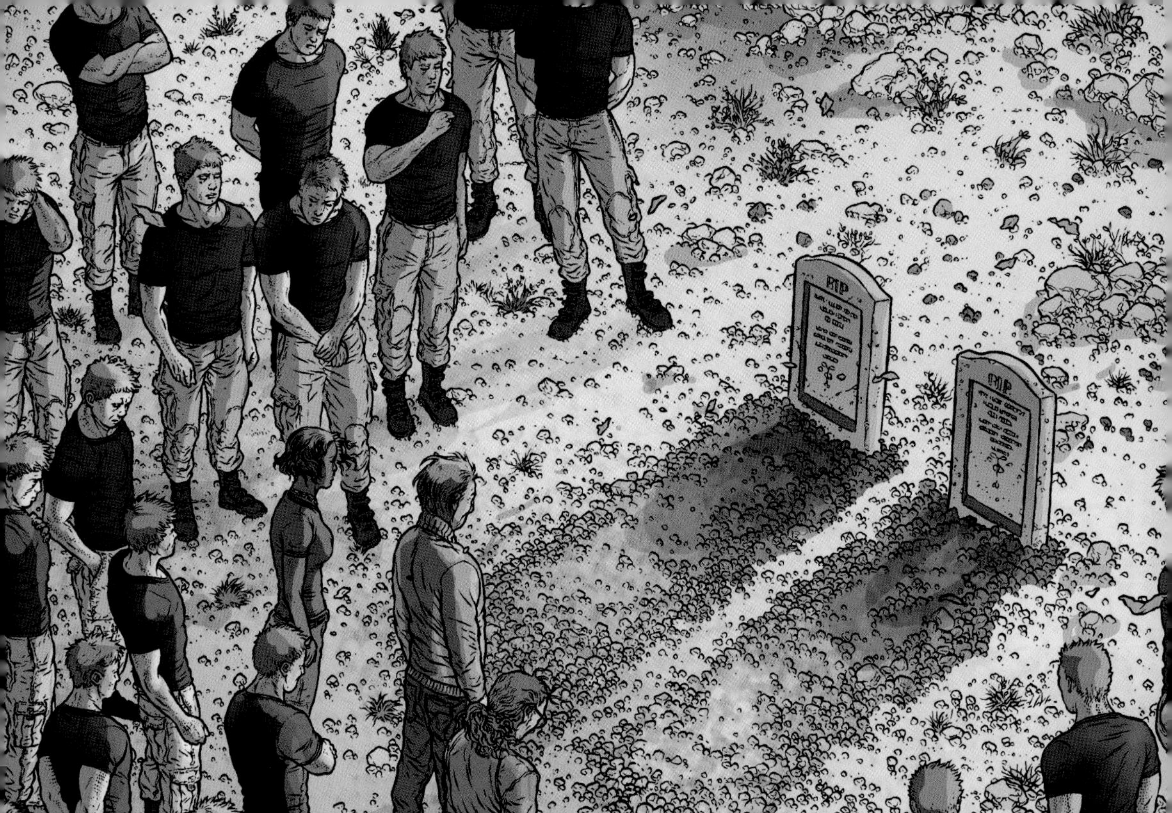

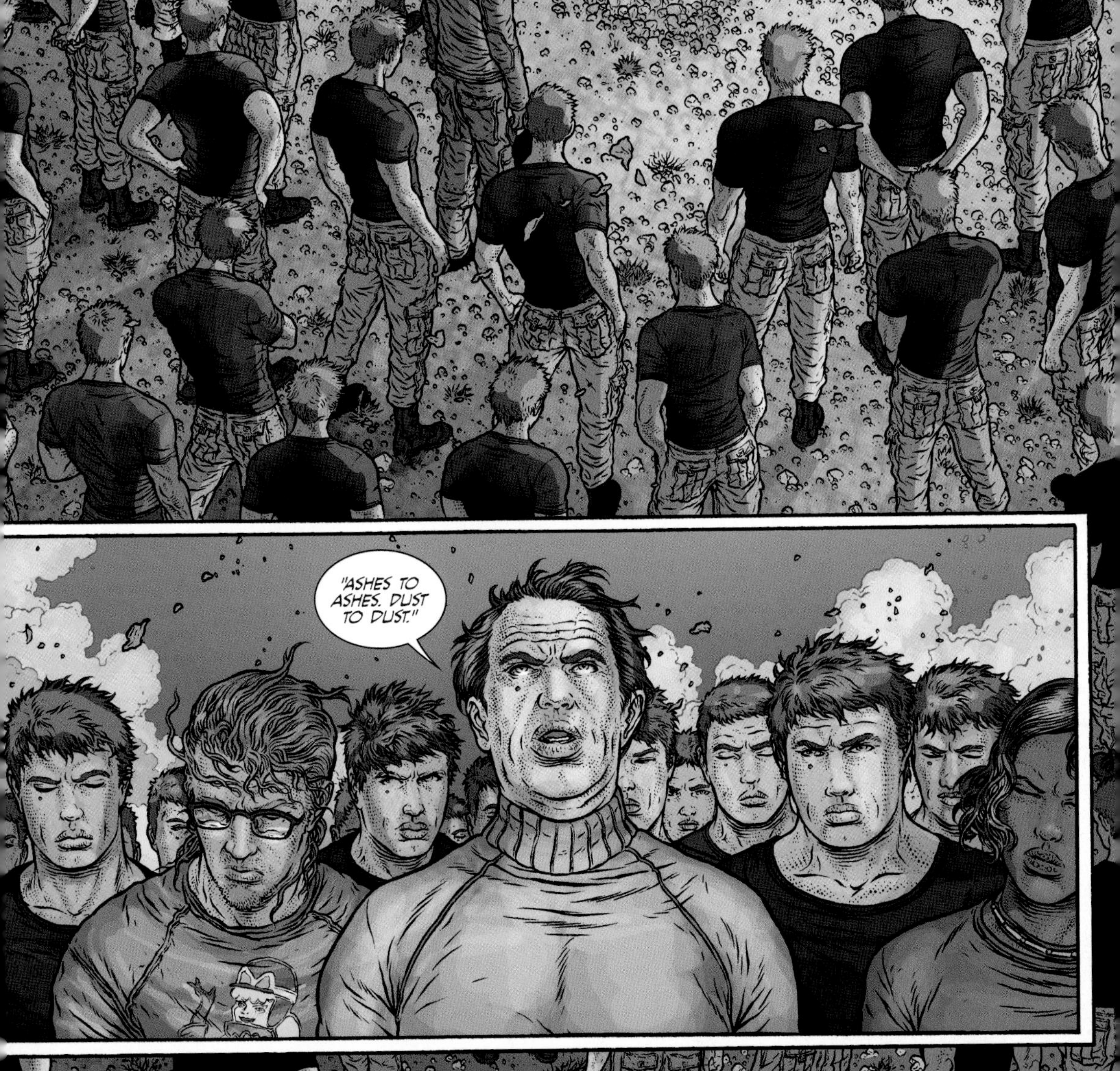
"ASHES TO ASHES. DUST TO DUST."

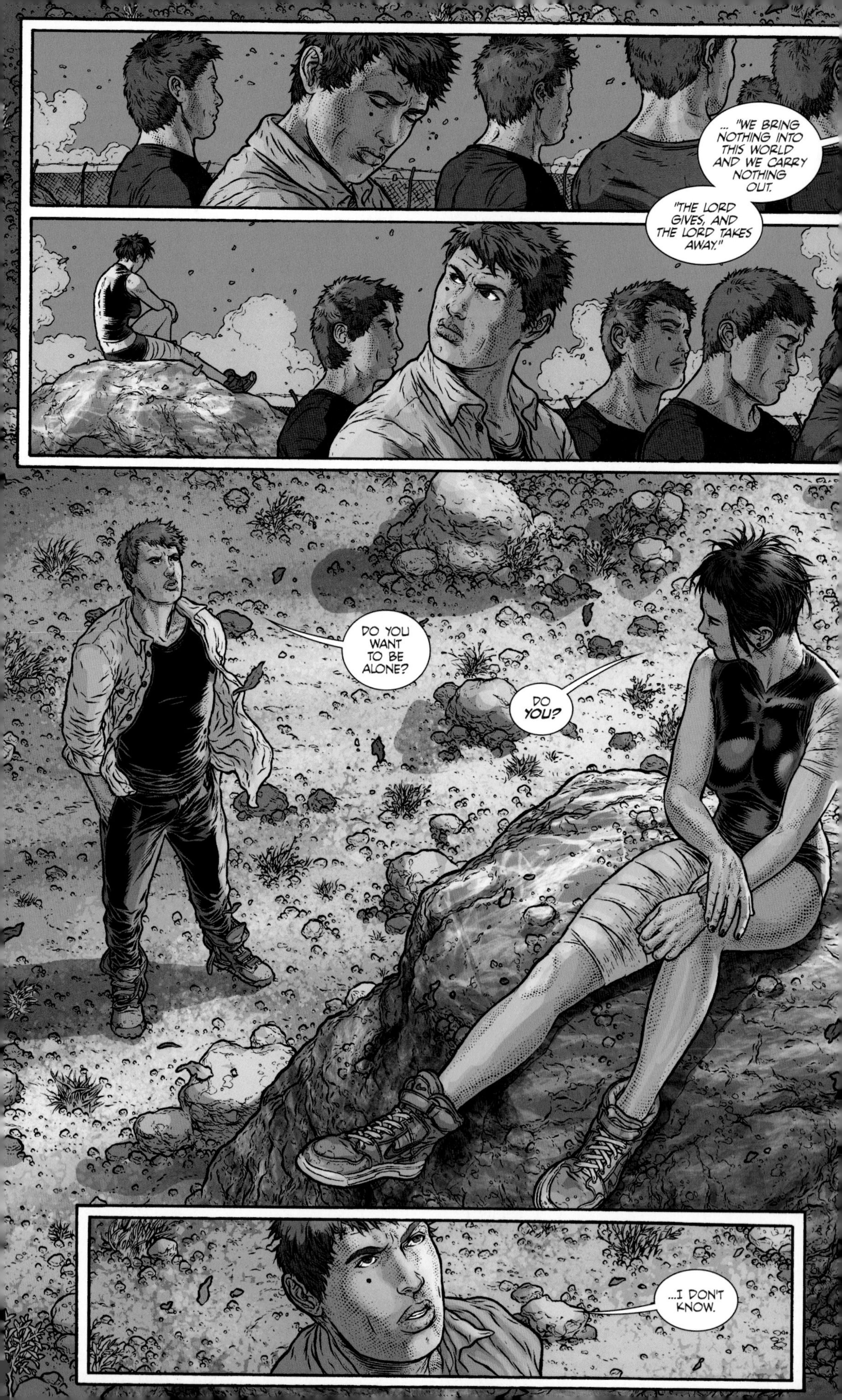
... "WE BRING NOTHING INTO THIS WORLD AND WE CARRY NOTHING OUT.
"THE LORD GIVES, AND THE LORD TAKES AWAY."
DO YOU WANT TO BE ALONE?
DO *YOU?*
...I DON'T KNOW.

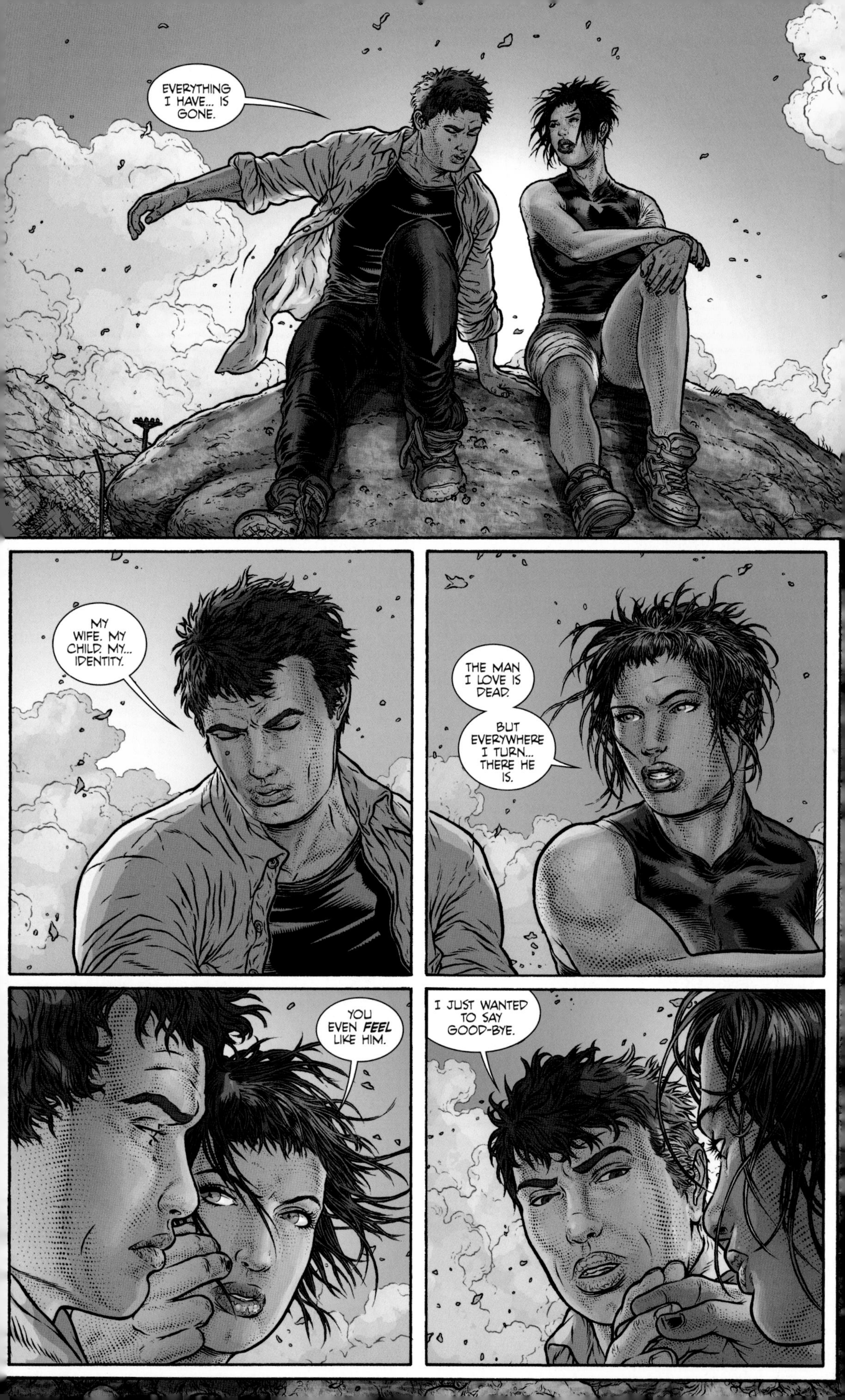
EVERYTHING I HAVE... IS GONE.
MY WIFE. MY CHILD. MY... IDENTITY.
THE MAN I LOVE IS DEAD.
BUT EVERYWHERE I TURN... THERE HE IS.
YOU EVEN *FEEL* LIKE HIM.
I JUST WANTED TO SAY GOOD-BYE.

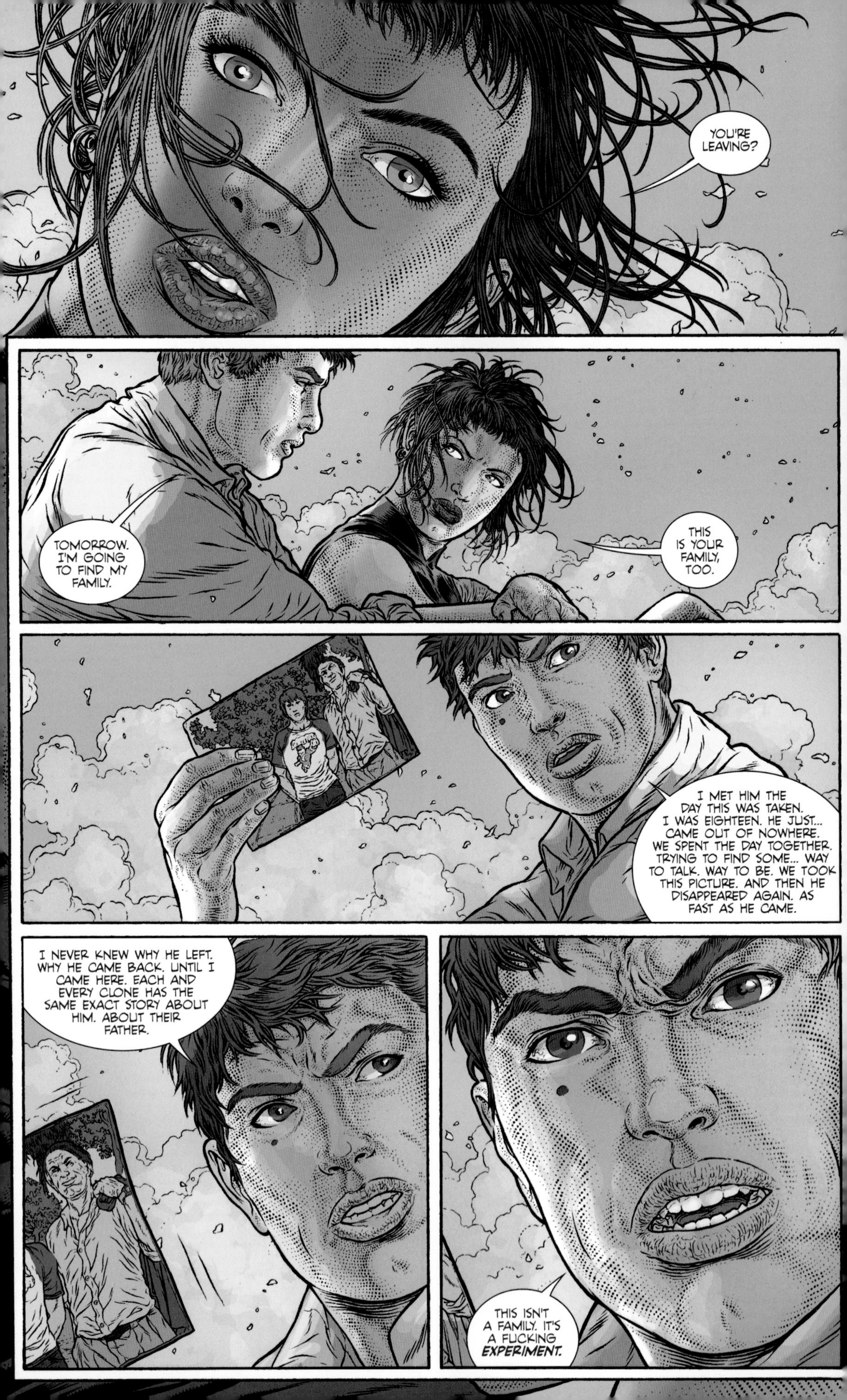
YOU'RE LEAVING?
TOMORROW. I'M GOING TO FIND MY FAMILY.
THIS IS YOUR FAMILY, TOO.
I MET HIM THE DAY THIS WAS TAKEN. I WAS EIGHTEEN. HE JUST... CAME OUT OF NOWHERE. WE SPENT THE DAY TOGETHER. TRYING TO FIND SOME... WAY TO TALK. WAY TO BE. WE TOOK THIS PICTURE. AND THEN HE DISAPPEARED AGAIN. AS FAST AS HE CAME.
I NEVER KNEW WHY HE LEFT. WHY HE CAME BACK. UNTIL I CAME HERE. EACH AND EVERY CLONE HAS THE SAME EXACT STORY ABOUT HIM. ABOUT THEIR FATHER.
THIS ISN'T A FAMILY. IT'S A FUCKING *EXPERIMENT.*

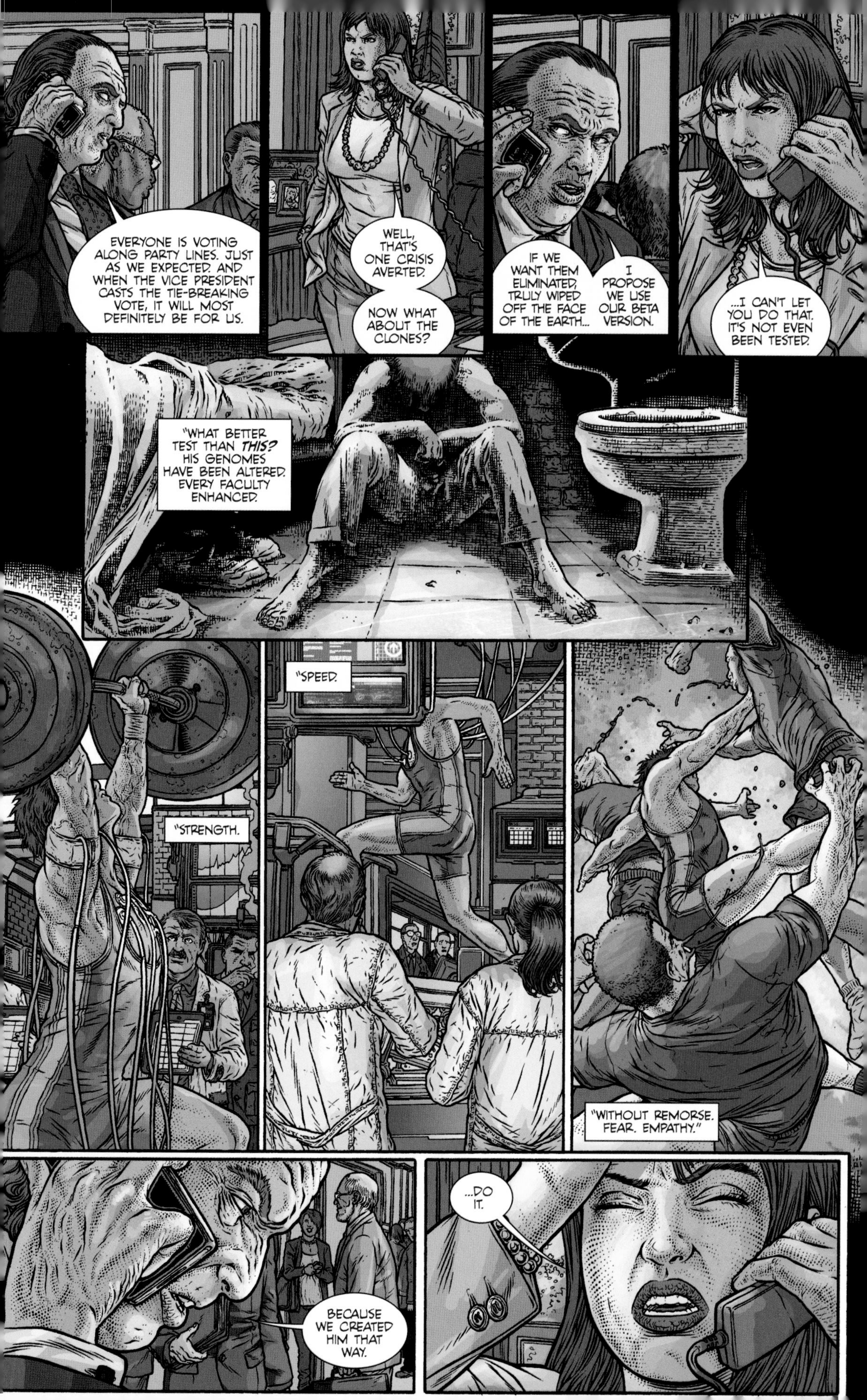
EVERYONE IS VOTING ALONG PARTY LINES. JUST AS WE EXPECTED. AND WHEN THE VICE PRESIDENT CASTS THE TIE-BREAKING VOTE, IT WILL MOST DEFINITELY BE FOR US.
WELL, THAT'S ONE CRISIS AVERTED.
NOW WHAT ABOUT THE CLONES?
IF WE WANT THEM ELIMINATED, TRULY WIPED OFF THE FACE OF THE EARTH...
I PROPOSE WE USE OUR BETA VERSION.
...I CAN'T LET YOU DO THAT. IT'S NOT EVEN BEEN TESTED.
"WHAT BETTER TEST THAN *THIS?* HIS GENOMES HAVE BEEN ALTERED. EVERY FACULTY ENHANCED.
"STRENGTH.
"SPEED.
"WITHOUT REMORSE. FEAR. EMPATHY."
BECAUSE WE CREATED HIM THAT WAY.
...DO IT.

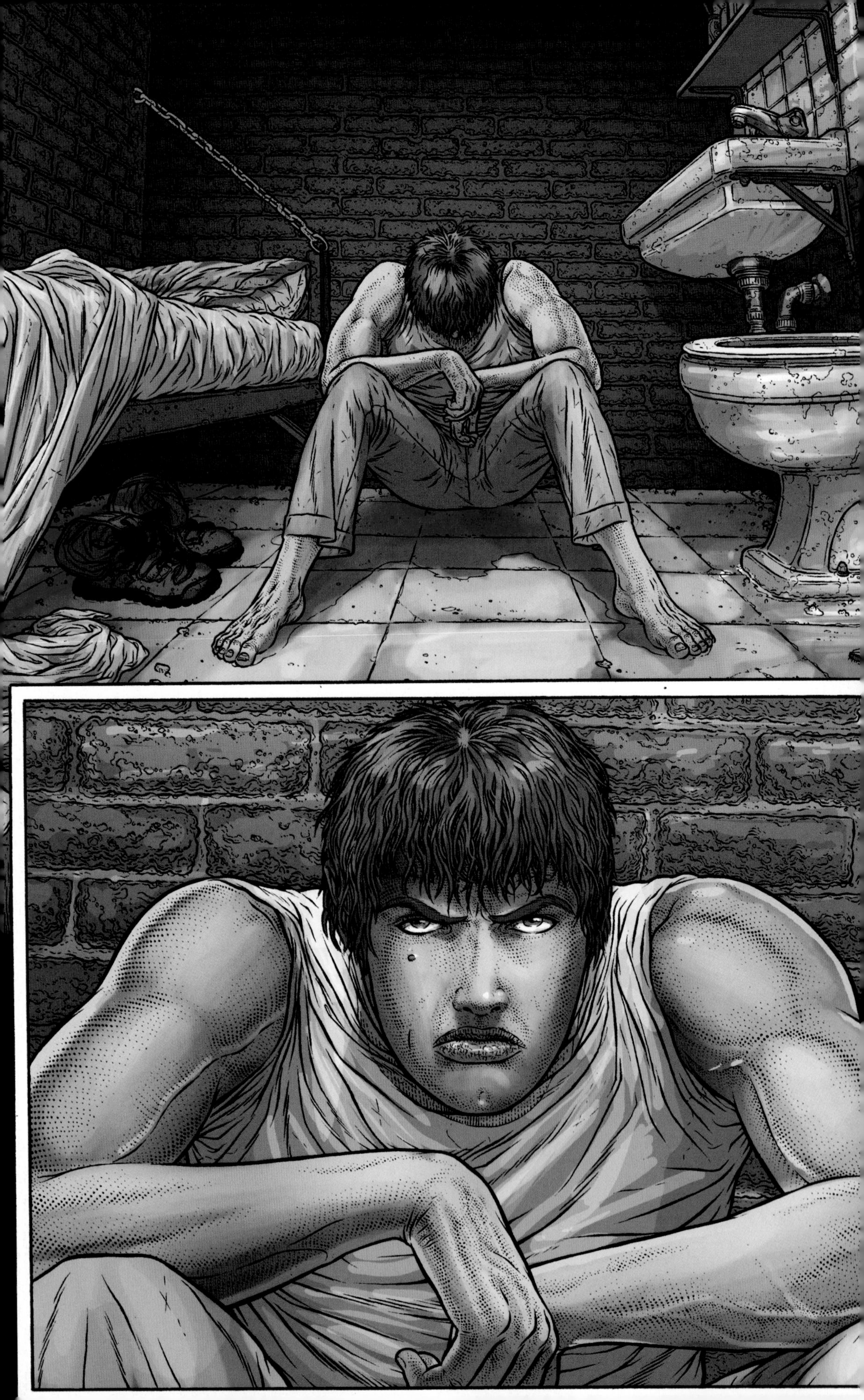

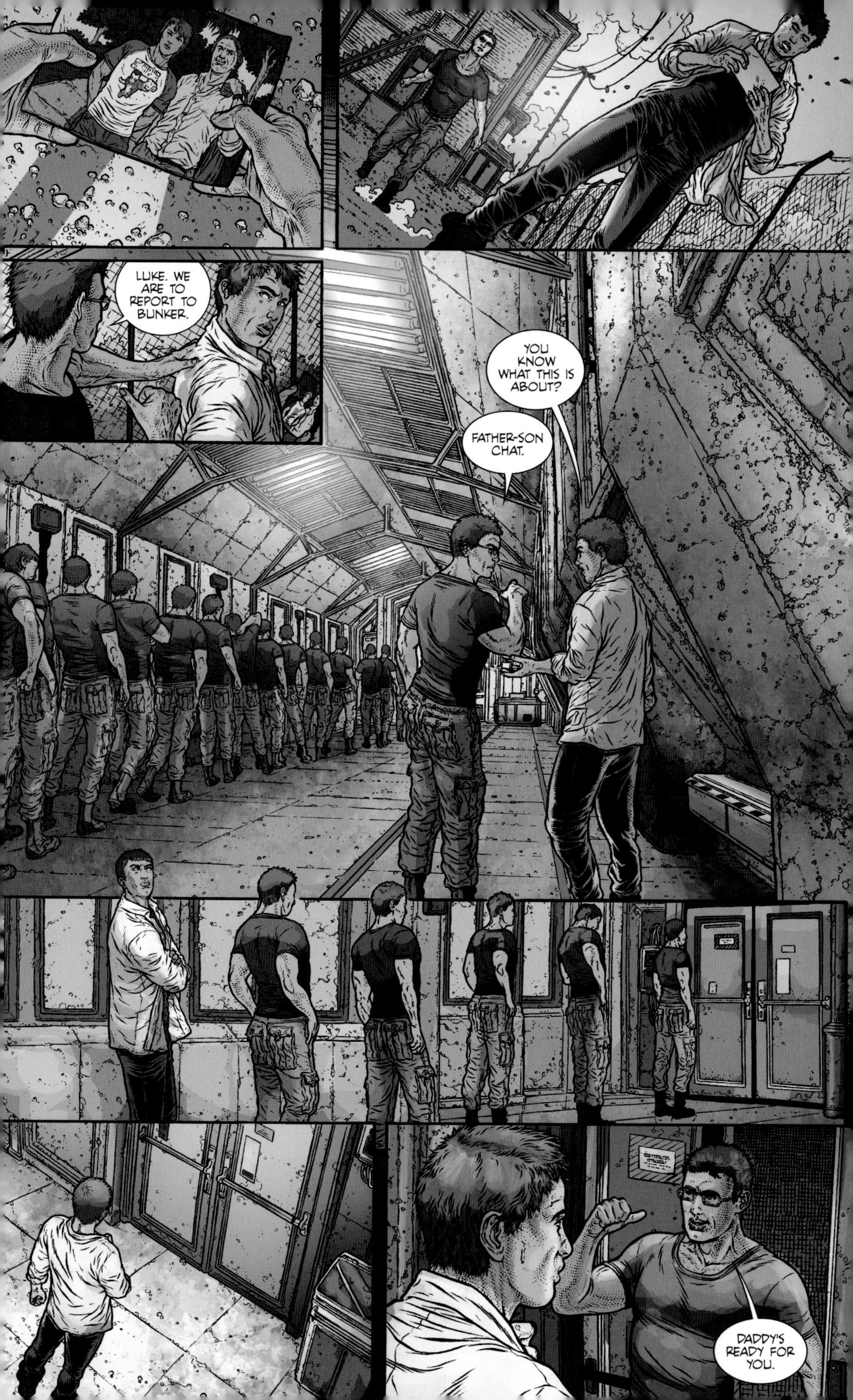
LUKE. WE ARE TO REPORT TO BUNKER.
YOU KNOW WHAT THIS IS ABOUT?
FATHER-SON CHAT.
DADDY'S READY FOR YOU.

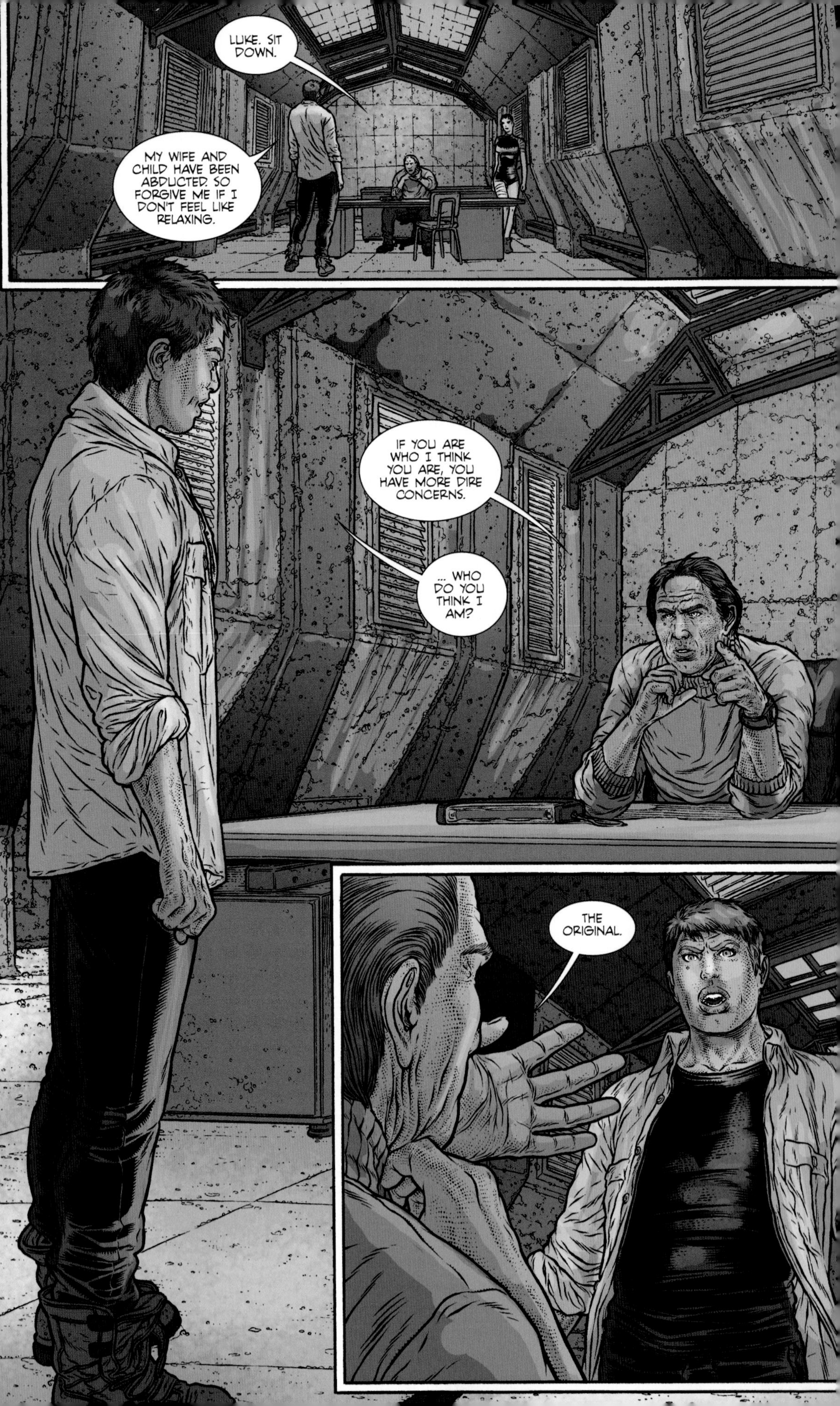
LUKE. SIT DOWN.
MY WIFE AND CHILD HAVE BEEN ABDUCTED. SO FORGIVE ME IF I DON'T FEEL LIKE RELAXING.
IF YOU ARE WHO I THINK YOU ARE, YOU HAVE MORE DIRE CONCERNS.
... WHO DO YOU THINK I AM?
THE ORIGINAL.

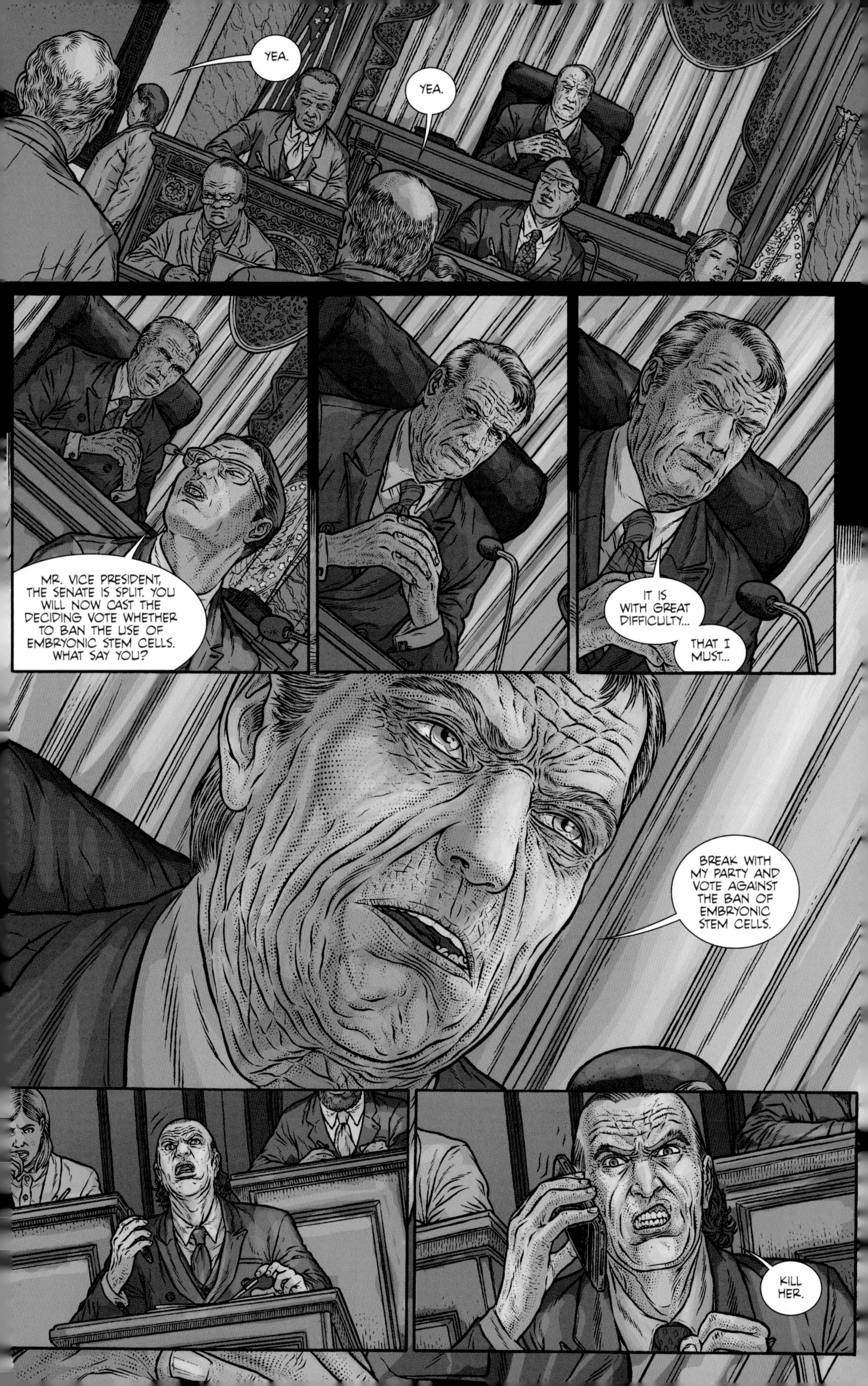
YEA.
YEA.
MR. VICE PRESIDENT, THE SENATE IS SPLIT. YOU WILL NOW CAST THE DECIDING VOTE WHETHER TO BAN THE USE OF EMBRYONIC STEM CELLS. WHAT SAY YOU?
IT IS WITH GREAT DIFFICULTY...
THAT I MUST...
BREAK WITH MY PARTY AND VOTE AGAINST THE BAN OF EMBRYONIC STEM CELLS.
KILL HER.

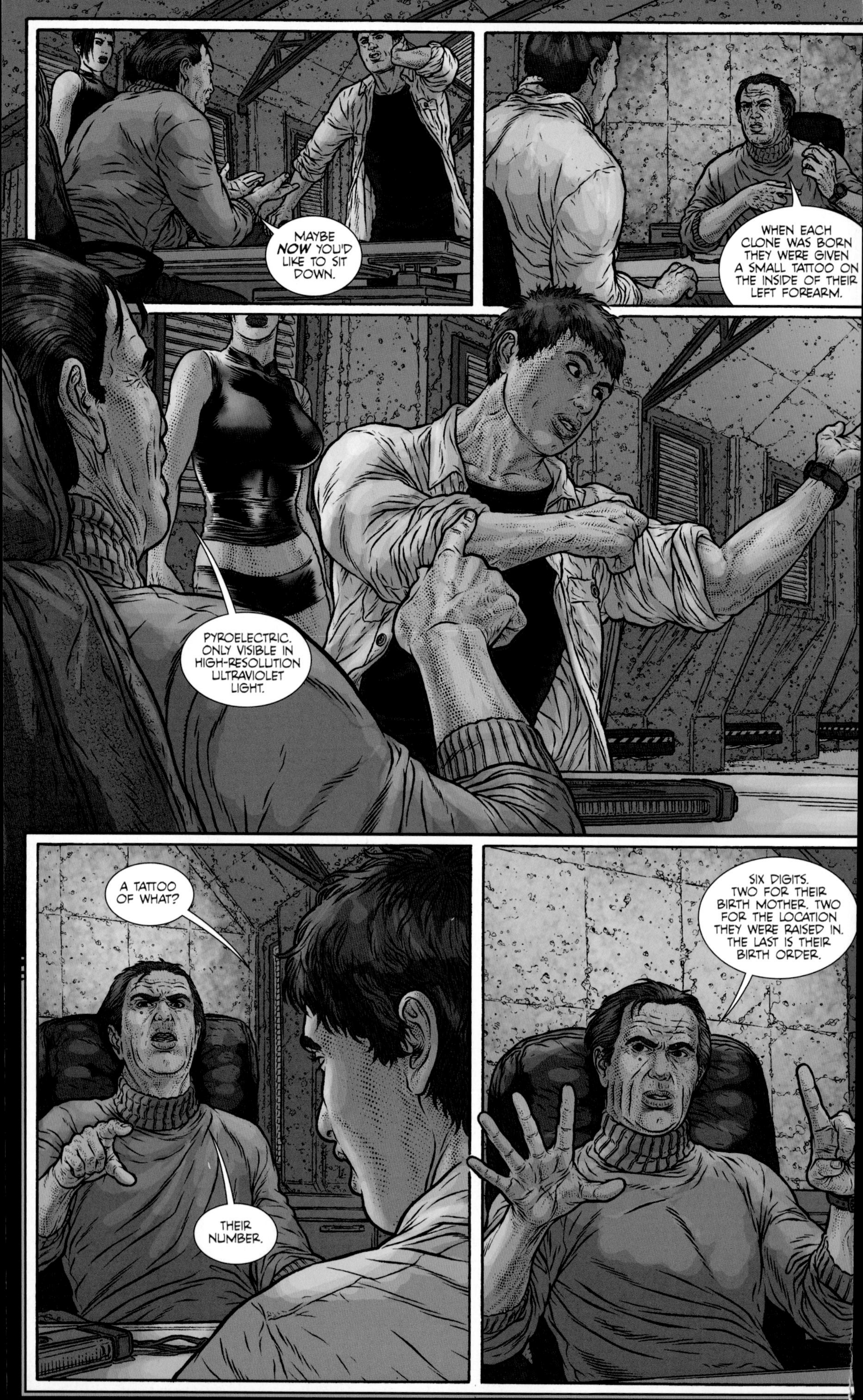
MAYBE *NOW* YOU'D LIKE TO SIT DOWN.
WHEN EACH CLONE WAS BORN THEY WERE GIVEN A SMALL TATTOO ON THE INSIDE OF THEIR LEFT FOREARM.
PYROELECTRIC. ONLY VISIBLE IN HIGH-RESOLUTION ULTRAVIOLET LIGHT.
A TATTOO OF WHAT?
THEIR NUMBER.
SIX DIGITS. TWO FOR THEIR BIRTH MOTHER. TWO FOR THE LOCATION THEY WERE RAISED IN. THE LAST IS THEIR BIRTH ORDER.

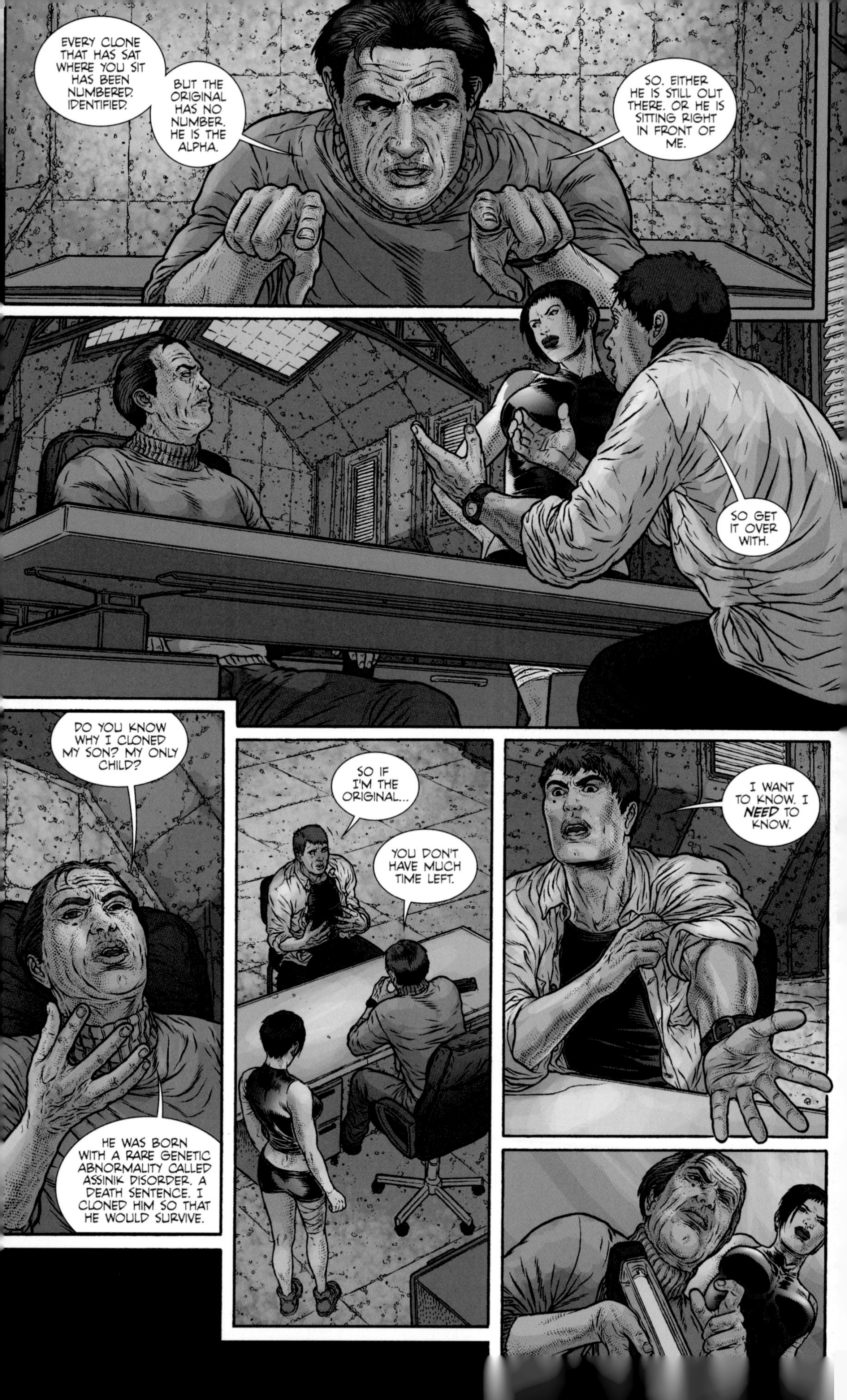
EVERY CLONE THAT HAS SAT WHERE YOU SIT HAS BEEN NUMBERED. IDENTIFIED.
BUT THE ORIGINAL HAS NO NUMBER. HE IS THE ALPHA.
SO. EITHER HE IS STILL OUT THERE. OR HE IS SITTING RIGHT IN FRONT OF ME.
SO GET IT OVER WITH.
DO YOU KNOW WHY I CLONED MY SON? MY ONLY CHILD?
HE WAS BORN WITH A RARE GENETIC ABNORMALITY CALLED ASSINIK DISORDER. A DEATH SENTENCE. I CLONED HIM SO THAT HE WOULD SURVIVE.
SO IF I'M THE ORIGINAL...
YOU DON'T HAVE MUCH TIME LEFT.
I WANT TO KNOW. I NEED TO KNOW.

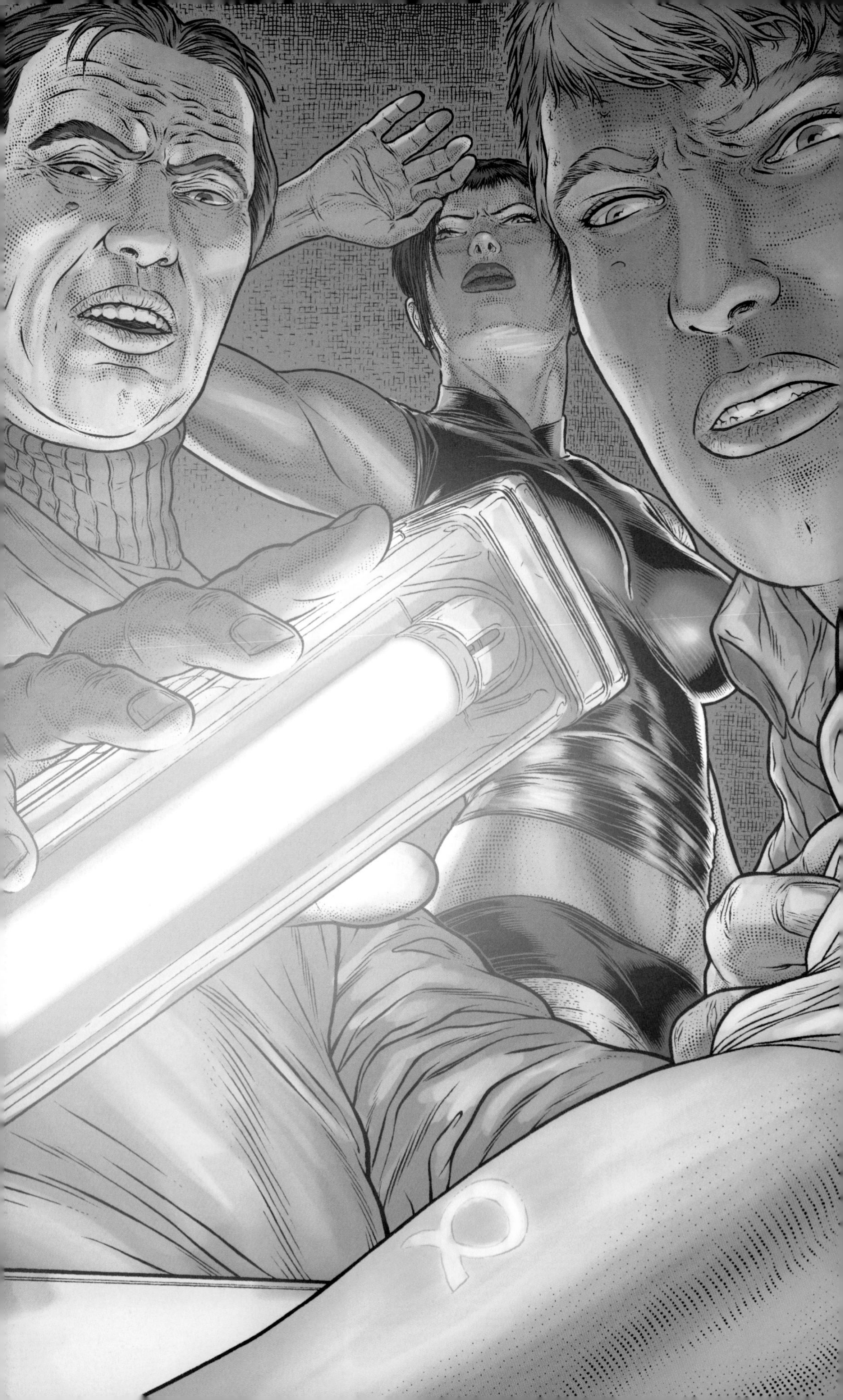

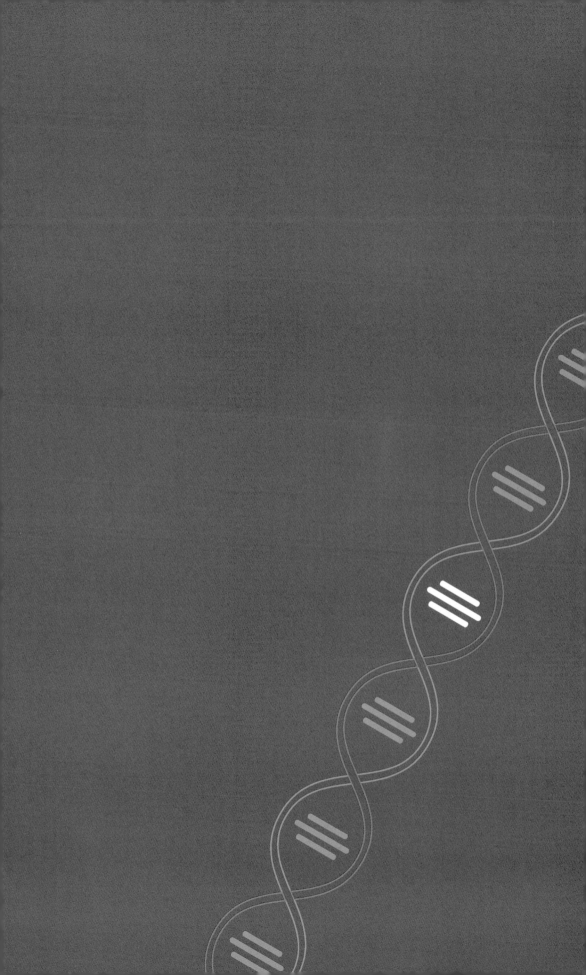

SEAN MACKIEWICZ: We got the cover to this first trade started the same way we get every cover started: we kick Juanjo (Juan Jose Ryp to you!) a concept, and he gave us a crazy amount of creative energy back. He sends us a selection of sketches and we pick the best. They're all pretty damn good, especially since we just wanted him to riff on the cover to #4, which was damn good the first go-around. We went for layout #1, but had him give Luke a more determined expression. It's hard work telling someone else what to draw...

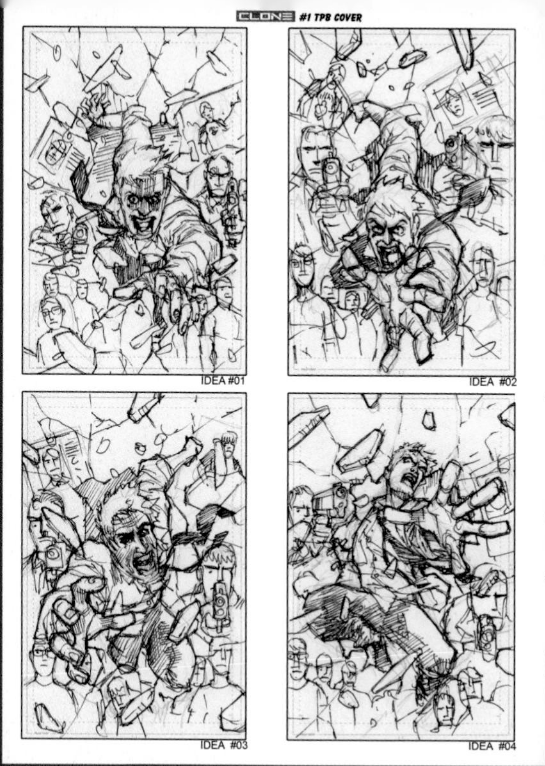
CLONE #1 TPB COVER
IDEA #01
IDEA #02
IDEA #03
IDEA #04

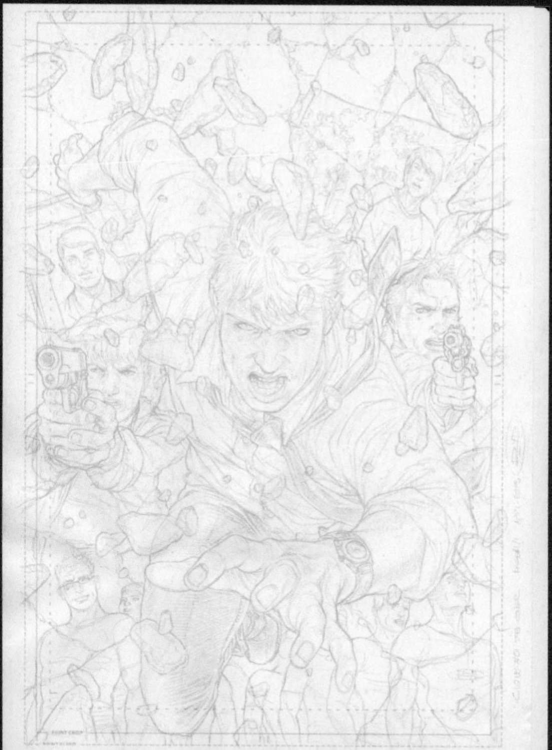

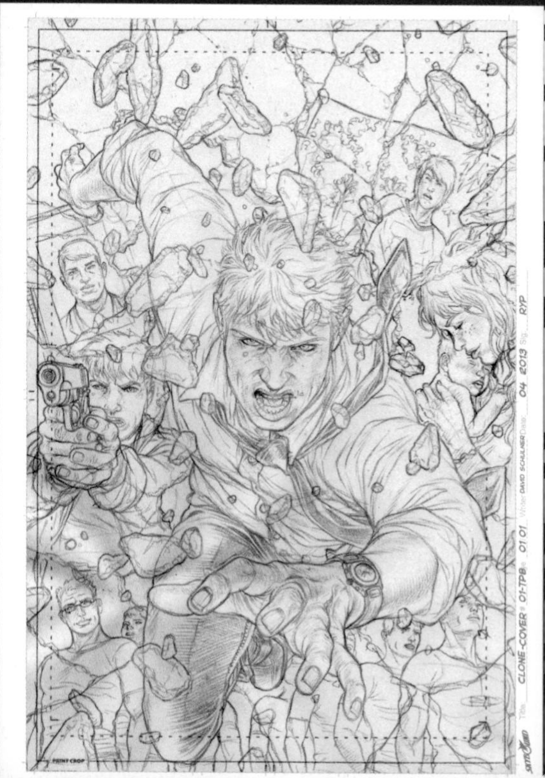

So Juanjo gets back to us the next day with pencils. We'd give him more time, but he wouldn't take it. It seems like he's always still awake in Spain while I'm sending out the last emails of the day from Los Angeles. David wanted Amelia on the cover, so we had Juanjo sub out Patrick... and then he inked it and it's an amazing cover.

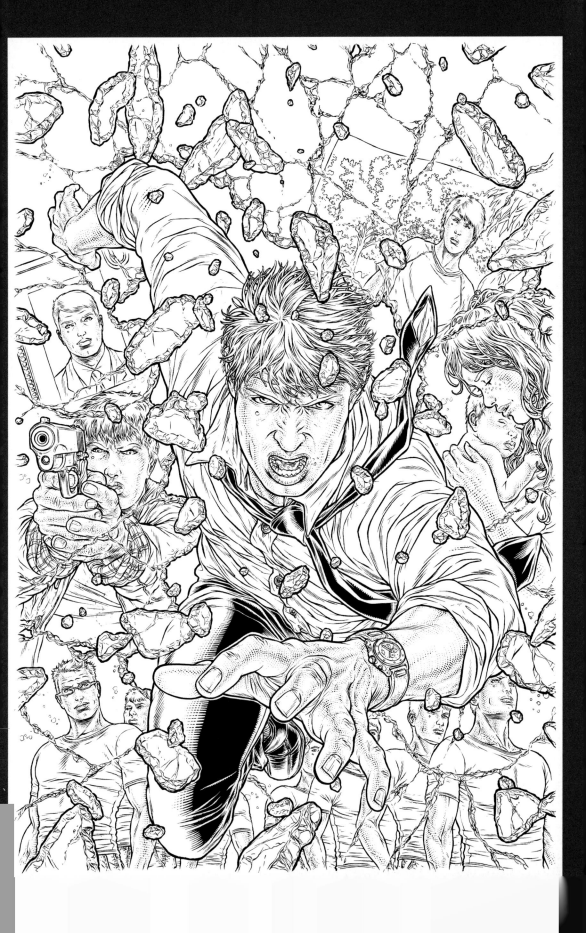

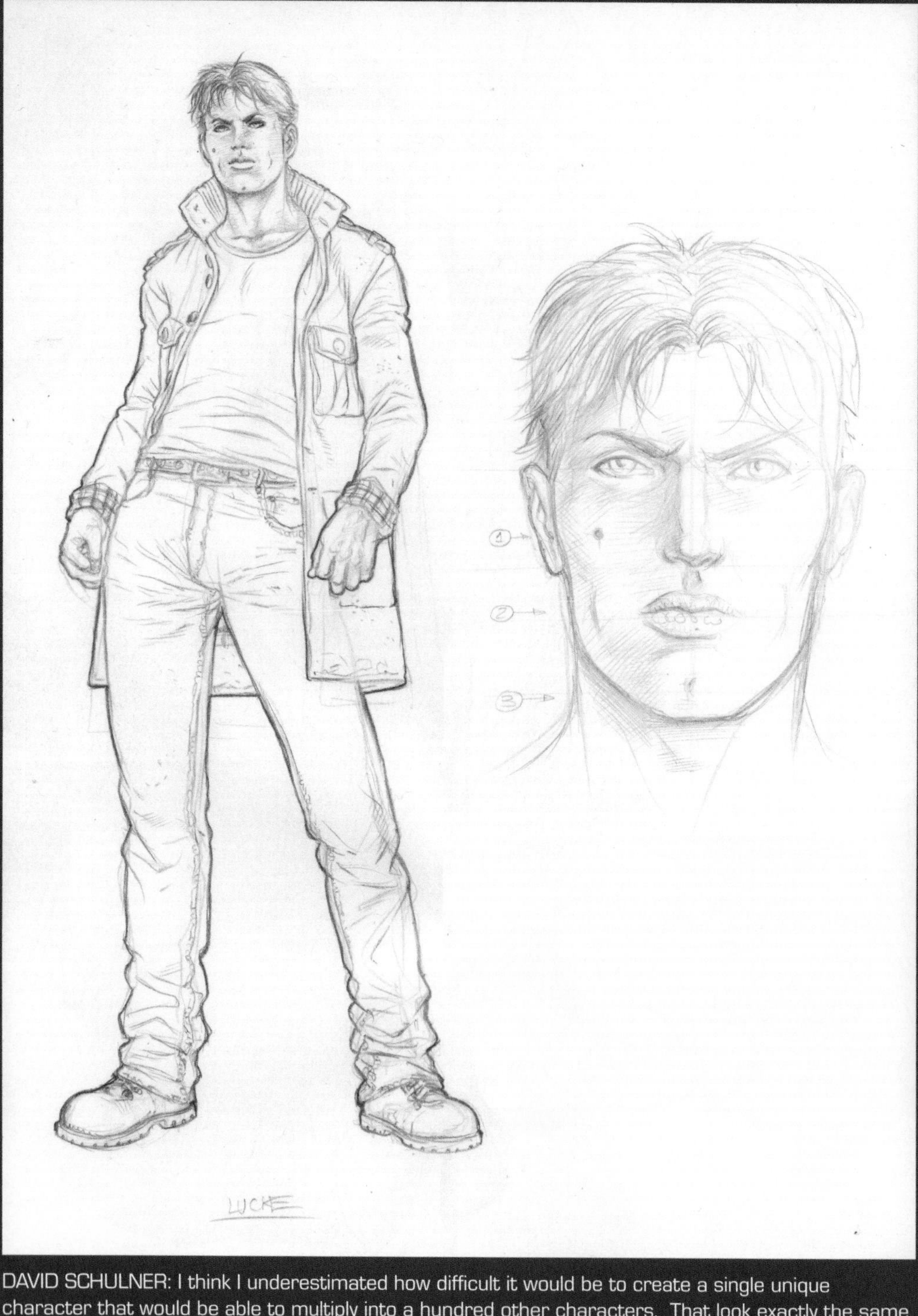
LUCKE

DAVID SCHULNER: I think I underestimated how difficult it would be to create a single unique character that would be able to multiply into a hundred other characters. That look exactly the same. But Juan created a real person in Luke that could be transformed many times over.

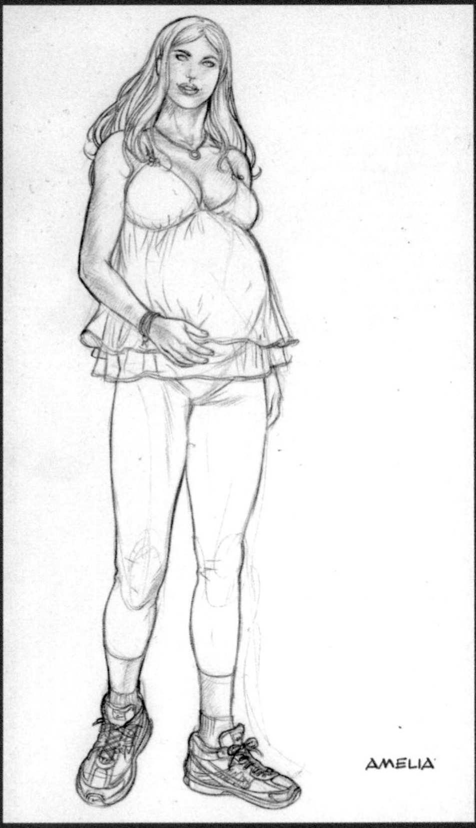
AMELIA

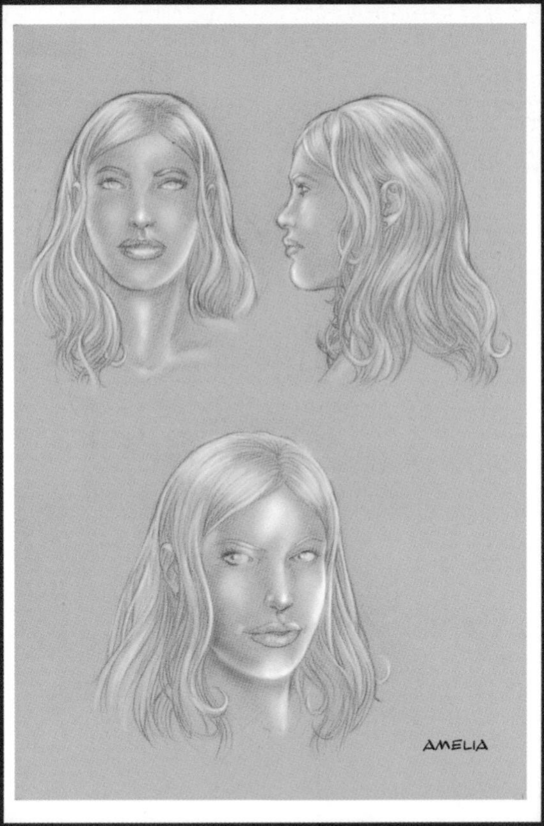
AMELIA

DAVID: So I gave very little to no direction to Juan in terms of how I wanted the characters to look. If I wrote them well, I hoped Juan would be able to visualize them and bring them to life. That and I'm a little lazy. So a crazy thing happened when I saw Amelia. She looked exactly like my wife. Red hair. Beautiful. Freckles. Thank you, Juan. I earned big points at home.

Isn't Jennifer a total badass? I love how tough Juan made her look because when she becomes vulnerable after losing Foss, it's truly heartbreaking.

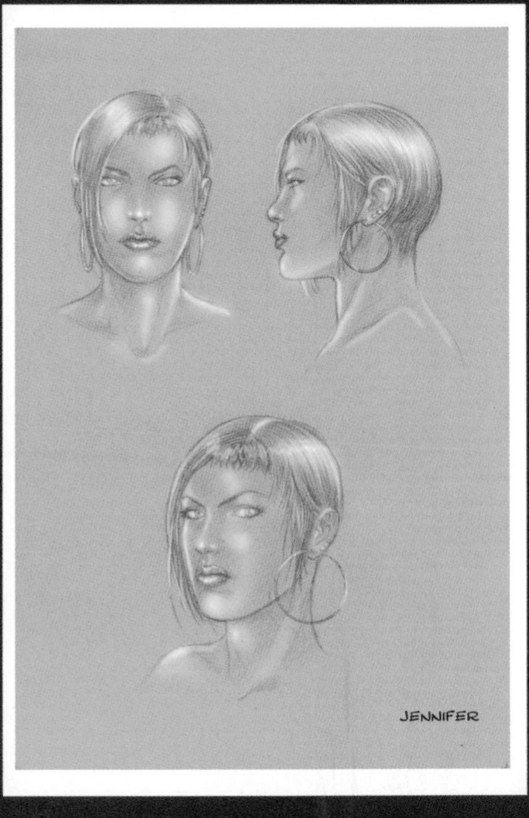
JENNIFER

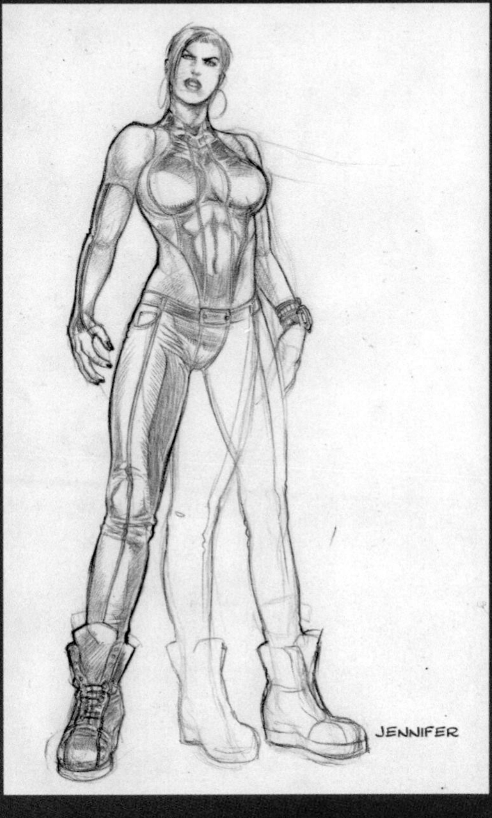
JENNIFER

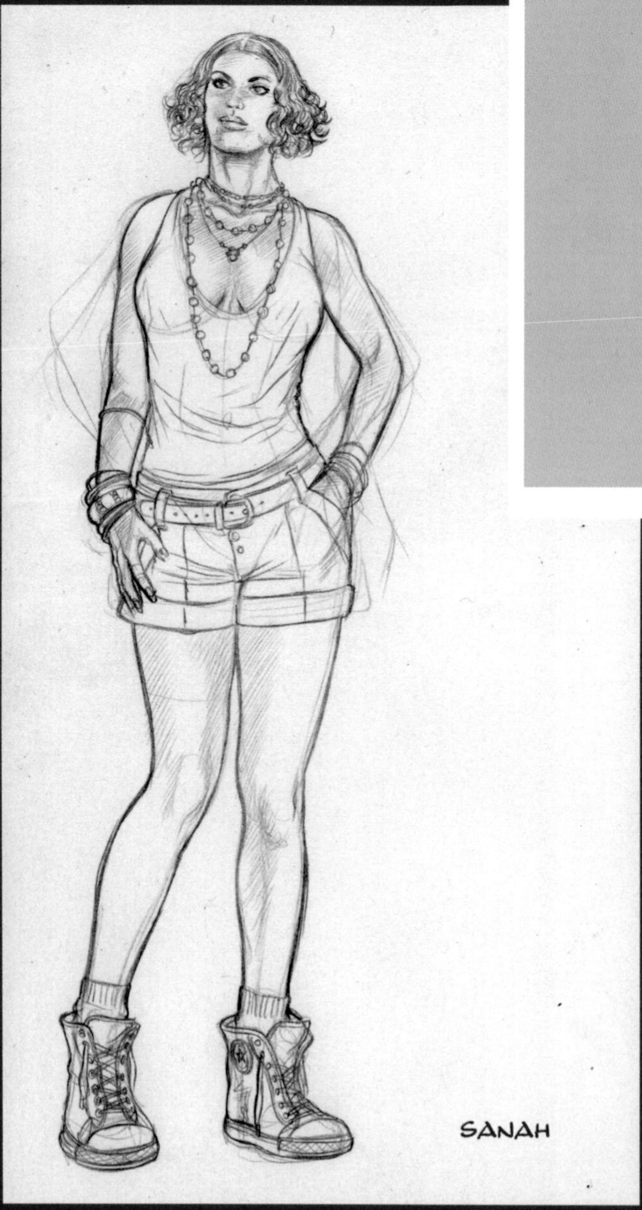
SANAH

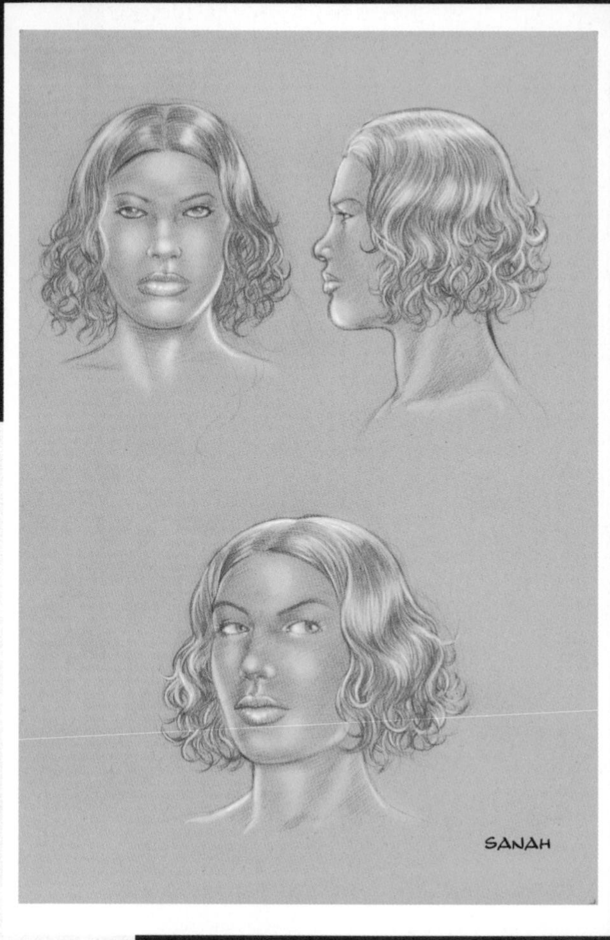
SANAH

DAVID: Sanah. As hot as she is, she still looks like a real woman. There are no frail waifs in these pages. All the women Juan drew are strong and sexy and still eat three meals a day.

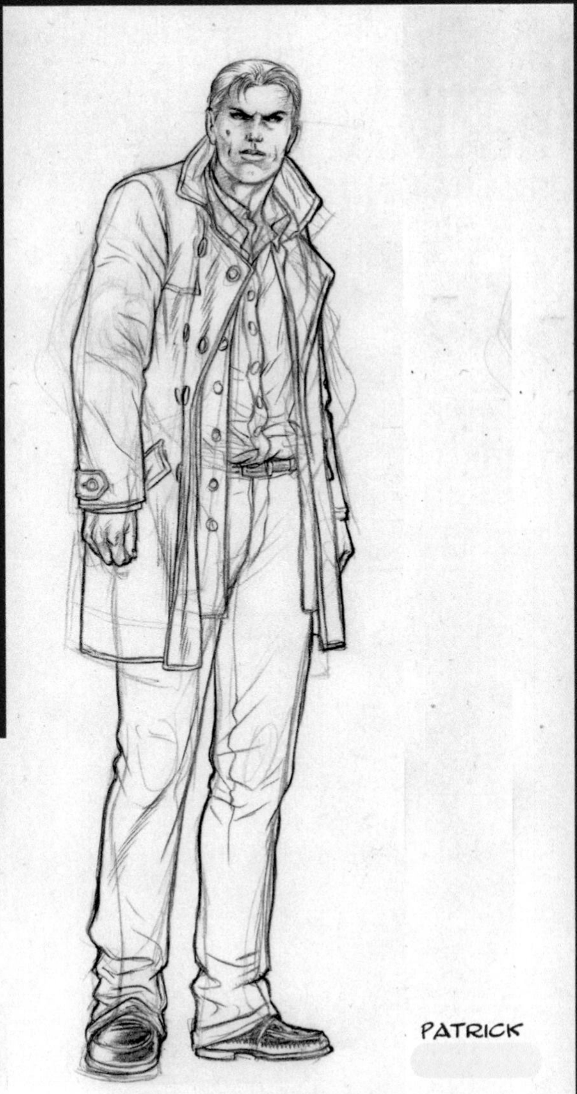
PATRICK

DAVID: Again, with no to little direction Juan came up with this early look for Foss. I guess he sounded homeless in my initial draft. I did a non-homeless pass at the script and Juan went back to the drawing board to create the Foss we know today. R.I.P. Foss. I miss him.

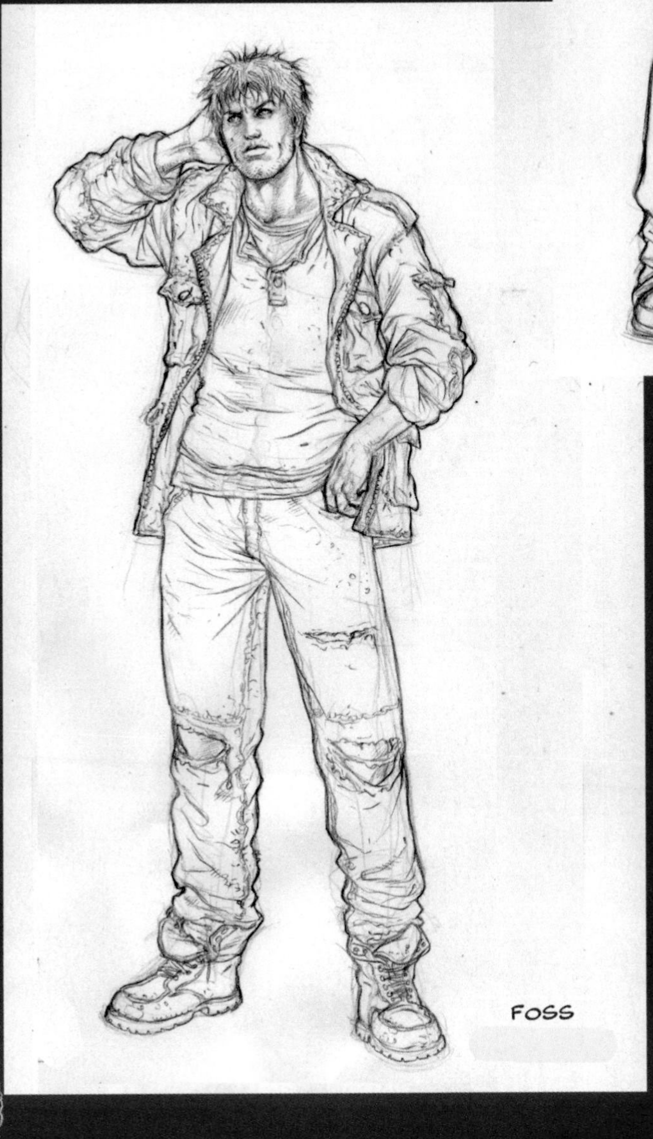
FOSS

Patrick is made of ice. And Juan really captured that. His body language is different. The way he cocks his head. It's that subtle, and Juan completely distinguishes him from Luke. It would be easy to have a clone with a beard and an eye patch to distinguish him, but Juan went for a brilliant, subtle and chilling characterization here. R.I.P. Patrick. I miss you, too.

MORE BOOKS FROM ROBERT KIRKMAN AND SKYBOUND!

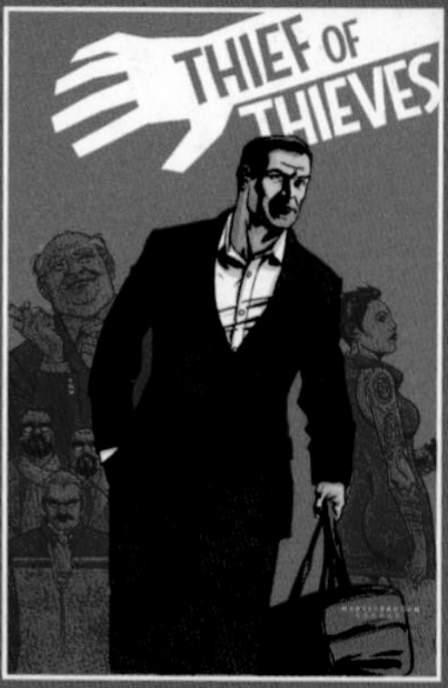
THIEF OF THIEVES

THIEF OF THIEVES
VOL. 1: "I QUIT."
ISBN: 978-1-60706-592-0
$14.99
VOL. 2: "HELP ME."
ISBN: 978-1-60706-676-7
$14.99

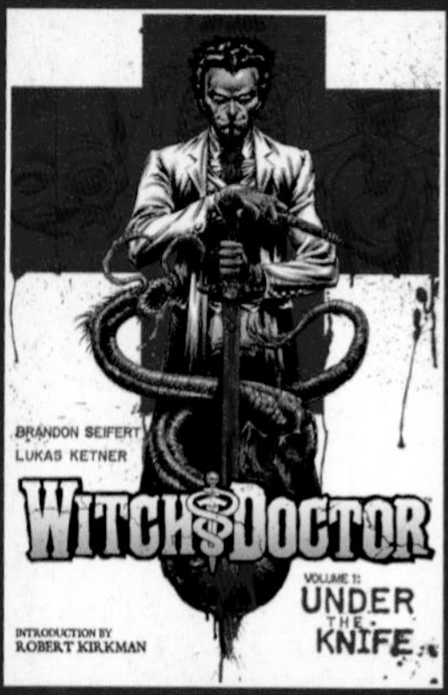
BRANDON SEIFERT
LUKAS KETNER
WITCH DOCTOR
VOLUME 1: UNDER THE KNIFE
INTRODUCTION BY ROBERT KIRKMAN

WITCH DOCTOR
VOL. 1: UNDER THE KNIFE TP
ISBN: 978-1-60706-441-1
$12.99

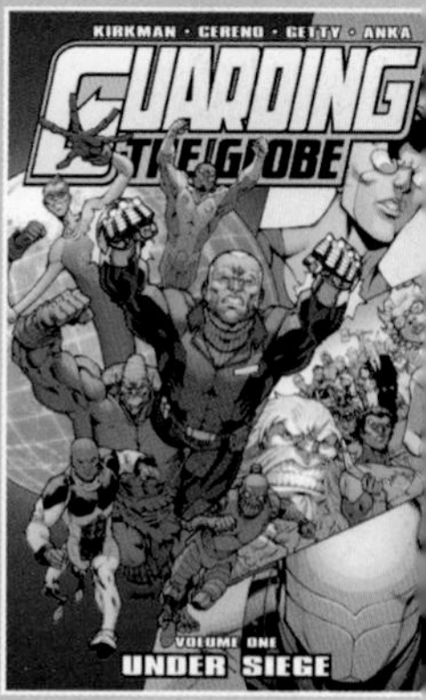
KIRKMAN · CERENO · GETTY · ANKA
GUARDING THE GLOBE
VOLUME ONE
UNDER SIEGE

GUARDING THE GLOBE
VOL. 1: UNDER SIEGE TP
ISBN: 978-1-60706-356-8
$16.99
VOL. 2: HARD TO KILL TP
ISBN: 978-1-60706-673-6
$16.99

TO FIND YOUR NEAREST COMIC BOOK STORE, CALL:
1-888-COMIC-BOOK

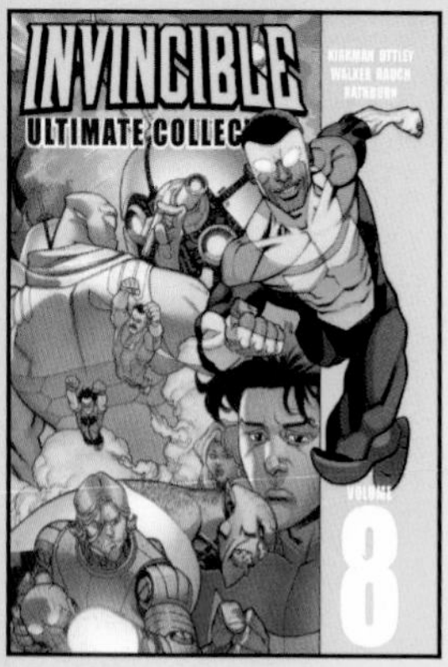
INVINCIBLE
ULTIMATE COLLEC
VOLUME
8

INVINCIBLE
VOL. 1: FAMILY MATTERS TP
ISBN: 978-1-58240-711-1
$12.99
VOL. 2: EIGHT IS ENOUGH TP
ISBN: 978-1-58240-347-2
$12.99
VOL. 3: PERFECT STRANGERS TP
ISBN: 978-1-58240-793-7
$12.99
VOL. 4: HEAD OF THE CLASS TP
ISBN: 978-1-58240-440-2
$14.95
VOL. 5: THE FACTS OF LIFE TP
ISBN: 978-1-58240-554-4
$14.99
VOL. 6: A DIFFERENT WORLD TP
ISBN: 978-1-58240-579-7
$14.99
VOL. 7: THREE'S COMPANY TP
ISBN: 978-1-58240-656-5
$14.99
VOL. 8: MY FAVORITE MARTIAN TP
ISBN: 978-1-58240-683-1
$14.99
VOL. 9: OUT OF THIS WORLD TP
ISBN: 978-1-58240-827-9
$14.99
VOL. 10: WHO'S THE BOSS TP
ISBN: 978-1-60706-013-0
$16.99
VOL. 11: HAPPY DAYS TP
ISBN: 978-1-60706-062-8
$16.99
VOL. 12: STILL STANDING TP
ISBN: 978-1-60706-166-3
$16.99
VOL. 13: GROWING PAINS TP
ISBN: 978-1-60706-251-6
$16.99
VOL. 14: THE VILTRUMITE WAR TP
ISBN: 978-1-60706-367-4
$19.99
VOL. 15: GET SMART TP
ISBN: 978-1-60706-498-5
$16.99
VOL. 16: FAMILY TIES TP
ISBN: 978-1-60706-579-1
$16.99
VOL. 17: WHAT'S HAPPENING TP
ISBN: 978-1-60706-662-0
$16.99
ULTIMATE COLLECTION, VOL. 1 HC
ISBN 978-1-58240-500-1
$34.95
ULTIMATE COLLECTION, VOL. 2 HC
ISBN: 978-1-58240-594-0
$34.99
ULTIMATE COLLECTION, VOL. 3 HC
ISBN: 978-1-58240-763-0
$34.99
ULTIMATE COLLECTION, VOL. 4 HC
ISBN: 978-1-58240-989-4
$34.99
ULTIMATE COLLECTION, VOL. 5 HC
ISBN: 978-1-60706-116-8
$34.99
ULTIMATE COLLECTION, VOL. 6 HC
ISBN: 978-1-60706-360-5
$34.99
ULTIMATE COLLECTION, VOL. 7 HC
ISBN: 978-1-60706-509-8
$39.99
ULTIMATE COLLECTION, VOL. 8 HC
ISBN: 978-1-60706-680-4
$39.99
COMPENDIUM VOL. 1
ISBN: 978-1-60706-411-4
$64.99
THE COMPLETE INVINCIBLE LIBRARY, VOL. 2 HC
ISBN: 978-1-60706-112-0
$125.00
THE COMPLETE INVINCIBLE LIBRARY, VOL. 3 HC
ISBN: 978-1-60706-421-3
$125.00
THE OFFICIAL HANDBOOK OF THE INVINCIBLE UNIVERSE TP
ISBN: 978-1-58240-831-6
$12.99
INVINCIBLE PRESENTS, VOL. 1: ATOM EVE & REX SPLODE TP
ISBN: 978-1-60706-255-4
$14.99

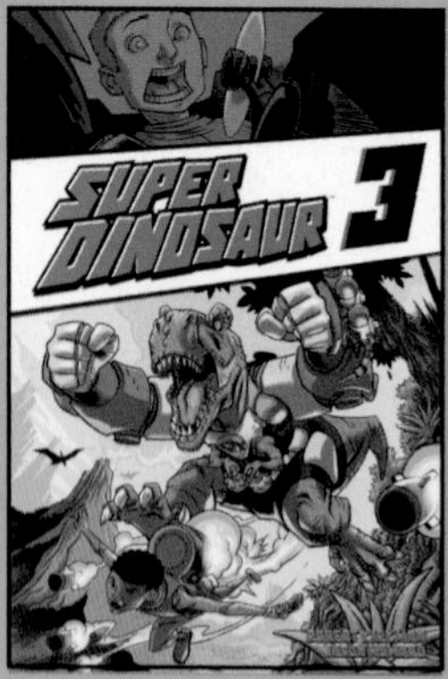
SUPER DINOSAUR 3

SUPER DINOSAUR
VOL. 1
ISBN: 978-1-60706-420-6
$9.99
VOL. 2
ISBN: 978-1-60706-568-5
$12.99
VOL. 3
ISBN: 978-1-60706-667-5
$12.99
DELUXE COLORING BOOK
ISBN: 978-1-60706-481-7
$4.99

THE ASTOUNDING WOLF-MAN
VOL. 1 TP
ISBN: 978-1-58240-862-0
$14.99
VOL. 2 TP
ISBN: 978-1-60706-007-9
$14.99
VOL. 3 TP
ISBN: 978-1-60706-111-3
$16.99
VOL. 4 TP
ISBN: 978-1-60706-249-3
$16.99

BATTLE POPE
VOL. 1: GENESIS TP
ISBN: 978-1-58240-572-8
$14.99
VOL. 2: MAYHEM TP
ISBN: 978-1-58240-529-2
$12.99
VOL. 3: PILLOW TALK TP
ISBN: 978-1-58240-677-0
$12.99
VOL. 4: WRATH OF GOD TP
ISBN: 978-1-58240-751-7
$9.99

BRIT
VOL. 1: OLD SOLDIER TP
ISBN: 978-1-58240-678-7
$14.99
VOL. 2: AWOL
ISBN: 978-1-58240-864-4
$14.99
VOL. 3: FUBAR
ISBN: 978-1-60706-061-1
$16.99

CAPES
VOL. 1: PUNCHING THE CLOCK TP
ISBN: 978-1-58240-756-2
$17.99

HAUNT
VOL. 1 TP
ISBN: 978-1-60706-154-0
$9.99
VOL. 2 TP
ISBN: 978-1-60706-229-5
$16.99
VOL. 3 TP
ISBN: 978-1-60706-552-4
$14.99
THE IMMORTAL EDITION, VOL. 1 HC
ISBN: 978-1-60706-241-7
$34.99

THE INFINITE
VOL. 1 TP
ISBN: 978-1-60706-475-6
$9.99

SUPERPATRIOT
AMERICA'S FIGHTING FORCE
ISBN: 978-1-58240-355-1
$14.99

TALES OF THE REALM
HARDCOVER
ISBN: 978-1-58240-426-0
$34.95
TRADE PAPERBACK
ISBN: 978-1-58240-394-6
$14.95

TECH JACKET
VOL. 1: THE BOY FROM EARTH TP
ISBN: 978-1-58240-771-5
$14.99